Soviet Militar

Soviet Military Intervention in Hungary 1956

edited by
Jenő Györkei and Miklós Horváth

with a study by Alexandr M. Kirov
and memoirs of Yevgeny I. Malashenko

Central European University Press
Budapest

No. 100 "Atlantic Studies on Society in Change"
Atlantic Research and Publications, Inc.
P. O. Box 568, Highland Lakes, NJ, USA
Editor in Chief Béla K. Király
Associate Editor in Chief Kenneth Murphy
Editor László Veszprémy

First published in Hungarian as *Szovjet katonai intervenció 1956*
in 1996 by Argumentum Kiadó, Budapest

English edition 1999 by
Central European University Press
Október 6. utca 12
H-1051 Budapest, Hungary

400 West 59th Street
New York, NY 10019, USA

Translated by Emma Roper Evans
Maps by Béla Nagy

© 1999 by Atlantic Research and Publications, Inc.
English translation © 1999 by Emma Roper Evans

Distributed by
Plymbridge Distributors, Ltd., Estover Road, Plymouth PL6 7PZ, United Kingdom

All rights reserved. No part of this publication may be reproduced, stored
in a retrieval system, or transmitted, in any form or by any means,
without the permission of the Publisher.

ISBN 963 9116 36 X Cloth
ISBN 963 9116 35 1 Paperback

Library of Congress Cataloging in Publication Data

Szovjet katonai intervenció, 1956. English.
 Soviet military intervention in Hungary, 1956 / edited by Jenő
Györkei and Miklós Horváth: [translated by Emma Roper-Evans].
       p.   cm.
 Includes bibliographical references and index.
 ISBN 963911636X (cloth) – ISBN 9639116351 (pbk.)
  1. Hungary—History—Revolution, 1956—Sources. 2. Hungary—
Military relations—Soviet Union. 3. Soviet Union—Military
relations—Hungary. I. Györkei, Jenő. II. Horváth, Miklós. III. Title.
DB956.7.S9613 1998
943.905'2—dc21   98-48738
                                                                   CIP

Printed in Hungary by Akaprint, Budapest

Contents

Preface to the Series and Acknowledgements xi

Abbreviations 2

Additional Data on the History of the Soviet Military Occupation
Jenő Györkei and Miklós Horváth

Soviet Troops in Hungary after World War II 5
"Soviet Troops Must Enter Budapest" 8
The Hungarian Revolution and Events in Poland 9
Comrade Hegedűs Makes a Request 10
"The Hungarian Army Has Done Badly" 14
The First Shots and the Occupation of the Radio
    Station 15
What Was Known in Moscow of the Hungarian Events 20
The Hungarian People's Army and the Revolution 22
The "Division of Labor" Changes 28
The Policy for the Peaceful Liberation of the Captive
    Nations and Its Failure 30
Forces Brought to Budapest Prove Insufficient 32
Soviet Tanks Open Fire–Kossuth Square,
    October 25, 1956 36
"We Increase the Number of Troops Active
    in Budapest" 40

Further Reasons for the Divisions in the Hungarian
    People's Army 42
"The Military Viewpoint Overtakes the Political
    Viewpoint" 44
"Two Possible Routes Lie Ahead of Us" 49
The Final Attempt 54
The Attack Begins 57
"The Situation is Deteriorating" 61
Counter-Revolution? National Democratic Revolution? 63
"How Can We Master the Situation? Real Power:
    the Army!" 68
Soviet Troop Withdrawal from Budapest 70
"At Present the Number of Soviet Troops Stationed
    Here is Adequate" 71
"Troops Must Stay in Hungary" 74
Mikoyan's Unsuccessful Attempts 76
Imre Nagy Demands an Explanation–Kádár Speaks
    in Support of Nagy 78
"Nobody Wanted a Counter-Revolution" 79
Murders, Atrocities and Kádár's Propaganda Intrigues 83
Central Leadership of the Revolution 85
"Revolution is Revolution" 90
The Command of Budapest Public Safety Forces
    is Formed 93
The Soviet Embassy "Siege" 94
National Guard Supreme Command is Formed 96
Polish "No," Yugoslav "Yes" 99
"This Government Should Not Be a Puppet
    Government" 103
The Revolution Turns into a War 105
A Mosaic of the Resistance 109

Notes **115**

Soviet Military Intervention in Hungary, 1956
Alexandr M. Kirov

Questions are Increasingly Being Raised 129
The Hungarian Workers Party Proves Unable to Lead
    Society 130
The "Wave," a Plan for Armed Intervention 132
How It Began 133
The Plan Is Set in Motion 135
Soviet Troops in Budapest 137
"A Friendly Message to the Workers of the Hungarian
    People's Republic" 140
Re-evaluation of the Situation 143
Command to Cease Fire 146
Refugees and Hosts 148
Troop Invasion Continues 151
Preparations for a New Military Operation 153
The Beginning of Operation "Whirlwind" 157
UN General Assembly Decision 161
"Who Represents the Will of the People?" 165
The Organization of the Soviet City Commands 167
The End of the Suppression of the Uprising 169
Rearguard Actions 171
"Sepilov Lied" 176
"There Have Been, and Will Be, Arrests" 179
And What Happened Afterwards 182
The Hungarian October and the Present 183
The Old View Is No Longer Valid 186
Soviet Troop Losses 187
Troops Withdraw, the Graves Stay Behind 189
After Nearly 40 Years 190
The Price of the Khrushchev–Kádár Agreement 191
Conclusion 193
Notes 195
Tables 201

The Special Corps under Fire in Budapest – Memoirs of an Eyewitness

Y. I. Malashenko

To the Reader **209**

Chapter I–On the Eve of the Events
In Hungary–in the Special Corps Staff 211
Mistakes and Consequences............................. 216
The Drafting of the Plan for Restoring Social Order......... 217
The Protests and the Armed Uprising in Budapest 222

Chapter II–Soviet Troops in Budapest
The Hungarian Government Requests Help 224
The Beginning of Combat Operations 227
The Arrival of Soviet Political and Military Leaders
   in Budapest... 232
The Arrival of New Formations and the Soviet Troop
   Operations in Budapest 234

Chapter III–Soviet Troop Withdrawal from Budapest
The Fight Continues................................... 244
Kádár Requests Military Aid 247
Preparations for Combat Operation 248
The Arrest of the Hungarian Delegation 253

Chapter IV–Operation "Whirlwind"
Special Army Corps Troops in Budapest Once Again 259
The Destruction of Armed Groups in the Country 263
The Direction of Soviet Troops in Hungary 265
The Final Destruction of Armed Groups in the Capital....... 266
Béla Király, Commander in Chief of the National
   Guard 269
Soviet Troop Losses in Hungary 273
Nikita Khrushchev, Imre Nagy and János Kádár............ 275
The Historical Tragedy 278

Afterword

    The History of the History 283
    Y. I. Malashenko's Letter to Jenő Györkei 285

Notes 288
Appendices and Maps 291

Biographical Notes 297

Preface to the Series and Acknowledgements

The present volume is part of a series which, when completed, will constitute a comprehensive survey of the many aspects of East Central European society and history. The series deals with the peoples whose homelands lie between the Germans to the west, the Russians, Ukrainians and Belarusians to the east and north, and the Mediterranean and Adriatic seas to the south. They constitute a particular civilization, one that is at once an integral part of Europe, yet substantially different from the West. The area is characterized by a rich diversity of languages, religions and governments. The study of this complex area demands a multidisciplinary approach and, accordingly, our contributors to the series represent several academic disciplines. They have been drawn from the universities and other scholarly institutions in the United States and Western Europe, as well as Eastern and Central Europe.

The editors, of course, take full responsibility for ensuring the comprehensiveness, cohesion, internal balance, and scholarly quality of the series they have launched. We gladly accept this responsibility and intend the volumes we publish to be neither a justification nor a condemnation of the policies, attitudes, and activities of any persons involved. At the same time, because the contributors represent so many different disciplines, interpretations, and schools of thought, our policy in this, as in past and future volumes, is to present their contributions without modifications.

This editorial policy has been rigorously observed. Since, however, there are completely contrary interpretations on some fundamental issues among the contributors' presentations, the editor in chief considers it his obligation to express the editorial board's views–based on extensive research–on the following issues:

– Did a revolution or a counter-revolution occur in Hungary in 1956? If it was a revolution, was it successful or did it fail?

– Was the declaration of neutrality on November 1 the cause or the effect of Soviet aggression?

– Did armed combat amount to a war or was it aid given to the Hungarian nation?

– Finally, was the armed conflict conducted between "socialist" states against each other?

The clarification of these issues is necessary since all these standpoints are represented by one or another contributor.

Revolution or counter-revolution? Revolution is a forceful act in which the old–usually oppressive, exploitative, and inefficient–regime is defeated and its institutions replaced by a–usually progressive–political force, which then establishes new social, political and/or economic institutions of its own.

In Hungary in 1956, one of the two pillars of the party state, the ÁVH, was abolished on October 29 by a decree issued by the Communist Minister of the Interior Ferenc Münnich. The other pillar, the Hungarian Workers (Communist) Party, dissolved itself on November 1, and under a new name, the Hungarian Socialist Workers' Party, accepted the idea of a multi-party state and parliamentary government elected by universal suffrage and secret ballot. By November 1 a multi-party government under Imre Nagy had taken the helm. There was no person, organization or party in Hungary at that date which might have, could have or would even have wanted to replace this government. The revolution was victorious. The new regime was suppressed not by domestic forces but by foreign aggression. This international act could not alter the fact that the Hungarian Revolution, as a domestic historical event, was victorious.

Was the declaration of neutrality on November 1 the cause or the effect of Soviet aggression? Retired Soviet Lieutenant General Malashenko, who in 1956 as a colonel was the acting chief of staff of the Special Corps, operating in the Greater Budapest area–states below that November 1 "sealed the fate of Hungary." This would mean that the declaration of neutrality was the cause of Soviet aggression. But on that day Khrushchev had already informed the leaders of the Warsaw Pact in

Bucharest, and subsequently told Tito on the island of Brioni, of the new Soviet military operations. In the meantime, during the night of October 30/31, a massive invasion of new troops into Hungary began. Imre Nagy protested against the invasion to the USSR. He also informed the UN secretary general and appealed to the permanent members of the UN Security Council to halt the aggression. But all in vain. The fact is that, at the time of the declaration of neutrality, aggression was already taking place. Thus it was the cause rather than the effect of the declaration of neutrality.

Was the armed conflict conducted between "socialist" states against each other?

The idea that the Soviet Union helped the Hungarian government by military means still persists. But Nagy, the head of the Hungarian government, declared at 5:20 a.m. on November 4:

"Today at dawn, Soviet troops attacked our capital with the obvious intention of overthrowing the legitimate Hungarian democratic government..."

In the Clausewitzian sense, that is exactly what war means: the continuation of politics by other means, in which one party forces its political will upon another. That is exactly what happened in Hungary: a war was waged.

The size of the forces invading Hungary–according to Alexandr Mikhailovich Kirov, one of the contributors to this volume–amounted to 17 divisional size units. As far as the intensity of the fight is concerned, the Soviet troop losses were 722 men killed, 1251 wounded. For "other" reasons 15 men lost their lives and 67 disappeared without a trace. We know that many of them deserted to the West. The intensity of the fighting was also demonstrated by the fact that 26 Soviet soldiers won the highest war decoration: the title and the golden medal of the Hero of the Soviet Union. In addition 10,000 soldiers and officers were decorated with combat medals.

It was a war in every sense of the word.

Finally, was the armed conflict conducted by two "socialist" states against each other? It is not our intention to define what socialism is. But the fact is that both the USSR and the Hungarian People's Republic considered themselves socialist states and societies. In fact, during the revolution of 1956, no stated program nor serious person or group demanded the instant abolition of socialism. Hungary in 1956 was a socialist state and society that was attacked by another socialist state. True, a democratic election by secret ballot to establish a multi-party government was the official policy of the last Nagy government and unmistakably the desire of the majority of the Hungarian people. Had Hungary been left alone, what would have happened? The freely elected Parliament surely would have secured the rights of the citizens, governed democratically and introduced private property and a free market. But this would not have been part and parcel of the events of 1956, but merely a distant result of the revolution. For without 1956 the radical changes of the "lawful revolution" that commenced in 1989 and is still in progress would not have happened, or if it had, it would not have been what it is today.

Atlantic Research and Publications, Inc. is grateful to military historians Jenő Györkei and Miklós Horváth on the Hungarian side as well as Alexandr Mikhailovich Kirov on the Russian side for their pioneering and successful research which unearthed hitherto unknown elements of Soviet military operations in 1956. Special thanks are due to retired Lieutenant General Y. I. Malashenko, who put at our disposal his memoirs, a fundamental document of the issue in question. He protests his non-historian status, which we respect. He also protests his unshakable belief that there was a lot of good in the Soviet aggression, that basic elements of the Hungarian events were of a counter-revolutionary nature, that Horthyist officers and many émigrés participated in events and that masses of Western weapons poured into Hungary. None of these claims have ever been proved. They are simply not true. But naturally, not being a historian, the general did not conduct research but relied on his memory. He believed and still believes in what he wrote. On October 22, 1992, at a reception given at the Hungarian Embassy in Moscow, he faced Árpád Göncz, president of the Hungarian Republic, who after an extended conversation with the general said, "...(in 1956) the Hungarian and the Russian people did not go to war against each other, but that one fought for its leaders, the other against its leaders." "I did not challenge this very questionable statement," writes the general at the end of his memoirs. In other words, more than four decades after the events, he still does not see the light. Yet he deserves our respect, since he seems to be an impeccably honest man, and we fully agree with his final words:

"Between our peoples reconciliation, understanding and peace should prevail."

If this volume, in addition to its academic merits, contributes even one bit to such an evolution, it was worth the labor we invested in it.

Highland Lakes, New Jersey, U.S.A., March 15, 1998

Dr. Béla K. Király
Editor in Chief

"Without the whole truth I cannot bring prime elements of progress, such as the examination of conscience, remorse and forgiveness, into play."

(*Russian President Boris Yeltsin,*
from his November 11, 1992,
speech to the Hungarian Parliament)

Abbreviations

ÁVH — State Security Authorities
ÁVO — State Security Intelligence
CP — Communist Party
ELTE — Eötvös Loránd University of Sciences
HAS — Hungarian Academy of Sciences
HSWP — Hungarian Socialist Workers Party
HWP — Hungarian Workers Party
MEFESZ — Hungarian University and College Student United Organization
MoD — Minister of Defense
NÉKOSZ — National Alliance of People's Colleges
UN — United Nations

ADDITIONAL DATA ON THE HISTORY OF THE SOVIET MILITARY OCCUPATION

Jenő Györkei and Miklós Horváth

Retired Lieutenant General Yevgeny Ivanovich Malashenko writes, "...the opinion of those on the other side of the barricades will always remain somehow subjective, and there will be certain inadequacies... but this is understandable..."

In our introductory study, which points out the inadequacies resulting from subjective elements, lack of sources, and the wear and tear that 40 years have wreaked on the memory, as well as concentrating on questions surrounding the presence of Soviet troops in Hungary and the circumstances of their deployment, we seek the truth.

Soviet Troops in Hungary after World War II

The stationing of Soviet troops in Hungary after 1945 was allowed for by the agreement of the Allied Powers. It was then confirmed by the peace treaty concluded between Hungary and the victors on February 10, 1947. One clause of this treaty allowed for troops, whose composition and size was decided by the Soviet Union, to stay in Hungary while there were still occupying troops in Austria, and until Hungary's western neighbor had regained its full sovereignty.

From 1947 until 1955 there were about four divisions in Hungary, securing suitable road and rail links for the continual supply of the "remaining forces." So the command and staff of the 17th mechanized division was deployed in Szombathely, while the troops under its command were deployed in various garrisons in Transdanubia. An air division was stationed in Veszprém, consisting of fighter-bomber units; subsequently an independent bomber division was stationed in Debrecen.

All three divisions came under the supreme command of the Central Army Group Command headquarters in Baden, Austria.

After the Rajk trial and the deterioration of relations with Yugoslavia, Mátyás Rákosi, Hungary's Communist leader, found the number of Soviet forces stationed in the country insufficient and asked for reinforcements. In the autumn of 1949, the 2nd division of the Soviet Army, stationed in Romania under General Golikov, was ordered to Hungary. The headquarters of this division was in Kecskemét, while units from the division were deployed in garrisons in Cegléd, Szolnok and other towns situated between the Danube and Tisza rivers.

After his request had been fulfilled, Rákosi calmed down. He then called the commander of the 2nd mechanized division and his political deputy in to see him and said: "I was very nervous until you arrived. I was afraid! I did not know what to do, as we were living under Tito's threat, and I only breathed again easily after you had arrived."[1]

During the negotiations held in Moscow between April 12 and 15, 1955, concerning the conclusion of the Austrian treaty, Austria committed itself to a Swiss-type neutrality. Accordingly the Soviet Union vowed to withdraw its troops from Austria when the treaty came into force, at the very latest before December 31, 1955. During this period three infantry divisions and one air defense division, that is 60,000–70,000 soldiers, carried out their duties as an occupying force in Austria.

On May 15, 1955, the occupying powers signed the treaty for the return of an independent, democratic Austria, but after the withdrawal of Soviet troops from Austria the situation in Hungary–contrary to expectations–only changed inasmuch as the presence of Soviet soldiers was regulated and made possible by the Warsaw Pact, concluded on May 14.

In this international military/political situation–following the dissolution of the Central Army Command–the Soviet political and military leadership decided that the size and composition of troops stationed would be altered in accordance with the objectives and tasks set down in the Warsaw Pact's military doctrine.

Two mechanized guard divisions (the 2nd and the 17th), the 20th pontoon bridge regiment, as well as air defense and other branches and special troops were transferred to the Special Army Corps set up in September 1955.

The object of the Special Army Corps was to close and defend the Austrian border in cooperation with Hungarian troops and, in the event of Soviet troop withdrawals, to secure lines of communication. The corps was under the command of the Soviet Union's minister of defense via its General Staff.

The Hungarian party and state leadership offered Budaörs, its airport and barracks, to the Special Corps command. This would have been, from many points of view, much more advantageous than Székesfehérvár, but the Soviet military leadership, weighing its strategic importance, decided on the latter.

The fact that the Army Corps command and staff were stationed in Székesfehérvár meant that it was more difficult to house the officers and their families. Nearly half of the officers were billeted with Hungarian families or in rented accommodation in a town which had suffered serious losses during the war (40 per cent of its apartments had been damaged).

The deployment of Soviet military formations was determined by strategic considerations, which reasoned that in the event of an attack on the West or on Yugoslavia, the mechanized divisions in Hungary would break through enemy defenses, advance rapidly behind them and, like an "iron fist," higher tank units would then strike at the heart of the enemy. In such an event the Special Army Corps would have represented the first echelon, while the tank troops on Soviet territories, such as those in the military districts in the Carpathians and the Baltics, would have carried out the final phase of the plan.

The commander of the Special Corps was Lieutenant General Piotr Nikolaievich Lashchenko. In July 1956–long before the actual revolution–Lashchenko was ordered to prepare a plan so that Soviet troops could "maintain, defend and, in certain cases, restore the socialist social order."

The plan was given the code name "Volna" ("Wave"), while the code word signaling the start of operations was the word "Kompas" (compass). The commanders of the Soviet divisions were briefed and given the opportunity to gather any necessary data for the operation. But the special preparations for the higher units, units and sub-units did not take place.

The leadership of the corps, in a report sent to the Soviet General Staff at the beginning of October, had already drawn attention to the possibility of demonstrations. Counting on a deterioration in the situation, Lieutenant General Lashchenko already ordered the commanders to be ready at their stations in their garrisons in the middle of October. The Soviet corps chief of staff, Colonel Malashenko, arrived in Budapest on October 22 to become personally acquainted with the situation. It was then that the colonel learned that a demonstration was planned for the next day.

Since the Hungarian leadership, particularly Ernő Gerő, now head of the Hungarian Workers Party, could not rely on an definitive action by the Hungarian People's Army, Gerő asked the Soviet leadership to introduce the Special Corps forces to help put down demonstrations.

"Soviet Troops Must Enter Budapest"

The circumstances of the political and military decisions to introduce Soviet troops on October 23 can be reconstructed on the basis of currently available sources.

The Presidium[2] of the Soviet Central Committee was informed of a "massive demonstration" in Budapest and the events at the Radio[3] through Zhukov's reports. The majority of the members of the Presidium–Bulganin, Molotov, Kaganovich, Perukhin, Zhukov, Saburov, Sepilov, Kirichenko–all thought that this was sufficient to support Khrushchev's claim that "...troops must enter Budapest..."[4]

Mikoyan, who knew the Hungarian situation best of all, was the only one who believed that a Hungarian application of the Polish solution was the only expedient means available. He believed that without Imre Nagy's help the "movement" in Hungary could not be taken in hand. "This will be the cheapest way for us. There are doubts surrounding the sending of troops. Let the Hungarians restore order. If our troops go in, we will ruin things for ourselves. Let them try by political means, and only then let us send in our troops."[5] But Mikoyan's argument fell on deaf ears.

Khrushchev only went along with Mikoyan's proposals[6] insofar as he realized that Imre Nagy had to return to political life to restore order.

Khrushchev's decision–"But let's not make [Imre Nagy] president"[7]– is a striking example of how the Soviet leadership arranged cadre affairs in the countries of the "socialist camp." Because many members of the

Presidium stressed that the Hungarian situation—and its possible solution—was quite different from the Polish one, it was decided to send Mikoyan, Suslov, Malinyin and Serov to Hungary.[8]

The Hungarian Revolution and Events in Poland

Events in Poland affected the Hungarian situation in several ways. News of the situation in Poznan, the repression that followed, and the events in the second half of October all reached Hungary.[9] It also became known that the Presidium of the Soviet Communist Party had been informed on October 17 that the Central Committee plenum of the Polish United Workers Party, scheduled for October 19, wanted to make fundamental personnel changes—without the knowledge or consent of the Soviet leadership. In order to prevent this decision, the Soviet leadership readied its troops on Polish soil and its Baltic fleet for action on October 18. And on the same day, on orders from Marshal Konyev, the tank troops engaged in a show of force.

On the following day, October 19, the soldiers employed in the Baltic Military District and the 7th paratroop guard division, which would later take part in suppressing the Hungarian Revolution, were made ready for action. On the same day a delegation from the Soviet Communist Party's Central Committee, led by Khrushchev, arrived in Warsaw. Mikoyan, who was to play such an important role in the Hungarian events, was also a member of this delegation.

Documents made public and published recently—some of which have been mentioned above—prove that events in Poland and Hungary in 1956 were not the results of an internal struggle within the Soviet party leadership that the "hardliners," those who wanted a return to Stalinism, tried to provoke in order to seize power. This is illustrated by the uncertainty of the line taken at the Twentieth Congress.

The Polish leadership made the Soviet delegation to Poland understand that the changes taking place in the country would not go beyond the limits accepted by the Soviet Union, but they did demand the cessation of a show of force.

The Presidium of the Soviet Central Committee at its October 20 session decided, "Only one solution is possible—to put an end to what is happening in Poland."[10] But the means to do so—military or political—

had not yet been decided upon. Only the next day was the unanimous position reached: "Taking the circumstances into account, armed intervention must be abandoned. Patience must be shown."[11] Of all the members of the Presidium, Mikoyan, who was to seek a "political solution" to the Hungarian affair not only on October 23 but on November 1 as well, was the only one to stick by this argument.

The changes in Poland, and Polish independence ambitions, received great sympathy in Hungary, where they were regarded as a model to follow.

The experiences the Soviet leadership gained during the "solution to the Polish crisis"–as the above shows–influenced the decisions and ideas in connection with the "resolution of the Hungarian question." And significantly, the alerting of Soviet troops on October 19 and the orders given to the Hungarian army at that time served, from a military point of view–primarily for the Soviet troops–as a good starting point for suppressing the unexpected uprising in Hungary.

The notes taken at the Soviet Central Committee Presidium's October 20 session show that, during the debate on Hungary, it was proposed that "Comrades Mikoyan and Zhukov should consider withdrawing military units" and calling home KGB advisers.[12]

Comrade Hegedűs Makes a Request

The Presidium of the Soviet Central Committee met at 21 hours Hungarian time, as is clear from the notes. Yet the operational documents show that some of the Soviet troops were made battle-ready before the decision was made. One such unit was the 128th infantry guard division in the Carpathian Military District, which received an order to go on the alert at 19:45 hours, while the order for Special Corps forces in Hungary to be ready for action was issued at 20 hours. The time given for the order to go on alert set down in Marshals Zhukov and Sokolovsky's October 24 report[13]–which was forwarded to the Soviet Central Committee Presidium–was (falsely) recorded as 21 hours on October 23. This shows that the army, with or without Khrushchev's knowledge, had prepared to move before the Presidium's decision was made.

What time did Soviet troops set off if the first column arrived in Budapest at 2 a.m. on October 24? The answer to this is that the time given to execute the order, six hours, was more than enough for the Special Corps forces designated–basically the units and independent sub-units of the 2nd mechanized guard division–to march to Budapest from their garrisons in Székesfehérvár, Sárbogárd, Kecskemét, Cegléd, and Szolnok. The alert order to the Special Corps was in fact just a repeat of that issued on October 19 in connection with the events in Poland, which is why it was not entirely unexpected by the Soviet troops.

Khrushchev, meeting with the leaders of the East German, Czechoslovak and Bulgarian Communist parties on October 24 in Moscow to discuss the precedents to the October 23 entry,[14] said that when he telephoned Gerő on October 23 to invite him to the October 24 briefing concerning the Polish events, Gerő had told him that "the situation is grave in Budapest, and that is why he would rather not go to Moscow."[15]

Following the telephone conversation, Zhukov told Khrushchev that "Gerő has asked the military attaché at the Budapest Soviet Embassy for Soviet troops to intervene to break up the increasingly large demonstrations, the like of which has never been seen before"[16] [at the time they were still only demonstrations; the armed struggle had not yet begun–authors].

According to Khrushchev's statement the Presidium of the Soviet Central Committee had not yet given the go-ahead for intervention, as no official request had yet been made by either Gerő or any other "leading Hungarian functionaries." Later the Soviet Ambassador to Budapest, Andropov, telephoned to say that the situation in Budapest was "extraordinarily dangerous"[17] and to ask for the intervention of Soviet units.

The Presidium then commissioned Khrushchev to talk the issue through with Ernő Gerő on the telephone. "This took place. Comrade Khrushchev informed Comrade Gerő that they would fulfill the request if the government of the Hungarian People's Republic would set it down in writing. Gerő answered that there was no way of calling the government together. Comrade Khrushchev then suggested that the request be made by Comrade Hegedűs as the President of the Council of Ministers."[18]

Following this Zhukov received the order to occupy Budapest with troops stationed in Hungary and Uzhgorod [part of the Carpathian Military District–authors].[19]

Khrushchev–perhaps as a result of the Polish experience–"suggested" to Gerő on the phone that the Hungarian Workers Party's Central Leadership not meet "before the suppression of the demonstration" in order to avoid undesirable changes in personnel. As we know they did meet nevertheless. To the new Political Committee, in addition to Antal Apró, András Hegedűs, Ernő Gerő and János Kádár, were elected Imre Nagy, József Köböl, Sándor Gáspár, Zoltán Szántó, György Marosán, Károly Kiss, Gyula Kállai, with Géza Losonczy and Sándor Rónai as substitute members. They replaced István Hidas, Béla Szalai, József Mekis, István Kovács, József Révai, Lajos Ács, István Bata (substitute member) and László Piros.

Imre Nagy, despite the by-no-means-clear Soviet view on this issue, returned to the leadership as a result of public pressure. The Central Leadership proposed Imre Nagy as president and András Hegedűs as first deputy of the Council of Ministers.

Khrushchev, on the basis of his intelligence from Hungary, informed the party leaders that in the Hungarian capital "...the interior law-enforcement troops have behaved extremely well; they have suffered the biggest losses: 25 dead and 50 wounded. A Soviet officer was killed and 12 soldiers wounded. The disturbances are confined to Budapest; there is calm in all other towns and in the villages."[20]

At this meeting Khrushchev spoke appreciatively of Imre Nagy's activities. According to Khrushchev, Nagy had demanded that the population restore order, and he had signed an order to establish martial law with the authority to take immediate action against anyone who resisted. Nagy had said that the government of the Hungarian People's Republic had invited Soviet troops to Budapest, and that the good movement that the students had started had been taken advantage of by bandits who had stirred up trouble and shootings in the crowds, and as prime minister he demanded that arms be laid down by 1300 hours.[21]

Based on information from Mikoyan and Suslov, who had in the meantime arrived in Budapest, Khrushchev declared that "... the situation is not so terrible as has been painted by the Hungarian comrades and the Soviet ambassador. There is more or less calm in Budapest. The enemy is only shooting here and there from rooftops and balconies. In general the forces have vigorously returned fire, and this gives the impression of conflict. By morning complete calm will be restored. The Soviet Embassy is surrounded, and 30 tanks are protecting the building."

"Within the Hungarian leadership, both in the party and the government, there was a complete consensus of opinion."

"Imre Nagy is acting decisively and bravely, stressing that on all points he is agreement with Gerő."[22]

Representatives arriving in Moscow from the German Socialist Unity Party, the Bulgarian Communist Party and the Czechoslovak Communist Party "all agree with the proceedings of the Presidium of the Soviet Communist Party's Central Committee."[23]

"It is not accidental that disturbances have occurred in Hungary and Poland, and not in Czechoslovakia. The reason is that living standards in Czechoslovakia are incomparably better. In the Soviet Union more than 10,000 party members have been rehabilitated, and more than a million people have been released from prison. These people are not angry with us because they see that we have done much to raise the national standard of living. People listen to the BBC and Radio Free Europe in our country too. But if their bellies are full, they won't listen to bad things,'[24] summarized Khrushchev at the end of the meeting.

According to Imre Nagy,[25] Khrushchev informed Gerő of the Soviet Presidium's decision to employ Soviet troops when he arrived at the Party building in Akadémia Street.

Imre Nagy's June 14, 1957, interrogation record states, "Ernő Gerő spoke on a direct line with the Soviet Presidium and informed them of the situation. Judging from the conversation I was of the opinion that this was not the first such conversation. Afterwards an agreement was made by which Soviet troops stationed in Hungary would help restore order. Indeed, I was convinced from the telephone conversation between Gerő and the Soviet leadership that they had negotiated this issue before and promised help. After the conversation was over, [Gerő] announced that the Soviet troops had received the order to march towards Budapest. Those present said not a word to Gerő upon hearing this announcement."[26]

The other person pulling the strings–according to Miklós Szűcs's memoirs–was Tihonov, the chief Soviet military adviser to the Ministry of Defense. At around 5 p.m. on October 23, Tihonov called General Antonov, the chief of staff of the Warsaw Pact, in the presence of Minister of Defense, Colonel General István Bata; Chief of Staff, Major General Lajos Tóth; Major General István Kovács; and Colonel Miklós Szűcs, and requested permission to order the Special Corps into Budapest. Szűcs states–contrary to Malashenko's records–that General Antonov gave Tihonov permission."[27]

Following this, Tihonov, according to Szűcs, alerted the Special Corps and announced to the Hungarian officers that the Corps would be arriving in Budapest sometime after midnight.[28]

Andropov, as is also clear from Malashenko's memoirs, did not wait for the go-ahead from above either but directly instructed the Corps leadership. However, citing his subordinate position, they refused to comply with the ambassador's orders.[29]

"The Hungarian Army Has Done Badly"

On October 24 Khrushchev, based his accounts on reports from Mikoyan and Suslov which read as follows:

"Following the meeting with army personnel[31]–in which it became clear that previous reports by the Soviet Military Command and the Command of the Hungarian armed forces had overstated the danger–we continued on to the Hungarian Workers Party Central Leadership building. Here we negotiated with Gerő, Imre Nagy, Kádár, Zoltán Szántó and Hegedűs...

"Our impression is that Gerő in particular, but other comrades also, overestimate the strength of the enemy and underestimate their own powers...The situation is summed up by the fact that here [at the Radio Station–authors] Hungarian colleagues, primarily the state security organs, put up bitter resistance against the insurgents, and only suffered defeat because they ran out of ammunition, and because a newly arrived battalion[32] from the Hungarian army disobeyed orders and turned against them and attacked them.

"The comrades are of the opinion that the Hungarian army has done badly, although the Debrecen division has performed well...[33] Now the task throughout the night is to finish suppressing the remaining groups, who have dug themselves into the apartment blocks. As there has been a turnabout, a decision was made to employ Hungarian soldiers as patrols, to take all suspicious elements and anyone breaching orders in this extraordinary situation into custody and to guard all important targets such as (stations and roads).

"The Hungarian comrades, especially Imre Nagy, strongly endorse the use of greater numbers of Hungarian soldiers, police, and state security organs, which will ease the task of the Soviet troops and increase the Hungarian role in the suppression of the disturbances...

"One serious mistake the Hungarian comrades made was to forbid the opening of fire on the participants right up until yesterday midnight. ... According to our agreement, they demand that the population hand in arms within 24 hours to prevent the civilian population from being charged with criminal acts.

"Imre Nagy said that if they had spoken to the masses earlier and had informed them before, or during, the rally about the changes made in the leadership, events would not have gone this far. The other comrades listened to Imre Nagy's statement in silence...

"In response to our question of whether we could tell our Central Committee that the Hungarian comrades are masters of the situation and are certain that they can deal with it, they answered yes... It is our impression that all the Central Committee members with whom we met accepted in a friendly spirit the fact that we have traveled here in this situation. We announced that the aim of our presence here was to aid the Hungarian leadership, that is to say that Soviet troops are taking part in suppressing the disturbances, furthermore without friction and to everybody's satisfaction. The Hungarian comrades, especially Imre Nagy, endorsed this."[34]

The First Shots and the Occupation of the Radio Station

Today many people, even Malashenko and Kirov, know that the first shots fired in the struggle between demonstrators and the agents of repression were fired near the Radio Station building. The police and the local organs of the ÁVH (State Security Authority)—on the afternoon of October 23–first opened fire in Debrecen on protesters marching outside the building of the Interior Ministry's County Department, during which four protesters were killed and many wounded.

The protesters gathering around the Budapest Radio Station building were not informed of the Debrecen events due to the lack of time. One of the factors leading up to the shooting on October 23 was that on

October 22 between 21 and 22 hours, when preparations were being made for the following day's demonstration in the Budapest Polytechnical University, the commander of the Radio Station Guard (a state security second lieutenant from the 1st battalion of the ÁVH interior forces) had reported to battalion HQ that a group of university students were preparing to go to the Radio Station to read out their demands. Then State Security Colonel Miklós Orbán immediately gave the order to reinforce the guard at the Radio Station with a platoon. The platoon in question reached the studio before midnight. When the university students were informed that a strong state security force was at the Radio Station, they postponed their plans.

On the next day, October 23, the day of the protest, at 16 hours 40 minutes, Colonel Orbán led two platoons from the guard battalion HQ to the Radio Station; the second platoon was equipped with machine guns and masses of ammunition as well as rifles and pistols. There were already about 260–280 soldiers from the guard battalion and state security soldiers from the special battalion defending it.

At first 96 soldiers from the Hungarian People's Army guard battalion were posted there to reinforce the Radio Station guard. The sub-unit went in through the back entrance. One hundred twenty soldiers from the signal regiment arrived at 20 hours 15 minutes but got caught up in the crowd.

Of the 150 officers sent from the Petőfi Academy at 8:30, only 35–40 officers armed with pistols reached their destination. "At around 21 hours you could see a lot of people teary-eyed and red-eyed from the tear gas around the Radio Station. The gate was protected by the guard with hoses and warning shots. In the gate to the studio even officers from the Petőfi Academy were met with warning shots and water hoses. ..." says the Academy report, which adds that the officers who managed to get inside the building were "given the task of trying to convince the crowd, which tried many times to break into the studio, to stop the violence..."[35]

The circumstances surrounding the use of arms around the Radio Station building–on the basis of archival documents–can be reconstructed from the following. The first use of arms is recalled by Police Captain Östör, an officer in the police special branch battalion: "On the 23rd at 19 hours the Mosonyi Street barracks were in a state of alert because of the events. An order was given for a 50-strong police detail and a fire engine from the Kun Street fire brigade to proceed to the Radio Station building to prevent any possible disturbance by protesters. The police were taken there in two squad vans, but they could not go down Bródy Sándor Street because of the crowds, so they had to stop in Gutenberg Square...

At around 19 hours 45 minutes the State Security Authority (ÁVH) issued the first warning shots from the Radio Station building. As the shots began the crowd started to run. These shots were just warning fire... It was obvious that within the Radio Station building there was complete confusion. The crowd demanded that the 16 Points be read out on the radio, while the ÁVH opened fire on the crowd, the result being that not only the crowd but also the police suffered numerous wounds and even loss of life... The second squad van went to the Vas Street hospital with eight to ten badly wounded civilians and police...Then Police Colonel Sándor Kopácsi gave the order for the police deployed there to return to police headquarters..."[36]

"Márton Megyeri, a former state security officer, states that (after 20 hours) Second Lieutenant Szigeti cleared Puskin Street with 30 men and rifle butts. Then shots were fired from the National Museum building or from one of the houses, and one of the ÁVH soldiers was killed. More shots and another soldier and a civilian were killed. The crowd lifted up the dead civilian and "went even wilder." After this Szigeti and his men went back into the building..."[37]

"Police Captain Károly Lasso, confirming Captain Östör's account, stated in his report that the "deployed police formations tried to put a cordon in front of the gates to the Radio Station. The protesters at that time were not armed. The police officers tried again to address the crowd, commanding them to disperse, but to no avail... At around 22 hours the first gunfire came from the Radio Station, which resulted in several dead and wounded among the police in the crowd, as well as civilians. When it became obvious that the deployed police forces could not break away from the crowd, the police battalion withdrew between 23 and 24 hours..."[38]

Colonel László Zólomy, who had been sent from the Ministry of Defense to the Radio Station with a chemical-weapons company and who was arrested after the revolution and imprisoned, provided this account in his confession: "Since I did not know what was going on, at the studio I sent the company commander to the studio entrance from the

National Museum garden with a vehicle while I, in another vehicle, came down from the other end of Bródy Sándor Street. When I got to the corner of Szentkirályi and Bródy Sándor Streets at about 21 hours I saw that the state security forces' soldiers were advancing in a chain, shooting and coming towards us, clearing Bródy Sándor Street. I told the soldiers to get out of the vehicle and gave the order to follow me, then I set out to the studio through the lines. Meanwhile I heard from the crowd that two of them had died..."[39]

At the time of the colonel's arrival no direct danger threatened the Radio Station.[40] "I did not experience any armed resistance from the protesters," confessed Colonel Zólomy during the investigation, "and since no permission had been given by the government or party to use arms against the protesters, I forbade the use of arms against the crowd around the building and only allowed the use of arms if the crowd forcibly entered the building. I thought this was necessary because I realized that there were several dead and wounded in the street, which intensified the tension in the crowd towards the studio guards...Until the arrival of the Piliscsaba regiment, there was no trace of armed resistance against the Studio..."[41]

In Police Captain Östör's summary report on the period following the arrival of the Piliscsaba regiment, he writes that Hungarian tanks arrived at the Radio Station at 21 hours. An officer carrying a national flag wanted to address the people from the atop one of the tanks, but he was shot down from the Radio Station building. "It is also possible that the shots were fired from elsewhere in the confusion of fire from all over the street..."[42] the police captain reckoned.

The direction of the shots that felled the officer on the tank becomes clear from ÁVH Captain J. M.'s report, in which he mentions that—on seeing that the tanks arriving at the Radio Station were on the side of the protesters—he personally gave the order to a rank-and-file soldier to shoot the major who was "giving a welcoming address" to the crowd from the top of one of the tanks. The state security soldier obeyed the order.[43]

To the question of "Who shot first?" the confession of Captain Gy. B. from the Budapest battalion may be decisive: "It must have been about 21:30 hours when several army and state security officers coming out from the entrance of the Radio Station fired warning shots, scattering the crowd from Bródy Sándor Street...I met Colonel Zólomy once during my time at the Radio Station, in the Radio Station's courtyard before the battle, and he asked me why the crowd was following me. I told him that it was probably because I had fired..."[44] Because of the captain's actions he was investigated by the guard battalion's Revolutionary Military Council after October 28.

During the battle the rebels entered the building through the fire wall in the attic of the neighboring building, and later by breaking through the scullery wall in the cellar. The crowd, recovering its wits from the gunfire and explosions which had also claimed lives at the Budapest Radio Station building, set off in search of weapons in order to enforce their demands and defend themselves from the violent authorities. The primary targets of this civilian search for arms were the barracks, munitions depots and arms depots in and around Budapest. They also soon took over and distributed weapons and ammunition from the large factories in Budapest as well.

When the Piliscsaba regiment arrived at the Radio Station, its commander, Lieutenant Colonel János Solymosi, stood on one of the tanks, said his name, and then announced that his soldiers would not open fire on the people. This announcement generated such enthusiasm from those present that several of them jumped up on the tank and embraced the lieutenant colonel. The soldiers got out of their vehicles and mingled with the groups of young people and civilians. The young people told them that before they had arrived, ÁVH men in the building on the Puskin Street side and at the Bródy Sándor Street gate had opened fire on them and that several of them had lost their lives. Not long afterwards shots rang out from the Radio Station and the neighboring buildings. It was then that ammunition arrived–the soldiers had not been issued ammunition on departure; instead, it had been transported separately. Ammunition was subsequently distributed to soldiers and civilians in Lieutenant Colonel Solymosi's presence. After this the lieutenant colonel ordered his soldiers to fire only at those firing at them. As fire was coming from the Radio Station windows the Piliscsaba regiment and soldiers from the Kilián Barracks fired on the Radio Station building. Both civilians and soldiers transported ammunition for those besieging the Radio Station in military ammunition vehicles after shooting had started.[45]

Following the intervention of Soviet troops, the fight at the Radio Station against the hard-line authorities became a freedom fight for a Hungary free from foreign interference.

What Was Known in Moscow of the Hungarian Events

In the following we will examine what the Soviet leadership knew and could have known about the Hungarian situation, on the basis of documents available to date.

Marshals Zhukov and Sokolovsky, in their October 24 report to the Soviet Central Committee, gave an account of how they had ordered an alert for the Special Corps as well as for the infantry division of the infantry corps stationed in the Carpathian Military District, as well as ordering them to cross the Hungarian–Soviet border and take over the main administrative and industrial sites in Hungary's eastern half, including Debrecen, Jászberény and Szolnok.

The Soviet military leadership also ordered one of the mechanized divisions of the independent mechanized army stationed on Romanian territory to enter Hungary. Its task was to control southern Hungary and to occupy the towns of Szeged and Kekcskemét.

According to Soviet sources 31,500 soldiers, 1130 tanks and self-propelling guns, 615 artillery guns and trench mortars, 185 air defense guns, 380 armored vans and 3930 vehicles were placed on alert and called in to "restore order" from five divisions.

At the same time the Soviet Armed Forces Ministry placed on alert forces stationed in Hungary–the fighter air force division and the bombers division belonging to the Special Corps–as well as a fighter and bomber division belonging to the Carpathian Military District. Therefore a total of 159 fighter planes and 122 bombers were on alert. Fighter planes protected troops as the Soviet military forces advanced. The bombers were on alert at their airfields.[46]

The Special Corps "seized the town's most important targets, continued restoring order, and cleared the protesters from the Radio Station district as well as from the editorial building of the *Szabad Nép* [Free People] newspaper and the Astoria Hotel. There is shooting in several areas of the town. A few dead and casualties have been suffered by both the military units and the population. A calculation of the losses is still being made. In the town the Soviet troops are cooperating with Hungarian state security and police forces..."[47] says the report.

October 25 had hardly dawned when, at several points in the town, the fight flared up again. The Soviet military leadership continued to sent its soldiers to certain death in tanks and rubber-wheeled armored vehicles which were open at the top (and thus were given the name "open coffins"), without any infantry support. A few times the Soviet tanks or mechanized sub-units experimented by employing Hungarian infantry to support them, but these trials ended in failure, as the following case shows

One of the Soviet tank sub-units in the Népliget (People's Park) and a company from the artillery military academy received the order to attack the Kilián Barracks in the afternoon of October 27 as well as to free the three Soviet tanks that were trapped near the Körút (Great Boulevard).

The commander of the school, Colonel Vilmos Koltai, ordered 50 of his cadets to carry out the attack by lying on the Soviet tanks. During the briefing several of the selected officers told Colonel Koltai that this would mean the certain death of those involved. They also said that without the reconnaissance data and without knowing the number of soldiers actually present in the Kilián Barracks, such an operation was irresponsible and could only end in failure and the loss of the personnel. But Koltai, absolutely determined to stick to the plan, was intransigent.

Reluctantly the officers carried out the order and lay on the tanks. They had hardly got as far as Nagyvárad Square when the rebels opened fire from Üllői Road. Then the officers, at the orders of Lieutenant Babják, jumped down off the tanks and refused to go any further. The operation had failed, and the officers went back to the school.

During the 1956 Hungarian intervention Soviet troops were trained and prepared to fight within civilian settlements in compliance with the experiences of World War II and the then-valid rules of war. However the highest political authorities decided that tactics "successfully" applied in the 1953 East Berlin events must be applied.[48]

The essence of this concept was that, by using technologically more advanced war techniques and a demonstration of force, it was possible to frighten and stop fighting groups which had come together spontaneously, were disorganized, had much less powerful weapons and were constantly changing position.

For this reason the Soviet Special Corps armored vehicles, T-34 tanks, arrived in Budapest on October 24 in the early hours, and began their "intimidating," but actually suicidal, maneuvers around the town's main roads and crossroads.

The Soviet and the Hungarian political and military leadership were not prepared for such a forceful, determined resistance. For a long time they did not understand why this already-tested method of combat could lead to a Soviet defeat in Budapest.

Later, as they recovered from their surprise and paralysis in the face of the serious losses sustained, they sought reconnaissance intelligence to prepare for an attack against the main centers of resistance and the armed groups. Intelligence would be able to tell what sort of forces they faced, and where. For example, they ordered tanks into firing positions which were relatively far from the resistance fighters' positions and then sent tanks to the endangered sections of the streets. The soldiers in the stationary tanks observed where the fire was coming from, which was aimed at the tanks going down the middle of the road as fast as they possibly could, and so worked out the density of the fire. This method caused heavy losses and furthermore was not always successful, especially in parts of the city such as Corvin Alley and its environs. The rebel fighters had formed a line of resistance down Üllői Road, from Nagyvárad Square to Kálvin Square, and along the Nagykörút, from Mester Street to Rákóczi Road, which was made up of more or less independent groups.

It became obvious to the Soviet military leadership that there was no hope of a quick victory while the revolution was concentrated in main bases, and so it was decided to quash these groups.

The Hungarian People's Army and the Revolution

"The Hungarian army was strong: it consisted of 120,000 men, approximately 700 tanks, 5000 cannons, and a few air force divisions and regiments. The Hungarians are not bad fighters, as we know from our experiences in the two world wars. This army ceased to exist in precisely five minutes," said Zhukov on March 15, 1957, at a meeting of Soviet armed forces stationed in Germany.

Kirov is no less critical in his study of the Hungarian People's Army. He reckons that a decisive part of the military formations and institutions in Budapest on October 24 went over to the resistance and did not carry out the order from Imre Nagy's government to suppress the fighters. Nor did they receive the order to continue active fighting from the military leadership.⁴⁹

Malashenko is more realistic about the army situation. He says that on the first days of the revolution, many rank-and-file soldiers and a few sub-units of the Hungarian army went over to the rebels, but that the majority of the Hungarian forces ordered to Budapest followed orders.⁵⁰

Given the sharply differing opinions on the activities of the army, it is legitimate to ask why the state and party leadership, frightened by the daring protest on October 23 and the resolve of the people, clung to a foreign power, to the armed might of the Soviet Union, to resist the people. Why didn't they or couldn't they use the entire Hungarian army against the people? Why was it that those forces which, even in their everyday life, belonged to the people did not fight for the people until October 28, until the victory of the uprising? And after November 4, why didn't the army defend the achievements of that revolution?

These are important questions which the authors cannot answer completely within the framework of this study, but which cannot be ignored nevertheless—in order to present a more complete picture of the circumstances surrounding the deployment of Soviet troops, and to examine the Hungarian army's activities and the practical effect the army had on the process of the revolution.

Obviously the "Communist Party's army" would not be unaffected by a social crisis that touched and mobilized the entire country. In the period running up to the revolution, changes had been made in the Hungarian People's Army that affected the events to follow. In 1955–56 there was a significant decrease in army effectiveness, and considerable reorganization took place. The Council of Ministers wanted to reduce the army of 150,000 men by a further 15,000, and within this, the number of officers by 4500.⁵¹

Only one military organization remained unaltered by the "Organizational Changes"⁵² made in the army during the autumn of 1956. Forty-nine of the higher units, units and institutions were closed, 290 were integrated into other staffs, while 21 were moved to other garrisons. During this period nine new military organizations were established.

Prior to the revolution the Hungarian People's Army consisted of two infantry corps–the 3rd and the 6th–containing 3 infantry and 2 mechanized divisions. A total of 12 infantry, 5 mechanized, 3 tank, 12 artillery and 5 assault gun regiments were in a state of war preparedness. Apart from the above, out of the framework of the 8th infantry division, 2 infantry, 1 mechanized, 1 medium tank, 1 artillery and 1 tank assault gun regiments could be mobilized if needed.

The situation was further confused by the fact that not all military organizations had been deactivated by the time of the revolution. Thus 18 of the remaining regiments wound up under the command of other divisions during this time. They were also significantly limited by the fact that the staff changes had only just begun. In most of the formations designated for closure, military service had come to an end, but new recruits had not yet been called up. This meant that the effectiveness in a regiment hardly added up to 5600 men, hardly more than a full battalion.

The officers from the military schools had just had their graduation, and newly appointed officers and cadets from military schools were on vacation. Part of the officer corps was being deactivated, while the other part was in a state of uncertainty because by October 10 only 55% of the planned reductions were completed.

These are important facts given that in Budapest the law enforcement forces depended on the military schools and academies. Apart from the above institutions there was no military force of any significance.

The approval in September 1956 of the order to create a new structure and reorganize the army shows that the outbreak of the revolution was unexpected among some in the highest political leadership. The army, which was in a complete state of reorganization, could not be deployed without certain limitations, even under the most unified and determined leadership.

One of the reasons for this was the great fluctuations in the officer corps, which meant that even in the highest-ranking officer circles, there was a permanent sense of insecurity. The life of a professional soldier, the formation of a military career, depended on decisions which ignored the law. The great bitterness in these military circles was also increased by the counter-espionage services' often arbitrary proceedings, which in many cases brought discredit on the commanders. The roots of the general hostility to the State Security Authority (ÁVH) during the revolution can also be found here.

Under such circumstances many previously active officers had become politically passive, watching the political situation, and within it the improvement of their own fate, as outside observers.

One of the basic tasks of the Hungarian People's Army was to defend the state and social order against "internal enemy forces," but public law enforcement was not part of the army's training. The army's plans concerning law enforcement–documents seen by Malashenko–have not yet come to light. Their contents may perhaps be revealed by the "Fundamental Proposal"[53] prepared by the General Staff for the Hungarian Workers Party Political Committee on October 17, 1953, in which the objective of the law enforcement forces earmarked for reorganization in the Hungarian People's Army had been designated as the following: "To support the armed forces of the Ministry of the Interior and to cooperate with them in cases when the Ministry's armed forces are not capable of fulfilling their duties to maintain law and order, protect the security of the People's Republic and defend the most important targets and locations."

In the proposal, "in the event of enemy movements inside the country," the law enforcement tasks of the Hungarian Army included:

— the increased protection and defense of barracks, military objectives, warehouses, premises, etc.,
— to relieve and reinforce the troops and guards belonging to the Ministry of the Interior which safeguard the operation of national and important local party and government buildings, as well as industrial, transport, communication and other plants in cases when "the special skills of the law enforcement forces are needed elsewhere."

The armed forces were to take part in the "liquidation of possible internal enemy movements" alongside the Interior Ministry's troops if:

"1. The force of the Interior Ministry's troops does not prove strong enough or
"2. The Ministry's troops are not expected to arrive at the site of the disturbance within a short time, and their tardiness means an increase in danger."

According to the proposal, the organization of the army's security services was carried out by the garrison commanders in Greater Budapest, and the country's important political, state, and economic centers by the chief of staff, in cooperation with the appropriate Ministry organs. The plan also stated that the "commanders of the Ministry's armed troops could not bring pressure to bear on the execution of tasks by army troops and their commanders."

The cooperation of the army in securing public order could be requested by the commanders of the Ministry's armed troops, by the community, city, district and local party and state organs and the leaders of the Ministry of the Interior's County Departments. But only the minister of defense, the chief of staff and the garrison commanders had the authority to give the go-ahead.[54]

On October 20, 1956, increased security regulations were introduced in the Hungarian People's Army, as a result of the fear that the events during the Polish United Workers Party Plenum would have repercussions in Hungary. Guards were reinforced and law enforcement plans were refined. Liaison officers belonging to the Political Department of the Hungarian People's Army were posted to the army corps and divisional commands, where they carried out orders until 17 hours on October 21. The liaison officers were given extraordinary powers; in certain cases they could even remove commanders from their posts. The necessity of restoring political officers to their previous posts as co-commanders also came up in the plan. The orders given then were retracted on the following day, October 21, as unnecessary.

We believe that the military leadership did not recognize the aims and significance of the processes and movements taking place in the country and did not fear any unexpected changes. That is why the army was surprised by the enormous dissatisfaction expressed in the demonstrations and the implacable hatred for those forces blocking basic social change.

Army officers, aware of the tense contradictions in society and knowing the objectives for social change adopted in the spirit of the reform-communist Soviet Twentieth Party Congress, became enthusiastic supporters of the movements that drafted the demands of the majority.

This is proved by the fact that, on October 22, delegates from the military academies and military schools in Budapest appeared at the university meetings, made contact with the organizers of the university protests and accepted the demands laid out in the points.

On the morning of October 23, an ad hoc meeting was held in the Petőfi Academy (Political Officer Training School), and an appeal was sent to the university students:

"We, the officers and students at the military academy named after the passionate freedom fighter Sándor Petőfi, agree with the Hungarian university students' legitimate and just demands and support them. In our oath we are the sons of the people, and we made an oath to the people. We will fight through hell and high water for the people."

This appeal was sent to the universities, where it was read out with great enthusiasm at the meetings. It was then that the slogan "The army is with us!" was born. At the same time demands for certain changes in the party and army leadership were made in the Zrínyi Miklós Military Academy: the students took up the issue of the Soviet troops' presence in the country and demanded a change in the uniforms. Delegates from the two academies sent a telegram to the Polish Military Academy expressing their sympathy with the changes taking place in Poland.

The Army leaders did not take the signs of protest seriously, accusing anyone who expressed anxiety of overreacting, and on the afternoon of the 23rd they decided that if the Army could not participate as an organization in the demonstration, individual soldiers could take part in the protest "to help calm the crowd."

They did not order any preparations during the preceding days, saying that "panic must not be provoked." Officers put down their service weapons, and it was only that afternoon that a few important leaders were ordered to the Ministry of Defense.

From the beginning of the initially forbidden and then "permitted" protest, history was on the side of the people. The students did not pay much attention to the Interior Minister's prohibition; indeed, the prohibition only strengthened the movement. The protest broke the barriers of fear.

The slogans of the reformers rang louder and clearer: "Into the Danube with Rákosi, into the government with Imre Nagy! Whoever is Hungarian is with us! Russkies out!" shouted the huge, swelling crowd gathered outside Parliament.

Thousands gathered at other points in the city. The protesters toppled Stalin's statue, and at around 21 hours the armed struggle started against the defenders of the Radio Station.

The "Division of Labor" Changes

The Hungarian political and military leadership–parallel with the appeal for Soviet aid–ordered the alert in the Ministry of Defense staff and the troops of the Hungarian People's Army.

At the beginning ammunition was not given to the formations in Budapest, and those ordered up to the capital–as we saw at the Radio Station–were forbidden to use weapons. Thus several waves of Hungarian soldiers were not capable of preventing the spread of the armed struggle and either watched the occupation of the Radio Station passively or helped the insurgents by passing out arms or changing sides at the beginning of the fight against the Soviet troops in Budapest.

The Military Committee[55] set up by the party leadership took over the control of the armed forces on the first days of the revolution and tried to "bring the army into public law enforcement," arming communists and workers, organizing and ensuring cooperation between Hungarian and Soviet troops.

The Military Committee influenced the activities of the army mainly by issuing ministerial orders that expressed the intentions of the political leadership. That is, it contributed in part to the planning and preparation of military actions carried out in Budapest. It also forwarded the requests and expectations of the Soviet and Hungarian military leadership to the political leaders.

Such "deployment" of military forces made it obvious to the upper leadership that the majority of soldiers were passive and that a few even supported the revolution. That reinforced the leaders' mistrust of the Hungarian People's Army. The disorganization of the police force meant that leaders relied on the ÁVH units and the weapons of the Soviet army to suppress the so-called "counter-revolution."

The low morale of the army, resulting from its close ties with the people and its obvious inner divisions, meant that it simply could not be deployed against the rebels. The political and military leadership could not be certain that the troops would obey orders.

That is why the "division of labor" between Soviet and Hungarian troops worked out and formulated during the first hours meant that the Hungarian army primarily posted sub-units, squads, platoons and company units to defend important party and state objectives, while the primany task of the Soviet troops was to patrol with mechanized forces, tanks and armored vehicles and fight the armed groups that were springing up around the city like mushrooms.

In fact during this period a few thousand people took up arms against the Hungarian and Soviet forces. They were present everywhere, not just at a few important crossroads and targets in Budapest. They attacked mobile Soviet and Hungarian armored vehicles and caused them many losses. The majority of the rebels were young workers with a smaller number of pupils and university students, but there were also a lot of teenagers. They resisted Soviet tanks with primitive combat weapons, handguns, Molotov cocktails and with a self-sacrifice which amazed the world. A decisive factor in their success was, of course, that the rebels knew that they had the practical and, above all, moral support of the population.

During this period the most active insurgents in Budapest were to be found in Districts VIII and IX on the Pest side, and in Buda around Móricz Zsigmond, Széna and Moszkva Squares.

Although a number of enlisted soldiers, and even officers, joined the rebels individually, no unified conditions for control and action came about. In the conflicts the soldiers drew on their own experiences, while the young people copied what they had seen in Soviet war and partisan films. Their leaders were chosen from their ranks on the basis of their bravery and organizational skill during fights. Later, in many places, members of the rebel units reinforced their leader's positions by voting for them.

Not even the use of force, threats, the introduction of martial law or promises could force them to give up the fight. They did not stop fighting but merely reorganized after they had been scattered.

Malashenko and Kirov are mistaken when they write that the insurgents were Horthyist officers. The majority of those in the armed uprising were young workers, intellectuals and students whose models were not the officers and gendarmes of the old order. Intellectuals were at the forefront of the opposition, followers of Imre Nagy, and at the forefront of the armed groups were party members and workers,[56] as János Kádár stated on November 2, 1956, in Moscow.

What can be read in Malashenko's memoirs and Kirov's study concerning armed émigrés coming over the Austrian border, policemen and

Horthyist officers, is all part of the political manipulation and misleading information fed to the Soviet forces until November 4, 1956, and later to the Hungarian population.

The émigré Ferenc Marosy, the "Royal Hungarian Ambassador to Madrid," writes in his memoirs:

"On Friday, November 2, Ottó Habsburg announced that sizable Soviet military forces were reported to be assembling in Galicia, obviously with the intention of invading Hungary. On November 4, His Highness rang me again and said that the Russian army had crossed the border and ordered that I go immediately to the Prado[57] and ask Franco, in his name, to send help to the Hungarian freedom fighters."[58]

Franco called his Council of Ministers that night. They decided to send a volunteer army to Hungary. Munoz Grandes, Minister of Army Affairs, commander of the former expeditionary force to the Russian front, the Blue Division, resigned from his post as minister, as he would have commanded the force sent to aid Hungary. Franco also ordered enough weapons and equipment for a division to be made ready at the airport so that American planes could take it to Sopron.

"Unfortunately," Marosy writes, "the generous plan was not carried out due to the shameful behavior of the Americans and the rapid succession of events."

In 1956 Spain was not equipped with planes that could fly from Madrid to Sopron without stopping for fuel. That is why American-loaned planes or a place to refuel would have been essential. The American government refused to lend planes, and the powers controlling the site for refueling in Germany forbade them to land. They could not have landed in Switzerland or Austria either because of those countries' declared neutrality. At the same time the American ambassador was ordered by Washington to do everything to prevent the Spanish government from interfering in Hungary.

The Policy for the Peaceful Liberation of the Captive Nations and Its Failure

The new U.S. administration, which had taken office in January 1953, had announced a "policy for the peaceful liberation of the captive nations," the aim of which was to force the Soviet Union to give up its

Eastern European conquests. Nevertheless, the U.S. administration was caught unawares by the Polish crisis and the outbreak of the Hungarian Revolution.

The propaganda organs serving this policy–especially Radio Free Europe and the Voice of America–fostered the illusion in the countries concerned, including Hungary, but also throughout the world, that the United States saw the restoration of independence to these nations as a central problem of East-West relations.

Yet in fact the United States's real ambition was to avoid an armed clash at all costs. The "massive liberation propaganda directed at Eastern Europe" misled most of the rebels in their quest to free the Hungarian people, because they believed that the West, and primarily the United States, "was just waiting for the moment when it could fulfill its promises and aid the freedom-fighting Hungarians or force the Soviet Union to recognize Hungary's independence by political means."

Instead, "Secretary of State John Foster Dulles had already rejected the possibility of armed American intervention during the Polish crisis. On October 21 he announced on the political television program 'Face the Nation' that the United States would not send troops into Poland even if the Soviets intervened."[59] In a presidential campaign speech in Dallas, the American secretary of state said about the Hungarian uprising: "The heroic Hungarian people... are resisting the deadly fire of the Red Army's tanks. These patriots value freedom more than their own lives. And it is the solemn duty of those people living in freedom to do everything possible so that these victims do not die for their freedom in vain."[60]

The United States did one useful thing by putting the Hungarian question before the UN Security Council. Yet at the same time it declared that the solution to the "Hungarian question" was unquestionably the concern of the Soviet Union.

"And so that no doubts are raised, let me make clear: The United States, when it speaks of the independence of the satellite states, has no hidden agenda Our greatest desire is that these nations, from which so many of the sons of our nation come, will regain their sovereign rights and can elect their governments freely. We do not see these nations as our potential military allies..."[61]

On the following day, October 28, at the UN Security Council meeting, the American UN representative–in order that the message would really get across to those for whom it was intended–quoted the part about the satellite countries in Dulles's speech. And on the next day, October 29, Charles Bohlen, the American ambassador to Moscow, confidentially drew the Soviet leaders' attention to the same speech, the most important part of which was, "We do not see these nations as our potential military allies." President Eisenhower even repeated this on television on October 31.

Christian Pineau, the French foreign minister, stressed in a speech to journalists in Paris on October 26 that "although it welcomes the Eastern European developments..., France does not wish by any means to get involved in the events of Poland or Hungary..."[62]

One of the representatives of the British government–on November 1 in Parliament–announced on Prime Minister Eden's behalf that "the British government has no intention of using the Eastern European events to undermine the security of the Soviet Union."[63]

So the Hungarian question was only really taken seriously by the UN. On October 25, the U.S. government decided that, along with its allies, it would raise the issue in the UN.

On October 27 the United States, Great Britain and France–despite the initial unwillingness[64] of the two latter states–proposed convening the Security Council to discuss the Hungarian situation. On October 28 the Hungarian question was put on the Security Council's agenda, but due to the lack of a draft resolution, a decision was not reached.

Forces Brought to Budapest Prove Insufficient

On October 24–25 the command of the Soviet Special Corps realized that they did not have enough forces in Budapest. The Soviet military leaders received no answer from any quarter when they asked why the police and the Hungarian army units were not capable of defending their own buildings and barracks.

As they arrived, Soviet units were sent straight out to fight and regained several objectives from the armed groups. Stations, bridges and some warehouses came under their control. The police force was disorganized and passive, the Hungarian units had received no decisive order to continue fighting, and many soldiers and a few sub-units had gone over to the rebels.

Even today the Hungarian People's Army is assumed to have been left mostly to itself throughout the revolution, and it is assumed that the troops simply never received any order or command.

But this is very hard to believe. General commands to the army were made during this period. The root of the problem is that the adjustment of these general commands to concrete situations and circumstances was very difficult. The commanders of units and superior units, in most cases, did not receive help from their superiors when it came to resolving real problems. To reach an individual decision, individual responsibility must automatically come into play. But this responsibility was not shouldered by many.

The situation of the formations directed to Budapest is well reflected in the report by the 33rd tank regiment, which states: "We are of the opinion that under no circumstances should the leadership of the army be (as) decentralized as it has been in recent times. Under no circumstances is it permissible that a unit should be as atomized as the 33rd tank regiment was recently."[65]

But the report written by the commander of the 7th mechanized division for the 6th Eger mechanized regiment speaks volumes: "... the 6th mechanized regiment's Budapest activities were controlled by the Ministry of Defense and certain unknown organs; therefore its activities were not known to the division staff..."[66]

The reports, commands and orders issued on the radio at this time, far from easing the situation, actually made it more difficult for the commanders.

One example is the Council of Ministers' report, read out on October 24 at 16:30–on Kossuth Radio–announcing a curfew, forbidding public meetings and saying that "the public law enforcement organs have been ordered to act with the full force of the law against any infringement of this decree...,'[67] only to be rescinded by the minister of the interior two hours later with the proviso that, because the "clean-up of the looting counter-revolutionary groups is still going on, people can go out onto the streets before 9 o'clock only on emergency business..."[68] The political and military leadership were completely misinformed if they imagined that the uprising could be suppressed by 9 o'clock.

On the same day–at 8:45–the decision to introduce martial law was announced, which decreed that "actions intended to overthrow the People's Republic, revolt, incitement, summoning and abetting revolt, murder, killings, arson, the possession of explosives or their use are crimes; violence against the authorities, possession of arms without a permit ... are crimes which must be punished on pain of death..."[69] Not quite four hours later Imre Nagy, in his address to the Hungarian people, said that those who laid down their arms and gave up the fight before 14 hours would not be court-martialed. At 14:08 the deadline was then modified to 18 hours.[70]

This behavior was further reinforced by the commanding staff's already great uncertainty and contributed to the breakup of the Hungarian army. In the first days the majority of commanders organized the defense of barracks and other objectives, increased sentries, organized patrols, organized the closure of main roads and made contact with the leading judicial, police and political organs. The higher command sent some of the staff officers into the ranks to help commanders.

On October 24 in Budapest, the forces belonging to the Hungarian People's Army units–approximately 6500 men–were sent into combat in three waves. In the first wave a total of 2429 men were sent out to defend and take back five military and nine civilian targets on 23 occasions. In the second deployment 2361 men were ordered to take five military and eight civilian objectives on 16 occasions. In the third wave–for three military and three civilian objectives–389 men were sent into action. The reserves at this time varied from between 100 to 400. The formation captured 360 people, 87 of them armed, between the morning of October 24 and the morning of the 25th.[71]

The number of Soviet troops in Budapest had still not exceeded a division. The 6000 Soviet soldiers, 290 tanks, approximately 120 armored vehicles and 156 cannons deployed against the rebels proved to be too little.[72]

On the morning of October 25, the 33rd mechanized guard division, ordered into Hungary from Romania, arrived in Budapest. The same night the 128th riflery guard division arrived in the same way from the Soviet Union. So by the end of the day, three guard divisions were active in Budapest–the 2nd and 3rd mechanized and 128th infantry. Their total number now reached 20,000 men.[73]

Lieutenant General Tihonov, chief Soviet adviser to the Military Committee, proposed ordering new Hungarian divisions into Budapest. Since it was likely that the uprising would spread to the provincial towns, this proposal was never carried out. In Budapest the numerous reports and false alarms coming through overheard telephone conversations created real chaos in the military leadership, which resulted in further disintegration and disarray in the ranks. At the same time the important armed centers were not being liquidated.

On October 25, of the 7400 soldiers in Budapest, 4638 men, in 65 places, carried out orders. The deployed staff generally defended party, state or military objectives. A smaller portion was on patrol, but there were also sub-units that received the order to fight independently or in cooperation with Soviet troops. Of the Hungarian fighting formations in the capital, there were four–6th, 8th, 12th and 15th–mechanized regiments and one–33rd–medium tank regiment. The make-up of the formations was typical in that the number of the above five regiments in Budapest hardly exceeded 2000 men. Of the formations ordered to the capital, even soldiers from the 37th pontoon brigade, and the Dózsa Mechanized and Tank Officer Academy represented a significant force (704 and 773 men, respectively). Half of the soldiers stationed there were equipped with old, obsolete weapons. During this period 64 Hungarian tanks carried out combat orders in Budapest. According to surviving sources 31 men died, 34 were wounded and 175 disappeared from Hungarian army ranks by the evening of the 25th. The interior forces and border guards–1767 men–primarily defended the Ministry of the Interior and their own commands.[74]

The intelligence of the commanders was further obstructed on October 25 by the fact that in the Council of Ministers' report, read out on the radio at 6:23, it was announced that "with the help of the army, the state security forces, the armed workers' guards and Soviet troops, the counter-revolutionary putsch attempt was liquidated on the night of October 25. The counter-revolutionary forces are totally scattered..."[75] It is not known who carried out this deception.

Apart from what was actually experienced on the streets, it was also contradictory that three hours later the Minister of Defense, István Bata, in an order also read out on radio, commanded that the soldiers of the People's Army "should with increased activity and total determination finally liquidate the counter-revolutionary forces still found in our capital before noon today..."[76]

The situation was further complicated by the fact that Major General Lajos Tóth, the chief of staff, in the communique he released at 14 hours, commanded the troops–contradicting the minister's order–to "ask the crowd to disperse and to shoot only if they attack the barracks with weapons ..."[77] In this order there was nothing whatsoever about active combat.

Soviet Tanks Open Fire
Kossuth Square, October 25, 1956

The Soviet Communist Party's Central Committee Presidium, with the participation of delegates from the Chinese Communist Party's Central Committee, debated Mikoyan's and Suslov's "reports" at an extended meeting on October 26, 1956. In their October 25 report Mikoyan and Suslov mentioned that, "following the calm on the morning of October 25, the situation again became tense in Budapest towards noon."[78]

Mikoyan and Suslov, in their report on the events in front of Parliament, wrote that the huge crowd on the square "did not disperse even when addressed by Soviet soldiers. Additionally, their units, which were posted on the roofs of surrounding buildings, fired several times and set one of our tanks alight with Molotov cocktails. As a result, shooting started, and reportedly, 60 Hungarians lost their lives, not to mention the wounded."[79]

Contrary to what was in these reports, Suslov informed the Presidium on October 28 that the relationship between the population and Soviet troops had fundamentally deteriorated as a result of the Kossuth Square events on October 25 [Suslov actually writes October 24–authors]. "They opened fire [the Soviet troops–authors] and 70 of the population died. Many black flags were flown."[80] announced Suslov.

The part of Malashenko's memoirs concerning the Kossuth Square salvo also supplements and clarifies the above. When working on this part of the book, the author also looked at the thorough research done by András Kő and Lambert J. Nagy.

Participants in the demonstrations, which had been initiated by university students, set off from Kossuth Lajos Street in front of the Astoria Hotel. On the way they were joined by workers from the outskirts of the city, who could not get to work because of the irregular public transport service, as they came in from the Budapest stations. The crowd of protesting students was also swelled by people walking to work in the city.

The first big groups came together on Blaha Lujza Square, demanding the removal of Gerő, the withdrawal of Soviet troops and the formation of a national government. They arrived at the Astoria Hotel just as two Soviet tanks approached from Kalvin Square. The tanks could not go forward because of the crowds and so came to a standstill.

Following this meeting, students who spoke Russian climbed onto the tanks to fraternize with the Soviet soldiers. They spoke about the aims of the revolution and asked them not to shoot at Hungarians. They also distributed bilingual flyers reading:

'Russian friends! Do not shoot!

' They have tricked you. You are fighting not against counter-revolutionaries but against revolutionaries. We fighting Hungarians want an independent, democratic Hungary.

'Your fight is pointless: You are not shooting at fascists but at workers, peasants and university students.

"Stop the fight!

"Revolutionary Hungarian Youth"

The tanks did not fire; indeed, the young people persuaded their drivers to go with them to Parliament. And they set off.

A third tank coming out of Szentkirályi Street at this time followed the crowd. The young people jumped up on this one too. Most of the crowd were now going down Bajcsy-Zsilinszky Road; they passed Budapest's main police station in Deák Square, then went down Arany János Street into Szabadság Square, where it filed down Vécsey Street into Kossuth Square and assembled in front of Parliament.

Another big group of protesters arrived in front of Parliament by going down Kossuth Lajos and Petőfi Sándor Streets. According to contemporary accounts about 4000 people gathered on Kossuth Square; they were then joined by about 3000 others who were working in the area's plants and offices, as well as by curious onlookers.

Some of the protesters amassed on Ságvári Square (now Mártírok Square), while the rest were in front of Parliament, which was guarded by Soviet tanks. At Parliament about 2000–3000 people were gathered who climbed onto the tanks stationed before Gates VI and IX and approached the main gates too.

A third group of protesters stood outside the arcades of the Ministry of Agriculture. Quite a few people watched the events from the area around the equestrian statue of Rákóczi.

Parliament's guards tried to stop and keep away from the building the delegates sent from the crowd to present their demands. Meanwhile several of the protesters spoke to, and befriended, members of the Soviet guard. They distributed leaflets there too or pushed them into the slits of the tanks. Protesters decorated the tanks with Hungarian flags.

During this time–as Mikoyan and Suslov's report states–in the building of the Hungarian Workers Party's Central Leadership in Akadémia Street, close to Parliament, the highest party leadership was sitting in the presence of Mikoyan and Suslov, as well as Serov, the KGB president. Serov left the chamber and the building during the meeting.

Hearing of the events going on in front of Parliament and the fraternization between Hungarian protesters and Soviet soldiers, he ordered the commander of the armored company guarding Parliament to clear the square, which meant opening fire.

At Serov's order tanks setting out from Akadémia Street to Kossuth Square fired warning shots and departed.

Before the departure of the tanks, a burst of gunfire was heard from the intersection of Akadémia Street and Kossuth Square, which was followed by warning fire–issued from a tank rifle–fired over the heads of the crowds who had sought shelter around Gates I and II.

Panic broke out on the square. The protesters fled, trampling on one another. Protesters sitting on the tanks near Gate VI were not quick enough, and they fell at the next volley. Many of them died or were wounded. A shell exploded in front of the Rákóczi statue. The Soviet tanks fired at Parliament from the corner of Alkotmány Street and Bihari Street. After this a Soviet tank appeared on the corner of Ságvári Square; it fired a shell towards the middle of Kossuth Square at the height of the Rákóczi statue and at the same time sprayed the square with bullets. Later a shell was fired point-blank at the small rise by the No. 2 tram stop, and then bullets rained down on the people who fell there. Many people died at this spot, but those who were able to run escaped into the gateway of Kossuth Square 9.

In their research, with the help of photos, András Kő and Lambert J. Nagy established that most of the protesters died from grenades, with a smaller number dying from gunfire. According to the official register of deaths, 54 people died, but Kő and Nagy have identified 61 people who died on the square. Two Soviet soldiers died in front of Parliament and one on Akadémia Street.

According to Kő and Nagy's research, 282 were wounded in the gunfire and, apart from the 61 who died immediately, 14 later died of their wounds in hospital. In the afternoon the river fleet sailors and trainee officers–under a government guard–picked up first 22 and then another three dead from the area between Parliament and the tanks. Undoubtedly this is where Lieutenant General Malashenko's figure of 22 dead comes from. The dead on the square and those collected in the Ministry of Agriculture and the house at Kossuth Square 9 were taken away by the state funeral directors.[81]

Kő and Nagy's research is reinforced and supplemented by the contents of a telex message[82] sent to the U.S. State Department on October 25 by the U.S. Embassy in Budapest. It reads:

"Today [October 25–authors]–at noon dead and dying Hungarian women and men lay everywhere on the square in front of the Hungarian Parliament. They had been mowed down by Soviet tanks...The Parliament massacre happened after a few hundred protesters arrived there on the top of vans, armored vehicles, even Soviet tanks. 'The Russians are with us! They say they do not want to shoot Hungarian workers,' they shouted at the reporter.[83] The guys in the Russian tanks seemed to confirm this–they smiled and waved...But this love was short-lived and had tragic consequences. About 10 minutes later a Russian tank rumbled onto the square and opened fire on the protesters. The reporter saw dozens of dead lying face-down, and watched as the ambulance men, dodging Russian fire, took many wounded men and women away. The tanks fired not only with guns but with cannons. Armored vehicles rumbled forth but fired shots into the air, obviously intending to terrify the fleeing crowds."[84]

In a telegram sent home by D. Soldatić, the Yugoslav ambassador to Budapest, on October 25 at 16:15, the Kossuth Square events are described thus: "The protesters resumed their demonstrations. At 12 o'clock a big group of protesters set off for Parliament to announce their demands, primarily for Gerő's removal. Soviet tanks entered the fray. There are victims too..."[85]

It is worth noting that I. A. Serov's October 25 report, which he treated as a secret document, is missing from among the reports which have thus far come to light.

However, we do have the report written in December 1956 by Major General Lajos Tóth, then chief of staff of the Hungarian People's Army.

It states: "The Soviet troops received the order to liquidate the protest in front of Parliament. This they did. The people climbed up onto the slowly moving [sic!] tanks. Soviet soldiers opened fire on the rebels on the Soviet tanks..."[86]

Those who were killed or wounded on Kossuth Lajos Square on October 25, 1956, were all the victims of the violence of Soviet troops. In concordance with Y. I. Malashenko's claim, Hungarian frontier guard units (the green ÁVH) also participated in the massacre.

"We Increase the Number of Troops Active in Budapest"

"Apart from this," says Mikoyan and Suslov's report, "Comrade Serov saw shooting start between our tanks and a Hungarian [border] company in front of the party center building itself, which had been sent there to reinforce the defense of the party headquarters. Our tanks thought that the soldiers were insurgents. Ten of the Hungarian company lost their lives in the exchange of fire, and one of their men was seriously hurt. This all happened as the Hungarian comrades were sitting in party headquarters. Meanwhile one of our tanks' gunners fired a round from a large-caliber two-barrelled gun at the windows of the chamber.

"Inside the plaster started to fall, creating panic among the leading Hungarian party functionaries. As a result they filed into the cellar, but it was not properly equipped, so they went up again and continued working. The heavy fire increased the tension in the capital. In the afternoon peaceful protesters took to the streets everywhere with national and black flags. ...

"Comrade Imre Nagy requested that the number of our troops be increased in Budapest, primarily infantry. Comrade Malinyin promised the Hungarian comrades that we would increase the number of troops restoring order in Budapest."[87]

The Soviet leaders–according to their report–considered "noteworthy" the suggestion of József Köböl, a Political Committee member, that "in the interest of calm the Hungarian government should ask the Soviet government to withdraw Soviet troops from Hungary"[88] after order had been restored.

"We announced," Mikoyan and Suslov say in their report, "that in no case should the question of Soviet troop withdrawal from Hungary be raised, as this would mean the entry of American troops. We said that it could be announced that the Soviet troops returned to their former barracks after law and order had been returned to Budapest. The other members of the Political Committee did not support Köböl."[89]

At this meeting the Political Committee decided that a radio speech by János Kádár and Imre Nagy would be appropriate, in which, apart from several important issues, they would also briefly analyze the events and touch on the Soviet troop question too.

János Kádár had been promoted to first secretary, replacing Ernő Gerő. On this day Kádár was the first to speak. He announced that on October 23, "the initially peaceful, and for the majority of participants dignified, procession deteriorated a few hours later into an armed attack on the state powers of the people's democracy, hijacked by anti-Hungarian counter-revolutionary elements ... It is the unanimous belief of our party leadership that the armed attack against the supreme power of our People's Republic must be beaten down with all possible means."[90]

At the end of his speech, Kádár, touching on general Soviet–Hungarian relations–not directly on the issue of Soviet troops–said that the Central Leadership had proposed to the government that after the restoration of order, "it continue its negotiations with the Soviet government for a suitable and judicial solution for both sides to the questions between the two socialist countries."[91]

Imre Nagy, evaluating the situation on October 23 and afterward, said, "A small number of counter-revolutionaries have incited an armed attack on the order of our People's Republic, which some Budapest workers have supported as a result of the bitterness over the situation in the country."[92]

Later in his speech Nagy announced as the president of the Council of Ministers–to Mikoyan and Suslov's great surprise–"the Hungarian government has initiated negotiations about the relationship between the Hungarian People's Republic and the Soviet Union, including the withdrawal of Soviet armed forces from Hungarian postings, the basis of Hungarian–Soviet friendship, proletarian internationalism and the equality and rational independence of the Communist parties and socialist countries."[93]

"The withdrawal of those Soviet troops, the intervention of which was made necessary by the disturbance of our socialist order," said Nagy, "will take place immediately after peace and order have been restored."[94]

When Mikoyan and Suslov received the exact translation of Imre Nagy's speech, they wrote the following at the end of their October 25 report:

"It is alarming that this speech did not say what had been decided upon at the Political Committee's meeting–in our presence–but just the reverse...In the morning we will continue our meetings on this issue."[95]

What happened after Mikoyan and Suslov's report was received can be read in the brief notes made of the Soviet Communist Party Presidium's meeting[96] in which Sepilov, Brezhnev and Furceva were given the task of reviewing the issue.

Further Reasons for the Divisions in the Hungarian People's Army

The divisions in the highest leadership–which also influenced the troops– are illuminated by the fact that while János Kádár, the new Hungarian Workers Party leader, announced in his already quoted speech made at 15 hours that "the armed attack against the supreme power of our People's Republic must be beaten down with all possible means..."[97] Imre Nagy, speaking directly afterward, stresses a partial fulfillment of the demands–e.g., the withdrawal of Soviet troops–and repeated the government's wish to make peace with an amnesty.[98]

The army was also further weakened by the fact that when military patrols arrested armed civilians, in most cases they were ordered to release them again later on. Often arrested civilians exchanged fire once again with soldiers after their release. Several formations regarded the fight and the government's contradictory measures as a mistake. The silence of the Central Leadership and the personal experiences of the soldiers convinced them that those fighting the authorities and the Soviet troops were right. But this was not the case with the 37th mechanized infantry regiment, which belonged to the 3rd army corps unit. The commander of the regiment, which was ordered to Budapest on October 26, shot in the head four of the rebels who had been caught on the edge of the city. In the fight with insurgents, the regiment lost one, while the insurgents lost 19.

Grave consequences arose from the lack of unity among armed forces all posted in one place but all subordinate to different commands–army, police, Soviet troops. Székesfehérvár is a good example.

A Soviet armored vehicle had opened fire on the crowd protesting outside the Interior Ministry's Main Department in Székesfehérvár on October 24. Before the shooting the Hungarian army and police patrol fired warning shots into the air; the shots were misconstrued by the personnel in the Soviet armored vehicles present. The Soviet fire resulted in seven dead and 13 wounded, including police and civilians. Some of the formations agreed with the people's demands but did not want to hand over weapons to civilians fighting against the Soviets, and they did not allow any group demanding weapons or anything else into their barracks. As a result there were several armed conflicts. Some formations announced that they would at all times represent the interests of the people and carry out its will, and that they agreed with the legitimate demands of the workers. "Our aim is to put a stop to, that is avoid, bloodshed, but we stand united in the defense of our district and objectives,"[99] reads the appeal by the 32nd infantry regiment.

But fire exchanged between the population and the armed forces happened for quite another reason: some of the population, despite several warnings, did not take seriously the army's basic duty to defend military objectives and the weapons therein.

However, there were also formations who, not satisfied with the organization of the defense, issued various regulations in order to avoid confrontation. For example, on October 25, unarmed soldiers and officers were sent onto the streets in Győr (in western Hungary) to try to persuade the crowd to disperse by talking directly to them. Officers gave speeches to small groups. In the same town on the 26th, in order to disperse the crowd gathering in front of the barracks, 50 unarmed soldiers and an orchestra were "positioned" in the crowd and managed to march it away from the barracks with music.

The outcome of events was also influenced by the methods and means used by the population in order to achieve its aims. The armed forces positioned to defend objectives often only followed events, reacting to the crowd's activities to try to prevent the use of armed force.

By October 26 and 27, it had become obvious that the army had split in two. In both Budapest and the provinces, the majority of the formations only encouraged and strengthened the revolutionary forces by their passive stance, until a few formations–independently of their commander–used excessive force against the often defenseless crowd who wanted to achieve their aims by peaceful means.

Revolutionary waves followed successively in the provinces as well. Between October 24 and 29, Hungarian People's Army formations–according to incomplete data–came into armed conflict with the population in more than 50 settlements, on 70–80 ocassions. The number of victims was about 300 people.

The term "armed conflict" also includes the parrying off of attacks and incidents concerning the defense of designated military and civilian objectives, fights between the military and armed insurgents, and violence used against unarmed crowds (volley fire).

"The Military Viewpoint Overtakes the Political Viewpoint"

From contemporary documents–the minutes of the October 26 session of the HWP Central Leadership and later those of the October 27–28 sessions of the Political Committee[100]–we can become acquainted with a slice of the 1956 revolution's reality by following the particular phases of political decisions that were to affect the whole country. Through these we can get a clearer picture of the persons taking part in decision-making.

At the beginning of the Central Leadership's October 26 session, the platform represented by Ferenc Donáth and Géza Losonczy was annnounced. The most vital element of this platform, from a debate standpoint, was the rejection of the evaluation of the events as a counterrevolution and the recognition of a "democratic mass movement." A change in attitude to the events after October 23 would have eliminated the use of force as a way of dealing with the problem. It would have also allowed for a political solution to the sharp differences between the authorities and society.

On that day Hungarian writers and artists had drawn up a leaflet in which they demanded that the party leadership declare a complete amnesty, the disarming of the ÁVH, an immediate ceasefire, the return of Soviet troops to their garrisons, and that they entrust the Hungarian People's Army with maintaining order, that Imre Nagy set up a national government of unity immediately, that the new government stand at the forefront of the national movement, and that workers' councils be elected in every factory. As will become clear, these demands affected the participants in the meeting both emotionally and intellectually.

The basis for this possible shift was the János Kádár and Imre Nagy declarations made on October 25 which were quoted above. Ferenc Donáth, in his address to the Central Leadership's meeting, declared that in Hungary "there is on the whole a democratic mass movement." He believed that there were two main policies supported by the leadership–use of arms to the bitter end and negotiations; and two main issues–the broadening of socialist democracy and achieving complete independence.

At the time Donáth thought that those present agreed with this, and announced that the withdrawal of Soviet troops could only take place "after the restoration of order." "What at the beginning was the action of a small enemy group became, in fact, a popular movement. My view is not to resist with weapons, because then we will be resisting the people with weapons," said Donáth.

Géza Losonczy added succinctly: "My view is that the Soviet army should go."

Jenő Hazai in his address stated, "If you see the anti-government uprising as legitimate... then that means that we see all those who have lost their lives for the People's Republic as illegitimate." He said that he would never see those "who burned the red flag, who tore the red star of soldiers" as democrats and that "if the Central Leadership condemns the soldiers, the ÁVH, who defend the regime, there will be no one who can maintain order."

According to István Kovács those present had to decide whether to "continue building socialism or diverge onto the path of bourgeois democracy." He then stated that it was not possible to win by conceding to the armed insurgents and that they would sweep away Imre Nagy and the other designated officials. He declared that the insurgents were against the working class and that the Central Leadership had been misled in this question. The party could not voluntarily hand over power.

"Let them destroy us, but I will not vote for them...," he finished.

András Hegedűs did not agree with either Ferenc Donáth's or Géza Losonczy's analysis of the situation. He said: "Why are the armed groups fighting? Is there really anybody who believes that they have to fight with arms for legitimate demands? This is not what they want: they want to completely destroy people's democracy. Many actually want fascism. Arms must be taken up against the bandits... We cannot see the armed bandits as fighters for social democracy. Those who condemn to death and murder ÁVH officers... I believe this is not only about Soviet troops. The workers must be confronted...The radio must be forced to report on the various foul crimes...The night must be made use of. The flood will sweep away Comrade Imre Nagy as well. Through Imre Nagy it will sweep away the state and our people's regime.

"It would be a crime not to turn to the working class... I agree with the people's government, if we immediately call on the workers to beat the revolution...If we do not turn to the party, then there's nothing left to do but to suppress it bloodily...There must be a clause in the decree which calls on the ÁVH, the soldiers, the armed workers' brigades, the workers we have armed, that they must fight to the bitter end against anyone who has not laid down their arms before 20:00... we simply cannot disarm and isolate the Soviet army and the party," Hegedűs said.

György Marosán in his address declared, "Comrade Gerő is responsible–the speech was bad! It is true they were shooting by 6 o'clock. They were shooting, but we had not given the order to shoot. You gave the Military Committee the power to operate, and then you did not let them act...When weapons are at issue, you can't sprinkle holy water– weapons must speak for themselves... There are military forces: let them become military organizations, immediately. When you put together the government, I said that I would not be part of it. If you allow the Social Democrats to re-form, then the other parties will come into being, and then there will be anarchy. I would rather turn to the army... If the Political Committee does not give five people complete power by this evening, then I will resign from everything, then the leadership deserves to be toppled. Let's go out and tell the proletariat what is going on...

"Comrades Donáth and Losonczy, this is not the time to debate minor issues. I dare say that this affair will be a great lesson," finished Marosán.

Sándor Rónai remarked, "I agree with Marosán. A fight for communist unity, a loyal, hard struggle for the Soviet Union means dying or living with honor."

"I am for negotiations, but we must never forget that we must accommodate the proletarian dictatorship. We must initiate a fight. There are two options, to capitulate or not," said Zoltán Vas.

Sándor Nógrádi said that the Political Committee had issued contradictory measures. If they had not withdrawn the curfew, stated Nógrádi, then the fight would have been over by the 25th. He said, "We need 24 hours. The situation is now at its gravest. If they continue to assemble, then we are facing more bloodshed."

Imre Nagy, responding to Nógrádi's address, said that he knew of no Political Committee decree that meant that the population could not buy food. It was not possible to prevent the entire capital from buying the most basic provisions. Taking issue with István Kovács, he announced that there was no state of siege and that he did not understand why the curfew was issued in his name.

"The military position is more important to you than the political position. You issued the order despite the Political Committee," Nagy said to Nógrádi.

László Földes said that he accepted Nagy's platform and completely supported its execution. He continued: "But let's not go any further. We are taking the party and people's democracy to the edge of an abyss which will take ages to climb out of. The demands are not trifling: the workers' right to strike and withdrawal from the Warsaw Pact have nothing to do with the workers' demands or the interests of the working class."

Földes, considering this, said: "The main reason is to be found in the terrible policy of the Political Committee. We have pursued a grave and criminal policy since March. This is the main reason for our present situation. It is right that Gerő is not first secretary, the other organizational regulations I deem proper...

"But to back down in this situation," he continued, "would be mad... What must be done? I believe the situation is extraordinarily grave. This fight is not only against armed youngsters; many unarmed young people are fighting against us. I can say with a clear conscience that the outer districts–Csepel, Angyalföld, Újpest–did not join the armed resistance; they did not join and do not support it... We must examine the behavior of the Hungarian troops. We stupidly allowed them to go among the masses, who disarmed them in a friendly way, but since then they have received the order to defend military objectives, and they defended everything, indeed they won them back. If we let the rabble off the hook, then there will be oceans of blood.

"Demoralized troops were let down by the party, that's why they will leave their posts and much more blood will be shed...," said Földes.

Károly Kiss in his address said, "We must in all events negotiate and separate by political means the working classes from the insurgents whom they joined yesterday afternoon."[101]

He went on to say: "The Central Leadership must oppose anyone who does not lay down their weapons. We still have the forces to do this. We must summon the army, the police, the former partisans and the ÁVH."

Antal Apró spoke in detail about how that night they had formulated a military plan which they could have carried out with the right amount of people and arms, if they had issued a curfew by noon or perhaps on the afternoon of the 26th. He said that they knew where the "counter-revolutionary bases" were. He continued, "The officers and generals were completely demoralized by the order (curfew). It is not possible to lead in this way... We asked you to praise the soldiers. It was not done. You did not allow us to operate... I proposed several times that the workers be armed, but for three days I have not been able to do it. I have even asked for help from the Czech government... I will not go one bit further than Imre Nagy and János Kádár's speeches yesterday. The situation is tragic. I agree with Donáth, the masses are on the streets, this is our fault, the fault of the old Political Committee, the fault of the factions. Polish events have urged it forward..."

At the end of the meeting, Ferenc Münnich said: "The Politburo is suffering from incomprehensible and criminal optimism. I am not talking about individuals. Complete powers were available and still the situation was ruined. Even if we liquidate the opposition in Budapest, we will face a counter-revolution in the provinces. We announced on the radio that to leave one's house was forbidden, and then this was changed by the Politburo. Anyone who knows anything about war will realize that by this step we aided the counter-revolution. ..."

Ernő Gerő, who could not decide whether this was an "internecine war or a counter-revolutionary attack," proposed the introduction of the following measures: "We must take the press and radio into our own hands, or at least give them to a supervisor. If they want to prevent us, then there are the armed forces, we arrest them. At the same time we need a broad policy, a broad national policy."

György Nonn proposed introducing a total curfew.

At the the end the participants elected Imre Nagy, János Kádár, András Hegedűs, Ernő Gerő, Ferenc Münnich and Antal Apró to the directorate.

Then Gerő asked to speak. He announced that he could not accept membership, because in the event of failure he would be blamed primarily. "I will gladly fight with arms, but do not elect me to it," said Gerő. Gerő was not elected the second time around.

István Kovács stressed again off the record, "If we write that they legitimately took up arms, then there will be no proletarian power. The Imre Nagy government will be swept away in a week too."

"Two Possible Routes Lie Ahead of Us"

In his October 26 report to the Soviet Central Committee, Mikoyan set down the following alternatives in his reaction to the demands to change the Hungarian government:

"Two possible routes lie ahead of us: one is to reject these demands, not to change the composition of the government and to continue the struggle relying on the Soviet army. If we do so, we will lose the trust of the peaceful population–workers, university students–and there will be further victims which will further enlarge the chasm between the government and the population. If we go down this road, we will lose.

"That is why the Hungarian comrades feel that the other road is acceptable: to bring a few democrats into the government, believers in people's democracy, from former petit-bourgeois parties, from intellectual, student and workers' circles–five or six people in a government of 20–22 members."[102]

The expansion of the Hungarian government–writes Mikoyan, referring to his conversation with Imre Nagy–would involve not the inclusion of other parties but "the individual nomination of various democrats."

"In reply to our warning that the inclusion of bourgeois democrats is a slippery slope, that we must be careful lest they fall and lose the respect of the masses, Nagy said that this step is being taken at its very minimum, as a last resort, so that the leadership will not fall from our hands,"[103] wrote Mikoyan.

Analyzing Hungarian policy and party leadership, Mikoyan believed that "since they [the Hungarians–authors] are afraid of taking certain steps, we must put hard facts before them. We have already informed you of the Soviet troop withdrawal. We were not informed of the changes in government by the leadership–it seems that they only inform us once they have made a decision. We have asked Comrade Nagy, and he has promised that they will avoid making any decision on this issue before we arrive [for the Central Leadership meeting–authors]."[104]

He evaluated the situation in Budapest on the basis of his personal experiences, saying that the Soviet "troops are behaving with exemplary decorum" and their morale and organization was good.

"The military opposition has been successfully liquidated," stated Mikoyan, who added: "The troops have no direct military targets, only small dispersed conflicts, shots fired from roofs at various points in the city. There are small partisan actions and small bands of counter-revolutionaries in certain houses. The job of capturing the counter-revolutionary bands hiding in houses and the disarming of the population has fallen to police and civic organizations. This is the job of local organizations, not the troops, who can at most just help.

"The local organizations are in a very bad state: they cannot carry out their duties. We are taking steps to make the Hungarian comrades strengthen this front."[105]

*

"Why did the promise to negotiate with the Soviet Union about the removal of Soviet troops come up in your speech yesterday, even though we had already told you that the Soviets do not agree to the withdrawal of Soviet troops from Hungary and the majority of the Politburo rejected this proposal"? Mikoyan and Suslov asked Imre Nagy during their meeting following the October 26 session of the Central Leadership.[106]

Mikoyan and Suslov–according to their October 26 report to the Soviet Central Committee–were especially offended that they were only informed of Imre Nagy's announcement, which he made without their permission, afterwards. The Hungarian leaders present at the meeting–

including Ernő Gerő, János Kádár, Imre Nagy and András Hegedűs–replied that, before the radio speeches by Nagy and Kádár were transmitted, members of the Central Leadership had debated this, and "taking into account the working masses, especially the biggest workers' centers, indeed a series of party organizations ... in order to be masters of the situation once more and preserve their practical influence on the workers, they were compelled to agree with this–in their opinion slight and not categorical–demand to withdraw troops."[107]

Gerő also agreed to this, after initial hesitation, "as he could see no other way out of the situation." After this, Mikoyan and Suslov announced that they saw this announcement "as the gravest mistake," as the withdrawal of Soviet troops, they said, would mean the "inevitable entry of American troops."[108]

"We have stated that we are against any sort of promise concerning the withdrawal of Soviet troops from Hungary being included in any sort of statement by the Central Leadership of the Council of Ministers and that we believe that the relationship between our countries is an essential issue... Imre Nagy and Kádár both promised that they would not include Soviet troop withdrawal in Central Leadership and government proclamations."[109]

The Soviet leaders noted in their report that Imre Nagy was uncertain about the absolute necessity of organizing a curfew, and the prohibition of demonstrations, for the use of military force to work. "We [Mikoyan and Suslov–the authors] were decisively for it and the majority of the Politburo supported us. Today, and whatever the situation tomorrow too, a really strict curfew must be imposed, not only at night but during the day too, to prevent all demonstrations," reads the report.

One of Mikoyan and Suslov's most emphatic conclusions was that the "majority of the members of the Central Leadership and the Directorate are firmly for the suppression of the counter-revolution," that they considered it acceptable and necessary for the sake of wider public support that "a certain number of influential petit-bourgeois politicians" enter the government. And the members felt that István Bata, who headed the Defense Ministry and did not have the "necessary knowledge and experience," had to be replaced by Ferenc Münnich. They also felt that the establishment of Workers' Councils in the factories was for the good.

"Regarding the danger of capitulation, we feel that the majority of the CL is not capitulatory. The danger is rather that capitulatory local governments will appear in Debrecen and Miskolc. We will take decisive political and military steps to prevent this... We believe that the most important task is not to employ military measures but to win over the working masses."[110]

In their report Mikoyan and Suslov quoted János Kádár's CL meeting speech. Kádár said, "We must differentiate between the counter-revolutionaries who want to destroy the people's democratic system, who must be fought until the bitter end" and the masses, who had to be separated from them and brought over to the communists' side. "The vast majority of the CL members angrily rejected Donáth's address and accepted a decree declaring that a ruthless struggle must be waged against the insurgents. At the same time political measures must be taken to gain prestige among the working class and masses..."[111]

Mikoyan and Suslov told the Hungarian leaders to warn Donáth: "If he sticks to his capitulatory position and does not abide by the CL decisions, then you must take the necessary measures against him."[112]

"We have decided," said Imre Nagy, according to the report, "that alongside the armed suppression of the uprising, we must continue a policy to win over the intellectuals and the masses, we must go to meet the people's movement and national feelings so that we can stand firm at the head of the people's movement, and by doing so beat the counter-revolutionaries and preserve the people's democratic system." The other route, Nagy said, would mean that the masses would remain opposed to the leadership. Thus the leadership would be forced to rely on the Soviet forces and that part of the party that was isolated from the nation. This, said Nagy, would be a tragic path to choose and would pave the way for American intervention.[113]

In a later section of their report, Mikoyan and Suslov note regarding Nagy: "We must keep an eye on Imre Nagy's swings of mood; because of his opportunistic nature, he does not know where to draw the line.

"For our part we warned them (the Hungarian leaders) that no other concessions must be made, otherwise it will lead to the fall of the authorities."[114]

The extent to which the Hungarian leaders took Mikoyan and Suslov's warning seriously is illustrated in the Hungarian Workers Party Central Leadership declaration to the Hungarian people[115] about Soviet–Hungarian relations and particularly about Soviet troops. The following was declared, according to a formula decided upon by the Soviet leaders: "The new government has opened negotiations with the Soviet government in order to arrange relations between our countries on the basis of independence and non-interference in domestic affairs. The first step of this is that, *after the restoration of order, Soviet troops will immediately return to their bases.* The complete equality of Hungary and the Soviet Union suits both our countries' interests, and only on that basis can true fraternal, eternal Hungarian–Soviet friendship be built. Relations between Poland and the Soviet Union are to be based on this principle once again..."[116]

The declaration–in accordance with the agreement with Mikoyan and Suslov–also spoke of a government formed along national lines, the election of factory workers' councils, and an amnesty for those who abandoned armed resistance before 22 hours on October 26. The Central Leadership also called upon "communists, Hungarian working people, workers above all, armed forces, former partisans, the guardians of people's power" to "ruthlessly destroy anyone who did not lay down his arms within the given time limit."[117]

*

In the first part of Mikoyan and Suslov's October 27 report,[118] they notified the Soviet Central Committee of the circumstances of the Hungarian government shuffle and expansion, and then noted the Politburo's agenda concerning military questions as well.

"The report on the military situation," says the second part of their report "was given by Comrade Apró in a very confident tone. He announced, among other things, that 3000 Hungarian wounded were in the hospitals, and 250 of them have died."[119]

Following Apró's address János Kádár referred to the "disturbing situation" in the provinces and asked Mikoyan and Suslov if "it would not be possible to increase the number of Soviet troops."

"We informed them that there are reserves and that as many of our troops will be here as is necessary. Members of the Politburo were very pleased upon hearing this."[120]

Apró later proposed launching further attacks in the city and announced, "A significant number of insurgents have begun handing in their weapons; we have taken 700 rifles so far." When Apró said that "the situation in the provinces has started to stabilize," Kádár and Hegedűs, according to the report, "were skeptical about this."

"The Hungarian comrades have began arming party activists, who, as a result, have started to become more confident. They have decided to introduce armed party members to the city's police stations. They have also decided to appoint military censors at the radio and daily papers," writes Mikoyan. They report also mentions that Imre Nagy, while negotiating with appointed ministers, fainted and had a heart attack because of the stress and was "restored" with Validol, which Suslov happened to have on him.[121]

In the interest of maintaining in power the highest political and military leadership–on October 27 and 28–the armed forces started a final effort. During this period some of the soldiers defending designated objectives lost all control and responded with force and the use of arms, even to civil actions which were not that violent. The orders issued at this time were interpreted as the introduction of military dictatorship. The order issued by Lieutenant General Károly Janza–who had taken over from István Bata on October 27 as the new Minister of Defense–might have played a role in the decisions made by the commanders at this time. He ordered troops to continue their fight against the armed groups. The minister's command said, "Military units should not cease liquidating the armed centers and restoring order."[122]

Lieutenant General Károly Janza, replying to a question from the Baja City Council, denied in his report on radio later that day that Soviet troops were carrying out large-scale military operations in Budapest. He announced that military activity was concentrated in only a few centers.[123] Naturally, the minister of defense could not say that preparations were being drafted for attacks on the most important insurgent centers–like the resistance groups around the Corvin Cinema–by Hungarian and Soviet forces.

The Final Attempt

After the initial confusion, the political and military leadership–as we have seen–received an increasingly precise picture of the rebels' strength. They concluded that the turning point in the struggle would come from a focused attack on the most significant armed groups' positions. The most important precondition to suppressing the uprising, they believed, was to crush the resistance forces in the Corvin Cinema and its environs–including the Kilián Barracks.

They had already begun preparing for the attack on October 25, when the Political Main Division Staff said that they had managed to make contact with the Corvin Cinema fighters from which they had extracted a promise for a cease-fire and to disarm. The preparations for the attack were canceled.

To this day we do not know whether the report was baseless or if the rebels simply changed their minds, but whatever the case, no weapons were laid down.

So on October 26 they continued with the plan. But over the issue of deployable forces and means, there were marked differences of opinion between the Military Committee members and the army, and the leaders of the Soviet forces.

Before the attack, when artillery preparations were being made, many people voiced the opinion that any heavy crossfire around the Corvin Cinema would mean huge civilian casualties and that they could not take this risk.

Since they could not decide, they rang Imre Nagy. His reply was recorded in Major General István Kovács's notebook:[124]

"Do not shoot (with artillery) at the apartment blocks, as it would create a very difficult situation. Please do not carry the plan out in this way; avoid mass bloodshed. I'm afraid of the consequences... I will resign. The new government cannot solve the situation; other methods must be used to influence the young people."

The above text was translated by Major General István Gábor into Russian for Malinyin. The Soviet general's reply to Imre Nagy contained the following:

"Artillery preparations will not begin without a separate order. But Malinyin will bring reinforcements in, including heavy weaponry. Please take into account the answer which they (insurgents) gave when summoned to capitulate. They refused to peacefully give up the fight. They demanded the disarming of the state security forces and that the [Hungarian] army restore order. Provisional government, elections by December 31 and a general amnesty. Restore order [that is the present government] otherwise he [Malinyin] will take a military path."

Malinyin thus informed everybody that if the government could not "create order" with its own methods within the time limit, then the Soviet troops stationed in Budapest would carry out the attack independently of the government's decisions.

Further "solutions" came up: technical forces should be sent in under the Corvin Cinema building through the sewers and then blow it up. László Földes, a member of the Military Council, strongly supported this plan,[125] but it was abandoned for lack of a proper map of the tunnels. There was also a proposal to fly over the cinema in a helicopter and to bomb it from the air. But the majority did not support this plan. In the end the units preparing the attack were left with the task of drawing up details for an attack without the use of artillery.

This work began in the Ministry of Defense on the 27th between 19 and 20 hours. The leader of the Soviet Special Forces operations division called Major General Kovács and asked him to help draw up the plans for the attack. As neither of them knew the exact positions of the insurgents in and around Corvin Cinema, or their strength, they sought out a "Corvinist" prisoner in the cellars of the Defense Ministry and made him draw a sketch of this data. They then drew up their plan accordingly.

They agreed to entrust the leadership of the operation to the commander of the Soviet division stationed on Dimitrov Square, who was also entrusted with the tanks and armored vehicles for the attack. The Hungarian command agreed to provide a sub-unit of 300–350 men to reinforce the infantry under the command of Lieutenant Colonel Zoltán Tóth, the commander of the 12th Kecskemét mechanized regiment. This regiment had arrived in Budapest on the 24th, and its main forces were stationed at the Zrínyi Miklós Military Academy.

Lieutenant Colonel Tóth was immediately summoned to the Ministry of Defense. At the briefing his deputy, Major László Takács, and the regiment's operations officer, Lieutenant Albert Szál, were also present.

Major General Kovács, in the presence of the Soviet general, pointed out on the map where the Corvin Cinema was and then made a sketch in which he marked out the probable lines of attack. They decided that contact would be made with the Soviet division by the Szabadság Bridge at 03:00 hours on the 28th and that the attack would be launched at 04:00.[126]

At 22 hours Lieutenant Colonel Tóth arrived back at the Academy, where he reported to Colonel András Márton, commander of the Zrínyi Miklós Military Academy, on the task ahead.

After the colonel had listened to the communiqué, he said that while Tóth had been at the Ministry, he had received the order from Colonel

Iván Trepper, the leader of the Minister's Secretariat, and Colonel Miklós Szűcs to form sub-units from the officers in the Academy who would take part in the liquidation of the Corvin Cinema groups alongside the Kecskemét regiment.

Lieutenant Colonel Tóth noted that he thought this was a completely unprepared operation which risked the lives of the men at stake and had no hope of success.

Colonel Márton listened to this argument and telephoned the chiefs of staff. Tóth and Major General Kovács were already asleep. He reported their observations to Colonel Szűcs and proposed that the operation be postponed. Szűcs then rang the minister of defense, Lieutenant General Janza, and in the presence of Antal Apró, head of the party's Military Committee, informed him of what he had heard from Márton. András Márton then received the message for the troops to depart as planned. Szűcs called Márton back; he did not accept this reply and said that if Szűcs was that hopeless, then he himself would go straight to Janza about the matter.[127]

Janza heard Szűcs out and then gave the order for Colonel Márton to be at the Boráros Square Bridge at a given time, where he would be met by Colonel Szűcs, without giving any explanation. Together they were to propose a plan of action to the Soviet division commander responsible, on whose authority they were obliged to act. Márton angrily replied that in Lieutenant Colonel Tóth's place he would not lead units to the slaughterhouse even if they strung him up. This type of operation, Márton continued, involving the destruction of civilians and soldiers, a massacre, had to be avoided at all costs.

Márton wanted to prevent the operation. He called Mária Nagy, the second secretary at the Budapest Party Committee, and asked for her help in stopping the attack. Indeed he wanted to inform Imre Nagy too. But he could not contact him, so he expressed his doubts to András Hegedüs and asked him to go to Nagy and get the plan stopped.

The Attack Begins

As no other order was given, a 360-man sub-unit was formed, from which six storm-groups were formed, each of 20 men. The rest were formed into reserve. The transport vehicles were lined up on the 28th at

2:30, and the column went down Hungária Boulevard through the Népliget (People's Park), Nagyvárad Square, Hámán Kató and Soroksári Roads, arriving at Boráros Square at 3 o'clock at the Pest side of the Petőfi Bridge.[128]

The Soviets accompanied the two Hungarian commanders to Dimitrov Square to see the divisional commander, who then held a briefing for the commanders of those going into action.

The orders called for them to launch the attack from two sides. Major László Tóth would have been in charge of the attack from Nagyvarád Square down Üllői Road, while Lieutenant Colonel Zoltán Tóth and Lieutenant Pál Kovács would have overseen the attack from Kálvin Square.[129]

The Soviet divisional commander drew up the battle order so that first the covering sub-group composed of officers would approach the Corvin Cinema with the task of protecting and covering the approaching tanks. The sub-unit composed of three T-34 tanks, escorting the infantry, would then get to the entrance of the cinema opening onto the Boulevard where–according to the plan–they would fire on the armed groups' positions in the cinema building and the surrounding houses. Then another sub-unit of T-54 tanks would have set off. The six tanks would have lined up before the cinema and covered it with heavy fire– instead of artillery fire–thereby giving the advantage to the Hungarian assault troops, who would have finished the job.

The divisional commander also planned to close the "arcade" opening onto Üllői Road with fire too.

When the commander told the Hungarian formations to get into the Soviet armored vehicles–the "open coffins"–to carry out the plan, Colonel Márton replied that the Hungarian soldiers had not been trained in the use of armored vehicles.[130]

The Soviet officers announced that, as far as they knew, the Corvin Cinema had several entrances, and therefore they deemed it necessary to modify the plan of action accordingly.

As the divisional commander did not say anything about the cooperation of the groups and forces engaged, Lieutenant Colonel Tóth asked how, and with what weapons, he could lead and control the attack. Then the Soviet division's signals officer reported that the tanks did not have the radios necessary for communication.

Lieutenant Colonel Tóth—who, according to the plan, would have led the assault troops—announced that in that case the plan was impossible, as without communications equipment the tanks, covering and assault troops would seriously endanger each other.

The other Hungarian officers—Colonel András Márton, Colonel Miklós Szűcs, and Lieutenant Colonel József Kovács—agreed. They also realized that six tanks could not possibly enter the narrow entrance to the Corvin Cinema at one time.

After this the divisional commander rang the commander of the Soviet Corps. Referring to these problems, he asked that the attack be postponed due to the lack of reconnaissance data.

But the Corps commanders did not accept this argument and gave the order to begin the attack.

Márton again asked Szűcs to ring Janza, but Szűcs was only able to talk to Major General Kovács, to whom he reported that he thought the operation had not been properly planned.[131]

Kovács called back a short time afterwards. He said that he had talked to Janza and the commander of the corps. They had to be ready for action but await the final order.[132]

Since the order did not come, the officers ordered into action from the Academy and the Kecskemét regiment got into the armored transport vehicles as originally planned and drove a column along the Belgrád Embankment.

At the head of the column were three T-34 and three T-54 tanks; these were followed by covering troops and then two other T-54s and two amphibious tanks. In the middle of the column were assault troop vehicles, and behind them four to six T-54s; another four T-34s closed the column from the rear.[133]

Then, diverging from the order, three T-34s set off down Üllői Road toward the Great Boulevard to survey the Corvin Cinema and its environs. But these tanks did not return after an hour and a half, so the three T-54s which had followed them in the column were sent out after them. After another hour's wait, two of the T-54s came back; one was intact and the other badly damaged. The Soviet tank commander reported that the T-34s were burning in front of the Corvin and that the third T-54 had been shot to bits. Then the Soviet officers withdrew to confer. For a long time no order was given to the Hungarian sub-units.

Colonel Márton later went back to the divisional staff. The Soviet commander told him that they were at a standstill because they were still continuing their supplementary survey. Márton reported that the Hungarian officers and soldiers were tired. Since the divisional commander was indifferent to this piece of information, he rang the chief of staff but again received the order from Major General Kovács to obey Soviet orders.

After many hours of waiting, Márton again appeared at divisional staff, where they told him that the attack was due to be repeated the following morning.

On the 28th, at around 19:20 hours, the Hungarian forces returned to the Academy. András Márton only found out later that András Hegedűs, in accordance with his request, had informed Imre Nagy of what he had said. Nagy had then phoned Lieutenant General Janza at dawn and strictly forbidden the liquidation of the Corvin Cinema base.[134] Imre Nagy's order did not reach the Soviet and Hungarian troops who were preparing, indeed beginning, the attack. The order to repeat the attack had not yet reached the Academy.

The rebels managed to inflict great losses on the Soviet troops. They made every effort to disarm the Soviet soldiers who were, in any case, acting either independently or in small groups. Lieutenant General Lashchenko gave the order to resist more decisively. He warned the commanders of the units and sub-units that they would be removed from their posts if they allowed troops to lay down their arms or give up weapons and ammunition.

*

In Serov's report[135] to Mikoyan on October 28, which he later expanded for the Soviet Central Committee, he says that secret agents in contact with the rebels informed them that "the rebels have their doubts about further resistance. Their most active forces are for continuing the struggle, but even if they stop fighting, it is only for a time, and they will do so only on the condition that they keep their weapons in wait for the next suitable moment to revive the fight."[136]

Serov also said in his report that some writers wanted to contact the insurgents in order to persuade them to give up the fight. Then he mentions the disarming of the provincial organs of the state security authorities, the Miskolc lynchings, the activities of the "National Guard" that had formed in certain places–consisting of students, young people and Hungarian army soldiers–and the activization of the state defense forces dressed in Budapest police uniforms under the leadership of the new interior minister, Ferenc Münnich.

Serov announced that two Americans had said–during a conversation with secret agents–"that if the uprising is not liquidated before the deadline runs out, then at the behest of the United States, UN troops will step in and a second Korea will start."[137]

"There is calm all over Budapest, apart from one or two rounds of fire. But there are three centers where the rebels have dug themselves in."[138] Serov says, closing his October 28 report.

"The Situation is Deteriorating"

The Soviet Central Committee's Presidium–according to the minutes of its sessions–focused on the "Hungarian situation" from October 26 until the next meeting on the 28th.[139] In Budapest the Hungarian Workers Party's Politburo meeting was still in session when the Presidium started its meeting.

Following the opening of the sitting, Khrushchev stated that "the situation is deteriorating... Kádár is willing to conduct negotiations with the opposition centers... The workers support the uprising (that is why they [the Hungarians] wanted to change the label 'counter-revolutionary uprising.')"

Zhukov's report on the situation did not satisfy the members of the Presidium, and so Khrushchev saw the return of Suslov as necessary in order to clear things up.

Voroshilov said that the Presidium was badly informed, then he stated: "We are in a bad situation. We must work out our own direction and must get a group of the Hungarians to join it. Mikoyan is not capable of carrying out this job. We must do what we set out to do... We cannot withdraw troops–we must suppress the uprising completely. Nagy is a liquidator."[140] For the first time the idea that a group of Hungarians had to be won over in order to suppress the uprising was voiced in Voroshilov's address.

"The situation is worsening, slowly it is creeping towards capitulation. Nagy has turned against us," intervenes Molotov, who goes on to say,

"We must agree on how far we will go in making concessions... They have shut Hegedűs out, that is, they do not deal with us anymore. Friendship with the Soviet Union, aid from our troops–this is the minimum... If they do not agree, then we must debate what will happen to the troops..."[141]

As becomes clear from the speeches, an increasing number of the Presidium placed their hopes in Kádár as a key figure. They expected, indeed demanded, a solution that would suit the Soviet leadership.

"The Hungarian Workers Party's Central Committee Politburo should act decisively; otherwise we will act instead of you. Perhaps we will have to appoint a government ourselves..."[142] announced Bulganyin. Khrushchev spoke up once more, saying, according to the minutes:

"We are responsible for a lot. We must face facts. The question is whether the government is with us, or is against us and requests the removal of our troops. Then what will happen?

"Nagy said that if we take action, he will resign.[143] Then the coalition will fall apart. There is no stable leadership there, either in the party or in the government. The uprising has spread to the countryside. The army could go across to the insurgents...

"There are two choices. The government acts and we help it. Then all will come to an end quite soon. Or Nagy turns against us, demands a cease-fire and the withdrawal of troops; after that comes capitulation."[144]

Khrushchev believed that the worst possible solution would be the formation of a new government or "committee," and he proposed continuing to support the Imre Nagy government and the liquidation of the armed insurgents. At the end of his address, he asked a rhetorical question: "Should we support the present government if they make such a declaration?" He then answered it by saying, "We must support it. There is no other solution." [145]

The majority of the members present at the Presidium agreed with supporting the Imre Nagy government.

"Let's not argue about their (the Imre Nagy government's) evaluation of events, let's not oppose the withdrawal of troops, let's not do it right away...," proposed Saburov[146] then Zhukov said concerning concrete military measures:

"The withdrawal of troops from Hungary: this question must be discussed with the entire socialist camp...Let's take the troops out of Budapest, off the streets and concentrate them into definite areas. Perhaps the command should issue a declaration..."[147]

The issues discussed at the meeting were summed up by Khrushchev in the following:

"I agree with the comrades. We must support the government, we must work out the right tactics. Let's talk to Kádár and Nagy, let's support them.

"A declaration, it seems, is all you are capable of. We will stop the fighting. We are willing to take our troops out of Budapest in return for the resistance centers stopping their fire..."[148] In the comments that followed, what Voroshilov said once again went beyond the stand taken by the Presidium at this time:

"If at least one group had been established, then it would have been possible to leave the troops there. There is no one to rely on. Otherwise there will be war..."[149]

Khrushchev spoke once more afterwards, expanding his arguments concerning avoiding military intervention:

"The English and French have started to stir up trouble in Egypt. Let's not get into the same boat as them. Let's not be deluded. We must preserve our image..."[150]

At this point Suslov, back from Budapest, entered the fray. He informed the Presidium of the Hungarian Politburo's October 27–28 sessions and the political decisions taken there.

Counter-Revolution?
National Democratic Revolution?

At the October 27–28 sessions of the Hungarian Politburo,[151] Kádár said the following: "...At midnight we learned that the Trade Union Council is negotiating with a student body ... and that they regard the whole uprising as a 'national democratic revolution.' The fact that the Trade Union Council and the students are making separate declarations without the party and government means the complete break-up of our political line. Comrade Gáspár was well-meaning, but it is certain that the opposition wanted it to be like this. A separate declaration means the separation of the working class and the party... This is in principle inconceivable; in practice it means that every concept of the Central Leadership and the government collapses."

"If we say that those who fought right to the last moment are revolutionaries, then the workers and students see our leading organs as not in the party's Central Leadership but in the trade unions. We feel the situation is serious; we must decide on the right position quickly."

Kádár stated, "It is not permissible to call the uprising a national revolution just like that, as that means that everybody who is against us is a revolutionary and that we are counter-revolutionaries. We must find the appropriate form."

In the trade union and youth agreement "there are good things too— but we must not let it get out. The party is completely absent from it. The party must have a role in it. The government does not necessarily have to have a role in the declaration..." Then, moving on to the question of the state security organs, he continued: "Some of the comrades were against disbanding them ... The state security troops are workers in soldiers' uniforms. They went to fight at our behest, they restored their honor; we cannot now feed them to the counter-revolution. Possibly... we could somehow slip into the emerging [government] declaration that we have reorganized the Interior Ministry."

Concerning Soviet troops he announced: "... we told the people that we invited the troops. We even gave the reason why we asked them to join the struggle. Can we also ask them to take their troops out? ...Whether they withdraw or not completely depends on the Soviet Union. If the formula which Comrade Nagy referred to in the negotiations[152] is good, then we accept it."

Kádár later went on to say: "Two members of the Soviet Presidium are here.[153] They have not given us any orders, but I, as a communist, believe it is my basic duty to take into account their advice, representing as it does the interests of our nation, the communists and international proletariat... that which I have sketched out here has been accepted by the comrades."

Kádár digressed to the fact that the greatest problem for the Soviet leaders was the divisions within the Politburo. They also said that a party directorate had to lead the party until elections were held. Kádár stated that the directorate elected the day before was now up and running.

Mikoyan asked to speak several times during the meeting. He mentioned that the Politburo and the Central Leadership were not divided; they had been called together to debate the question, but the decision would be made by the directorate. He proposed including in the declaration the formula saying that the government was determined to fight effectively against bureaucracy and autocracy for socialist legitimacy. Then he continued: "If we want to head the workers' movement, then we must call upon it to cease the struggle. We must not negotiate in the crossfire using street microphones, but we must hold meetings, factory meetings. The comrades must show resolution. If they make a new set of concessions tomorrow, then it will not be possible to stop it... if we let the trade union leadership out of our hands, then a parallel center will form and we play into the enemy's hands.

We respect Comrade Nagy; he is an honest man, but sometimes he is easily swayed by others. But if we are to be resolute, then we must have a final objective by which we stand."

András Hegedűs also spoke about this in his address, saying that it was wrong "to leave things unclear, that the struggle is basically a real struggle. If we are unclear at this point, then I believe we will make a very grave mistake." Later he said about the cease-fire question: "I am for a cease-fire, but in no way for the bandits and looters. I understand a cease-fire, a cease-fire for a thousand people who are surrounded in Budapest, but where there is stealing, murder, comrades killed, then I cannot vote for a cease-fire, and I believe nobody can. We must not go in for demands that we cannot fulfill later on and which go beyond the boundaries of the people's democracy. They [the insurgents] are negotiating with Apró: they want 1) a coalition government, 2) to withdraw from the Warsaw Pact, 3) the withdrawal of Soviet troops.

"If we go beyond the agreement, then there are two possibilities: either a bourgeois restoration with several parties, or fascism. Or a Soviet invasion, which would be very hard for both us and the Soviet government," stated Hegedűs. Later, concerning the state security organs, he said: "It would not be moral if we put them into the fight and then let them down afterwards. These comrades are in a very difficult situation. They are branded, their families are persecuted. I agree with the reorganization of the state security organs, let there be a separate police department. But I am afraid that we have not recognized in the declaration that they stood at their posts along with the soldiers and that we just talk of reorganization and then stigmatize them."

Later Mikoyan again asked to speak. He stated that the legitimate government could not negotiate with the rebels; the Trade Union Council had to negotiate with the young people, but the young people could not demand conditions from the government. "The question must not be tackled during armed struggle but afterwards," said Mikoyan.

Ernő Gerő, in his address, said that it was incredibly important that the backbone of the armed forces was a self-aware working class. "We must ensure that, from the beginning, this armed force is under party direction and must not slip from our fingers." He called for caution in regard to the amnesty as the following step would be legal proceedings against those who fought the rebels.

Antal Apró, after stating that there was no other solution but the one Kádár put forward, also said that they had to ensure that when the Soviet forces pulled out, the Hungarian law enforcement formations were able to act whatever the time and time limit of the cease-fire. Zoltán Szantó said: "What started as a peaceful protest is now the working masses demonstrating against the people's power. They have removed councils, and the workers who are not enemies of people's democracy watch passively as party functionaries are killed.

"We can go further along this road to where we fire on workers with guns and cannons. We are increasingly isolating the party, politically and morally, from precisely those masses who sympathize with and follow us. The fact that the Soviet comrades took on this, for them, really delicate and difficult role has had a seriously negative effect... I agree with a general cease-fire and with fighting against those who launch armed attacks on armed formations and state institutions... I agree with the reorganization of the State Security Authority, but we do not need to speak of this."

Then Sándor Rónai asked Imre Nagy to express his opinion.

"The need to raise such questions in such a tragic situation is precisely the bankruptcy of the party," said Nagy, who continued:

"Comrade Mikoyan turned to me and said that we must be steadfast. I will not stand steadfast when the party interests demand advance. ...There are two possibilities: if we call this broad-based movement counter-revolutionary, as we did at first, then nothing else can be done but to suppress it with the aid of arms, tanks and artillery. This is a tragedy. We have already seen that this is not our way...We have created an incredibly difficult situation for the Soviet Union and for the world, in that a counter-revolution has overrun us. This means that, if we are not careful, we will be open to imperialist aggression.

"We must stand at the head of the huge powerful people's force which is now moving. But we can only do so if we see events as they are.

"Cease fire as soon as possible. This morning there was the greatest uncertainty; at 6 a.m. they wanted to start military operations.[154] ... Soviet troops must be withdrawn from the fight, while Hungarian troops must be brought in; we must rely on the army, a democratic police force, workers and I don't even exclude students either... We must at all costs speak about the ÁVH. We must take them out of the field, however we evaluate them...An amnesty is all to the good," Nagy concluded, after many interruptions.

Ernő Gerő, referring to Nagy's remarks, repeated that legal charges must not be brought against those who fought [against the rebels]. Two types of amnesty were possible: 1) for participants in the struggle, and 2) for all political prisoners.

Károly Kiss emphasized the importance of friendship with the Soviet Union, saying that they had to be careful not to allow the murder of their best comrades during the cease-fire. "I agree that the ÁVH cannot stay in place, but we placed the best children of the working class in it and we must protect them, as they now want to kill them. I agree with amnesty," he said in closing.

Sándor Rónai asked Apró whether they could maintain order without the Soviet army. "There is only one guarantee: that is if there is unity among party members, workers and aware people who are against the looters and killers. Otherwise I'm afraid there will be a vacuum," replied Apró.

János Kádár, in his draft proposal, stated that the body had accepted the platform he had drawn up and regarded it as binding; they agreed that there should be a government declaration. They said that the government was operating and acting with the agreement of the party, that they agreed with all that which Kádár and others did to prevent the Trade Union Council resolution. The Politburo accepted the above and decided that the party's central leading organ should not be called a directorate but a party presidium.

Following the session events accelerated. On the 28th at 13:30, the government ordered a general immediate cease-fire over the radio. Imre Nagy in his government program at 17:25 tried to answer the question: counter-revolution, or national democratic revolution?

"The government condemns those views which say that the present mass movement is a counter-revolution. Undoubtedly, as in all great uprisings, unsavory elements have used the past days to commit crimes. It is also true that reactionary counter-revolutionary elements have joined in and are attempting to use events to overthrow the people's democratic system. But it is also certain that in these shifts a huge national democratic movement has emerged with elemental force embracing the whole nation and binding it together. This movement aims to ensure national independence, sovereignty, and self-determination, to develop the democracy of our social, economic and political life, as this is the only basis for socialism in our country."[155]

Nagy, after characterizing the activities of the previous days as a national democratic movement, announced the immediate withdrawal of Soviet troops from Budapest, that negotiations had started on the complete withdrawal of Soviet forces, the closure of the State Security Authority, the amnesty, the introduction of the Kossuth coat of arms, the declaration of March 15 as a national holiday, a general pay raise, price and norms balances, and the end of compulsion in the agricultural coop movement.

The reevaluation of events created a new situation in the Hungarian army. Those units that had supported the revolutionary forces up until October 28 were now justified in their behavior. The majority of those who had watched the events passively now accepted what had been said in the government declaration and actively joined the new phase, defending the victories of the revolution and carrying out tasks to help realize the government's goals and tasks.

"How Can We Master the Situation? Real Power: The Army!"

Suslov, who had been hurriedly recalled to Moscow, informed the Presidium–according to the minutes[156]–of the Hungarian situation, saying that following the entry of Soviet troops on October 23, only one resistance center remained, and that they had only found out on October 26 that in the Corvin Cinema there was "... a band under the command of a colonel[157] who served in Horthy's army who primarily fires at (Soviet) officers."

Suslov put the number of Hungarian wounded at 3000 and the number of dead at 350. "Our losses amount to 600 dead," he said, adding that the relationship between the population and the Soviet troops had deteriorated following the "dispersion" of the Kossuth Square demonstration.

Suslov also digressed to evaluate the activities of the Hungarian leadership. Imre Nagy–without their knowledge or participation–"has interpolated the notion of Soviet troop withdrawal..."[158]

Following a brief evaluation of the situation, Suslov answered the question, "How can we master the situation?":

"We must establish a relatively ruthless government. Our tendency is not to oppose the inclusion of a few democrats...if the government is already planning a cease-fire, our command can formulate the order to withdraw from Budapest... There is no need to hold elections."[159]

Following Suslov's speech and the anti-Mikoyan comments, the following propositions were made: "We must take a tough line..." (Bulganyin), "A revolutionary Military Committee[160] must be formed"[161] (Kaganovich)–to show that a decisive turn had been taken in the evaluation of the Hungarian situation and its possible resolution. Despite the stand taken by Zhukov a few hours earlier–"We must support the present government"–a "tough stand"[162] had been taken.

'The real power is the army. If we make concessions, then it will be seen as weak...,"[163] added Sepilov.

Despite Khrushchev's until now daringly different evaluation: "A new period has started. We do not agree with the government...," and his proposal: "Hegedűs and the others should be in contact with us. We must appeal to our troops... Let Molotov, Zhukov and Malenkov fly over there...," "We will fix everything later," the beginning of decisive changes can be felt here in regard to the fate of the Hungarian Revolution.[154]

Soviet Troop Withdrawal from Budapest

On October 28 General Korzenyevich, adviser to the Hungarian general staff, and Colonel Kromsov, adviser to the military operations staff, summoned Major General István Kovács and informed him that the Soviet command had entrusted them with preparing the plan to withdraw Soviet troops from Budapest. Major General Kovács ordered Colonel Zólomy to help with the plan.

The Soviet officers planned for every formation to leave the city along the shortest route at the same time: those in Buda to the west, and those in Pest to the east. Colonel Zólomy did not agree with this plan and proposed that the whole army go east, since otherwise the troops would have to go through Budapest when leaving the country, which could provoke the population once again.

Major General Kovács interjected, saying that the majority of the forces then in Budapest had their garrisons in the western half of the country and when they finally left the country altogether, they would go from there. Kovács instructed Zólomy that the Soviet command's standpoint in preparing the withdrawal plan was the proper one.

The Soviet officers planned to carry out the plan in two phases. They intended first to withdraw those troops in the outer districts and then in the second phase take out those in the inner city guarding the Party Headquarters, the Ministry of Defense, Parliament and the Ministry of the Interior.

Then the Soviet officers and Colonel Zólomy agreed to jointly establish which objectives were guarded solely by Soviet troops, as following their withdrawal Hungarian troops would have to take over from the Soviet forces in those places. The Soviet officers indicated that they would draw up the plan for troop withdrawal and would contact Zólomy shortly. But they did not appear until noon on October 29. Then Lieutenant General Janza, the minister of defense, summoned Zólomy and, in the presence of Lieutenant General Tihonov, requested a proposal on the technical arrangements of the Soviet troop withdrawal. Zólomy proposed that withdrawal start where there was no armed struggle and that only at the end should Soviet troops who were still fighting with rebels be taken out–in other words, those at the Corvin Cinema and at Moszkva Square.

Zólomy's proposal was again rejected, and they decided to do exactly the opposite, that is, start withdrawal from the Corvin Cinema area. Zólomy proposed that the replacement of troops at these sites take place from three directions. This task was to be given to the Zrínyi Military Academy, the Artillery Officers School, and the 12th mechanized regiment. According to the plan replacement troops were to be in position on October 29 from 20:00 until 06:00 on the 30th. The Soviet leadership made it a condition of withdrawal that Hungarian troops replace them in a reassuring manner. At the same time they attempted to make the rebels lay down their arms to the Hungarian army after the withdrawal at 9:00 on the 30th. But the negotiations concerning the handing over of weapons conducted by Major General Gyula Váradi in the Corvin Cinema were not successful.

At noon on October 30 the preparatory work for Soviet troop withdrawal took a new turn. Colonel Zólomy was summoned by the Soviet chief of staff in Budapest. The two officers established that the withdrawal in its first phase–between 15:00 and 24:00–would empty Budapest except for District V. Zólomy proposed that this only be started at 18:00 in Buda so that the 26th Kaposvár infantry regiment's entry into the city would not be impeded by Soviet troop movements.

They planned the second phase from 24:00 until 5:00 on the 31st, during which Soviet forces would depart from District V. Preceding this the 26th infantry regiment would replace troops guarding the Ministry of Defense, Parliament, Party Headquarters and the National Bank. Lieutenant General Lanza immediately approved the plan. Soviet troop withdrawal initially went according to plan, but the second phase was only over by the afternoon of the 31st.

"At Present the Number of Soviet Troops Stationed Here is Adequate"

The final decision was not long in coming. At the October 30–31 session of the Soviet Central Committee's presidium–according to notes taken by Malin–the circumstances leading up to the decision can be reconstructed as follows:

On October 30, preceding the debate on the Hungarian question, Serov's report–presumably from October 29[165]–and Mikoyan and Suslov's October 30[166] report were made.

In Serov's report, originally written for Mikoyan and Suslov and then forwarded to the Central Committee (and very exaggerated and even false on certain issues), he mentions the negotiations between the rebels and the government on disarmament, the release of prisoners on the 27th and 28th, the handover of weapons by the rebels, the persecution and murder of communists and the lynchings in Miskolc.[167]

Writing of the breakup of the ÁVH–on the basis of reports by Soviet advisers to this organization–he indicates that many groups of defense officers "will illegally enter the Soviet Union," or if they do not get quite that far, will "illegally continue the partisan fight."

Serov went on to say that 40 state defense colleagues had escaped to Romania and that many groups were awaiting permission to enter on the Czechoslovak and Soviet borders.[168]

Mikoyan and Suslov, in their report of October 30–influenced by Serov's report–established that the political situation in Hungary and Budapest "is not improving: on the contrary, it is deteriorating"... "The rebels have announced that they will only hand in their weapons if Soviet troops leave Budapest, and some of them have explicitly said: only if Soviet troops leave Hungary altogether. This means that the break-up of this center [the rebel groups in the Corvin Cinema area–authors] in a peaceful manner is quite impossible."

"We are trying to get the Hungarian forces to break up the center of resistance. But there is a great danger that the Hungarian army will take a wait-and-see position. Our military advisers tell us that the relationship between Soviet officers and Hungarian officers and generals has deteriorated recently; there is no longer the trust there once was. Hungarian units sent in against the rebels might go across to them, and then Soviet military operations will again be necessary...Until such time as Hungarian troops show antagonism, the present number of troops stationed here is adequate. If the situation deteriorates further, then of course we must look at this question again."[169]

Mikoyan and Suslov–on the basis of a meeting between Imre Nagy and Andropov–warned the Soviet leadership that the entry of more Soviet troops into Hungary "could mean a turning point in Hungary's policy in the Security Council."[170]

Imre Nagy had summoned Andropov and "asked him whether it was true that further Soviet military units were coming into Hungary from the Soviet Union, and if so why." "We did not agree to this," said Nagy to Andropov, according to the report.[171]

"Today we intend to inform Imre Nagy of the following: in accordance with our agreement our troops entered until today, but for the time being we do not plan to bring in any new formations on the assumption that the government is dealing with the situation in Hungary," write Suslov and Mikoyan, who propose that the Central Committee should order the "minister of defense (Zhukov) to stop sending troops to Hungary and to continue concentrating troops on Soviet territory."

"We believe that Comrade Konyev should come to Hungary immediately,"[172] their October 30 report ends.

After reading this, Zhukov informed the Presidium of the concentration [73] of military transport planes around Vienna; then, citing Malinyin's opinion, he said that Nagy was playing a double game. Zhukov said he supported Mikoyan's and Suslov's proposal: he felt it was necessary to send Konyev to Budapest.[174]

The comments voiced at the October 30 session of the Presidium display the divisions and uncertainties in the Soviet leadership.

Khrushchev, conveying the opinion of the Chinese party leadership, announced that on this day "we must accept the declaration on the withdrawal of troops from the people's democracies..." and the questions related to it, "taking into account the opinion of the country where our troops are stationed," must be debated at the Warsaw Pact session. According to Khrushchev a "separate document" had to be drawn up for Hungary and the rest of the Warsaw Pact member countries.[175]

Molotov, agreeing with this proposal, said that they should start negotiations immediately on the withdrawal of troops, but that this also had to be negotiated with the other countries of the Warsaw Pact.[176]

When Voroshilov said that the Soviet leadership should "really criticize itself" in the declaration, Kaganovich objected. "Self-criticism is not necessary in this document," he said.[177]

Sepilov's argument was full of contradictions—"We must eliminate regimentation elements...Let us not permit them to make use of the present situation...In agreement with the Hungarian government we are willing to withdraw...We must fight long and hard against national communism..."[178] After this Zhukov made a daring suggestion: "We must take troops out of Budapest, if necessary out of Hungary. This has been a military-political lesson for us."[179]

The most self-critical speech was from Saburov, who was in agreement with Furseva on the question of troop withdrawal and the declaration: "We did some good work at the Twentieth Congress, but afterwards we did not go ahead with mass development initiatives. We cannot lead against the people's will. We did not adopt true Leninist principles. We have been led by events...We must build relations on the basis of equality."[180]

In the debate that developed over the question of the declaration, Khrushchev's proposal is striking: he said that the Soviet leadership had to formulate its relationship with the Hungarian government, particularly concerning the roles of Imre Nagy and János Kádár.[181]

Khrushchev–on the basis of a telephone conversation with Mikoyan–announced that "Kádár behaves well," that out of the six members of the party directorate five were resolved, the debate on the withdrawal of the Soviet troops was taking place within the Presidium, and the minister of defense would order "the military suppression of the rebels in the theater [Corvin Cinema–authors]." He also said that the Hungarian "state defenders" had reached the Soviet troops.[182]

Zhukov also proposed that they express their sympathy with the people and demand an end to bloodshed.[183]

"Troops Must Stay in Hungary"

Interrupting the debate, they heard Yudin's information on the negotiations with Chinese party leaders, who had probably arrived at that moment.

"What is the situation? Has Hungary left our camp? Who is Nagy? Can we believe him?"[184]–Yudin repeated the questions he was asked by the Chinese delegation, questions and answers which meant a new turn in the evaluation of the Hungarian situation and the calculation of possible "solutions."

As the minutes make clear, Liu Sao-chi, who was invited to participate in the work of the Presidium sitting, was given pat answers to his questions.

Liu Sao-chi announced, in accordance with the latest viewpoint of the Chinese Communist Party's Central Committee, that "troops must stay in Hungary."[185]

Following this Khrushchev–despite the Chinese position–still proposed two alternatives: 1) a warlike occupation and 2) peace, withdrawal of troops, negotiations.

According to the minutes only Molotov spoke. He referred to the Chinese opinion and said: "The political situation has become clear. A counter-revolutionary government, a transitional government, has been formed... We must make our relationship with the new government clear. We should negotiate on the withdrawal of troops."[186]

A new and more decisive turn, and at the same time the final decision, was taken at the Soviet Central Committee Presidium's October 31 session.

"We must investigate the evaluation," Khrushchev stated. "Our troops must not be taken out of Hungary or Budapest; we must act decisively in order to restore order in Hungary. If we withdraw from Hungary, this will encourage the American, English and French imperialists. They will see this as our weakness and get ready to attack... In this event our party would not understand us. We would give them Hungary as well as Egypt. We have no other choice."[187]

As Zhukov, Bulganyin, Molotov, Kaganovich, Voroshilov and Saburov agreed with his proposal, Khrushchev stated possible measures with a drama worthy of a film script:

"We must state that we anticipated them, but there is now no government. What line should we take?

"We must form a provisional revolutionary government [under Kádár's leadership]. But the best would be if he were deputy. Let Münnich be the prime minister, minister of defense and interior minister.

"We will invite this government [the Imre Nagy government–authors], let's say, to negotiate the withdrawal of Soviet troops and then solve the problem.[188] If Imre Nagy agrees, let him be deputy prime minister. Münnich asks our help, we will give help and restore order.

"We must talk to Tito and inform the Chinese comrades, the Czechs, Romanians and Bulgarians. There will be no great war."[189]

Following this the Presidium decided that Zhukov should draw up the military plan and then report to the Presidium. Sepilov, Brezhnev,

Furseva, and Pospyelov were to work out the propaganda material needed to carry out the plan, in which "the government's appeal to the people" and "the provisional revolutionary government's appeal to the people" were to play a role.

Konyev was to draw up the general orders, and the Presidium was to send a group to set up Konyev's general headquarters in Hungary.

After this they also noted that Rákosi, Hegedűs and Gerő, who were in Moscow, supported Münnich's prime ministership and that Antal Apró, János Kádár, Károly Kiss, János Boldoczki and Imre Horváth[190] could be considered[191] members of the counter-government.

They also decided that in order to debate the Hungarian situation, Khrushchev and Malenkov would travel to Yugoslavia, and Khrushchev, Molotov and Malenkov would go to Brest.

Mikoyan's Unsuccessful Attempts

The Hungarian problem was again discussed by the Presidium on November 1–while Khrushchev was away–at the prompting of Mikoyan, who had returned to Moscow. When Mikoyan learned of the Presidium's October 31 decision in Moscow, he protested to Khrushchev, who was preparing to go to Brest. Mikoyan was against interfering in Hungary and demanded an immediate session of the Presidium. Khrushchev rejected this, saying that a unanimous decision had been taken and that the plan had already been set in action.[192] At the Presidium session, which was held nevertheless, Mikoyan–attempting the impossible–tried to convince the Presidium that it had to support the Imre Nagy government under the present circumstances, that the Soviet leadership would achieve nothing through force, and that they had to begin negotiations and delay the decision for at least 10–15 days.[193]

"...If the authorities weaken further, then let's decide what to do...If the situation stabilizes, then we can decide whether to take the troops out or not. Let's wait 10–15 days and support this government. If the situation stabilizes, then everything will be for the better,"[194] said Mikoyan.

Suslov, disagreeing with Mikoyan, announced that he did not think that Imre Nagy had organized the uprising but that his name was being used. "There is no certainty that this government can maintain itself. Only by an invasion can we ensure a government that will support us."[195]

Serov added that troop movements had been thoroughly worked out and that Imre Nagy was in contact with the rebels. "Firm steps must be taken, the country must be invaded,"[196] demanded Serov. The soldiers–Konyev and Zhukov–who spoke next in the debate expressed their opinions very forcefully. "Budapest is in the hands of the rebels. Anarchy rules. Reaction has the upper hand. The solution: invasion,"[197] Konyev announced.

"There is no reason to reexamine the October 31 decision. I do not agree with Comrade Mikoyan that we should support the present government. This is the time for decisive action. To catch all the scoundrels. To disarm the counter-revolution,"[198] said Zhukov.

"Everything must be done in the spirit of the October 31 decision,"[199] Bulganyin said, closing the debate.

On the same day, November 1, the Presidium sat once more, and the Hungarian question was touched on once again. Sepilov–according to the evaluation he gave then–saw two ways to solve the Hungarian "problem": first, to calculate the mass nature of the movement and not to intervene; second, the armed way. But there was also a third possible outcome: "We intervene and yet reaction wins."[200]

"The present situation is this: a counter-revolutionary putsch has been carried out, the state system has changed, the main tendency is against the Soviets and the main line is being organized from outside. If we do not take firm measures, things will fall apart in Czechoslovakia as well. We must restore order with armed force," Sepilov concluded.

Mikoyan, who followed, voiced his hopes loudly and desperately. "We still have three days to think it over; advice is still being given by the comrades."[201]

More important decisions were also made on this day: Soviet families were to be sent home, while the personnel at the Embassy were to remain in Budapest. Suslov and Brezhnev were to prepare measures with the "Hungarian comrades" in Moscow (presumably Gerő, Hegedűs and Bata); they were to consider what to do and "on which cadres it is possible to rely."[202]

Imre Nagy Demands an Explanation– Kádár Speaks in Support of Nagy

In the late hours of November 1, Andropov sent the following report[203] to Moscow in which he says that at 19 hours they "had invited him" to a sitting of the Council of Ministers of the Hungarian People's Republic, where Imre Nagy "in fairly angry tones had informed those present that he had already asked for information from the Soviet Embassy that morning concerning the fact that Soviet troops had crossed the Hungarian border and were heading for the center of the country."

From Andropov's report we know that, after Imre Nagy had "demanded an explanation," Zoltán Tildy noted, "if the Soviet troops continue to march towards Budapest, there will be a scandal and the government will have to resign."

He announced that "he demands that the Soviet troops, and at least those who had not come into the country on the basis of the Warsaw Pact, immediately leave the country."[204]

Andropov gave information in the spirit of the directives he had received from Moscow. This, according to Imre Nagy, did not answer the Hungarian government's questions.

"Given that the Soviet government has not stopped the Soviet troop march and has not given a satisfactory explanation for this step," reads Imre Nagy's answer to Andropov in his report, "he proposes that Hungary leave the Warsaw Pact, reinforcing the morning decree to declare Hungary a neutral country, and has turned to the UN so that the four great powers will guarantee the country's neutrality. If the Soviet government stops the advance of its troops and orders them back to their own borders (which the Hungarian People's Republic will ascertain from its own military intelligence), then the Hungarian government will immediately withdraw its request to the UN, although Hungary will remain neutral."[205]

Nagy's above announcement–according to Andropov–was "totally supported" by Erdei and Losonczy. Tildy agreed reservedly, while Kádár accepted it "without much joy."

An hour after Andropov left, the Hungarian Foreign Ministry's memorandum was leaked to the Soviet Embassy. The memorandum said: "Despite the strenuous protest of the government of the Hungarian People's

Republic, a large number of Soviet troops crossed the border today and entered Hungarian territory; the Hungarian People's Republic immediately withdraws from the Warsaw Pact."[206]

"Nobody Wanted a Counter-Revolution"

The Soviet Central Committee's Presidium held an extended session on November 2 with the participation of János Kádár, Ferenc Münnich and István Bata.

On November 1 Kádár had left Parliament late at night during a meeting between the Hungarian Workers Party's Action Committee and the Chinese ambassador, and had gone to see Ferenc Münnich. Münnich, probably because of his agreement with Andropov, attempted to convince János Kádár of the incorrectness of the political line taken by him and Imre Nagy after October 28. Kádár went with Münnich to the Soviet Embassy, where, getting into an armored vehicle, they were taken to the airport at Tököl. From here separate planes took them to Moscow. Malashenko writes of the events at Tököl Airport in his memoirs.

Kádár had already decided to leave and was on his way to Moscow when his appeal to the Hungarian people went out over the radio; the November 2 papers also covered it. "Our people have proved with their blood that they firmly support the government's demand for the complete withdrawal of Soviet troops. We do not want dependence any longer! We do not want our country to become a theater of war! We address all good patriots! Let's stand together for Hungarian freedom, for the victory of Hungarian freedom!"[207] ended Kádár's speech.

At the Soviet Presidium's sitting–according to Malin's notes–the Hungarian situation was discussed.[208] At the beginning of the session, János Kádár (reconstructing his words on the basis of fragmented notes) spoke about how at the spearhead of the movement in Hungary stood opposition intellectuals, Imre Nagy and his followers, and that the leaders of the armed rebels were also party members and workers who fought to get rid of the Rákosi clique, for the withdrawal of Soviet troops and a people's democratic system.

The aim of the mass protests in the countryside was not to overthrow the people's democratic system but to democratize it to achieve social demands.[209]

"At the beginning we did not see this," said Kádár. "We saw it as a counter-revolution and turned it against ourselves,"[210] as the participants in the action "did not feel they were counter-revolutionaries," as nobody wanted a counter-revolution, although within the armed groups "counter-revolutionary-type armed groups did form."[211]

"They demanded the withdrawal of all Soviet troops," which was the reason Kádár declared it to be "counter-revolutionary propaganda."[212]

Kádar also informed the Soviet leaders that the strikers, who had demanded the withdrawal of Soviet troops, had wanted to start work again upon hearing the declaration by the Soviet government, but this did not happen because of the news arriving about continued Soviet troop movements.

Kádár stated that the former coalition parties "are using all their strength to re-form their parties. Everyone wants to get their hands on power," and this was undermining the government's position even more.[213]

He used the Social Democrats as an example. By not designating actual people for the government, Kádár said, they were expressing that "they do not wish to show any solidarity with Nagy," in whose policy, continued Kádár, "there are counter-revolutionary elements."[214]

Later Kádár, returning to the coalition parties, said that "they did not want a counter-revolution." The main reason, as Kádár saw it, was Zoltán Tildy's and others' fear of the emigrés. At the same time he stated that the situation in Hungary was "moving rightwards hour by hour."[215]

Later he touched on the precedents leading to the declaration of neutrality, saying that the withdrawal of troops from Budapest and the Soviet government's declaration had had a calming effect on the population, but further Soviet troop movements, the entry of new forces into the country, had "agitated the government and the masses." "The Hungarian formations have dug themselves in, they were asking 'What should we do, shoot or not shoot?'"[216]

"We called Andropov in. Andropov said that these were railway workers. Hungarians had sent a telegram from the border saying that these were not railway workers. Then came the information that Soviet tanks were approaching Szolnok.

"This took place at noon. The atmosphere in the government was very tense. They called Andropov. He simply replied: regrouping. Then more news: Soviet tanks have surrounded the airports. We rang Andropov again. He replied: they are transporting wounded soldiers. Imre Nagy was convinced that an attack was being prepared on Budapest....The whole government was of the opinion that if troops came closer to Budapest, then Budapest had to be defended. It was in this atmosphere that the idea of neutrality came up. It was suggested by Zoltán Tildy. Everybody supported it.

"I was of the opinion," continued Kádár, "that we should do nothing until we had talked to Andropov. Apart from me the whole cabinet thought that the Soviet government had tricked the Hungarian government."

Two hours later–as the notes on the meeting reveal–the Soviet government's explanation had not reassured members of the cabinet. "They told Andropov that they would take that step." When Andropov went, they reached the decision on neutrality and to turn to the UN. It was also decided that if it became clear that Soviet troops were just holding military exercises, then the Hungarian government would withdraw its request to the UN.[217]

"When Andropov left, then Kádár also voted for neutrality,"[218] Malin noted. The name change of the Hungarian Workers Party–said Kádár, who had also voted for this–was necessary because the party had lost credibility "before the masses."[219]

From what he said later about possible solutions, it becomes clear that János Kádár still did not know about the Presidium's October 31 decision.

Kádár said that if Soviet troops left Hungary in two to three months, then the Communist Party "and the other parties could take up the fight against the counter-revolution." Then he weighed the possible consequences of party struggles, seeing them as a "real danger," and said, "the counter-revolution might perhaps overthrow these coalition parties."[220]

"I believe," said Kádár, "that there is another way. To hold onto Hungary with military force. But then there will be exchanges of fire. An armed suppression means bloodshed.

"What will happen then? The communists' moral stance will be good for nothing. It will harm the socialist countries. Is there any certainty that a situation like this will not arise in other countries?"

"The counter-revolutionary forces are not small. But this is a question of war. If the restoration of order takes place by force of arms, the prestige of the socialist countries [will be damaged]."[221]

Kádár also stated (on what basis is not known) that the intervention of a "35,000-man [West-German/Hungarian] fascist [Horthyist] organization" with Austrian support also had to be reckoned with, and–probably referring to the October 30 events at the Budapest Party Committee building on Köztársaság Square–stated that some of the party functionaries "had been murdered, while some had escaped."[222]

Ferenc Münnich, after stating that the "situation is grim," added to Kádár's analysis that the situation in Hungary was caused by the divide between the leaders and the masses and the conviction that the socialist system in Hungary "exists and can be maintained only with the support of the Soviet Union." He announced that if the Soviet troops withdrew, then "counter-revolutionary elements will gain greater strength and their activities will continue unimpeded.

"We have no more forces. ...It is not really possible to trust that a political fight would successfully win over events,"[223] Münnich concluded.

István Bata added to all this that there was a danger of "conflict" between Soviet and Hungarian troops which the "government wittingly or unwittingly created. Order must be restored with a military dictatorship. The government's policy must be changed."[224]

According to the notes the Presidium session then broke up. The Hungarians did not take part in the next session of the Presidium held on the same day to discuss Hungarian measures. The sketch notes show that–on the basis of Zhukov's, Serov's and Konyev's recommendations–the military operations "Storm" and "Whirlwind" were debated and accepted at that sitting. Konyev's priority order of the day was to plan the tasks to be carried out in Hungary, presumably under Serov's leadership–with the forces of the KGB.

Murders, Atrocities and Kádár's Propaganda Intrigues

János Kádár and Ferenc Münnich frequently made a connection between atrocities committed against communists and "counter-revolutionary danger." The two authors of our volume–Malashenko and Kirov–also deal with the issue of violence, regarding it as an important, if not the most important, reason for the Soviet intervention.

In his study Kirov writes, among other things, about "the violence perpetrated against the communists using terrible methods," "the bestial killings of many communists," the "desecration of the corpses of Soviet soldiers" and the "violent activities of released criminals."[225] Malashenko recognizes the events as a popular uprising[226] but, similarly to Kirov, explains the second military intervention primarily as a response to the atrocities committed against communists and Soviet soldiers.

We cannot deny that, as in any such social uprising, there were violent episodes in the Hungarian Revolution–primarily as a result of the crude steps taken by the authorities and the intervention of Soviet troops. But these atrocities were equally foreign and unacceptable, both to those who wanted to achieve the objectives of the revolution peacefully and to those who wanted to do so by force of arms. Writings and documents, radio broadcasts, newspaper articles, leaflets and placards all appealed, and not unsuccessfully, to people to obey the law throughout this extraordinary situation and to preserve the integrity of the revolution.

While studying the documents, we became convinced that during the revolution these atrocities were not nearly as frequent as Kádár's propaganda stated and that the majority of the people who committed them had absolutely nothing to do with the revolutionaries.

This being so, the organizations preparing and carrying out Kádár's reprisals also realized that they had to try and manipulate the masses and to fake information in order to misinform them.

One of the main methods for increasing the tallies of "counter-revolutionary" victims was to blame the rebels for some of the deaths of the Hungarian soldiers, police and civilians who were either killed in the fights against the Soviets or by Soviet soldiers.

In this way the police and civilians who died from Soviet fire on October 24 in Székesfehérvár became the victims of the "counter-revolution," as well as the army officer who was later crushed by a Soviet tank. István Farkas, a soldier, was also included in this list; at dawn on November 4 he was shot in the head without warning by Soviet soldiers occupying the town. Similarly, soldier János Bogár was shot in the head on his way home by a member of a Soviet patrol while getting off a bus near Gyulafirátót. This also happened with one of the students at the Kossuth Artillery Officer School who was shot by Soviet soldiers opening fire from the Népliget (City Park) in Budapest. Perhaps the most unscrupulous case of falsification was that of Colonel Sándor Sziklai. For decades it was claimed that Colonel Sziklai and his father-in-law "died in a fight with counter-revolutionaries" in a house at Vörös Hadsereg Road 12, Budapest. In the inquiry into the Sziklai affair, Dr. Gyula Ostoros, the local doctor who had examined the corpses in the Sziklai house, recalls the events thus:

"On October 26, 1956, we entered the house through the street door. We saw neither shards of glass nor broken furniture in the room. The windows were not damaged either. There had certainly not been a hand grenade explosion in there! Sziklai was not killed by a hand grenade [later official propaganda said that he was–Jenő Györkei]. I believe he took his own life; he shot himself in the head with a pistol...

"I examined the corpse. The body was still warm, but I could feel no pulse. A hole gaped on his forehead... We went out of the room into the kitchen, where we found a door opening onto the garden. Before this door lay Lajos Kiss (Sándor Sziklai's father-in-law) with a huge head wound. His body was already cold and stiff, the blood that had seeped out of his head had congealed and striated. He lay on his stomach; his right arm under his body, while his left was next to him. The right side of his face lay on the kitchen floor. His left leg was stretched out with the inner side of his foot turned out, and his right leg was slightly bent at the knee; his foot was also bent in, as if he had been running. The position of his body was such that it was certain that he did not take his own life. The bullet had hit him in the back of the head as he was trying to leave the room...

"In addition Júlia Porcsalmi, who lived in the house next door, had heard shouting before the gunfire. A suicide does not shout before killing himself! It is also important to mention that the furniture in the kitchen was completely undamaged and in place."[227]

This information and the inquiry documents seem to reinforce the view that the Sziklai house was not besieged by rebels but that Sándor

Sziklai had shot the 26-year-old László Marity, who had knocked on his door, then during an exchange of words with his father-in-law, Lajos Kiss, had killed him and finally turned the pistol on himself.

The organs of repression pronounced six death penalties in response to the Sziklai affair, two of which were actually carried out. The minimum sentence was 15 years, but the majority of the defendants got life.

Malashenko and Kirov emphasize this problem, yet at the same time seem to ignore atrocities perpetrated by Soviet troops, or else lay sole responsibility with the Hungarians, as they do with the massacre on Kossuth Square. But Hungarian archive sources show that many violent acts were committed by Soviet soldiers. These include the use of arms against unarmed protesters; some such acts were committed by Soviet troops after November 4 with Hungarian law enforcement forces. But it is also necessary to mention that Soviet troops shot captured rebels, officers captured instead of rebels or even Hungarian soldiers who gave themselves up voluntarily. Perhaps these events are not mentioned in the Soviet troop documents. That is why what Malashenko writes about this in his memoirs is food for thought:

"Officers and soldiers fulfilled their combat duties; they did not wonder whether their actions were legitimate; they did not question orders. Furthermore, many remembered that Hungary had fought on the fascist German side against our country in the last war, and when they saw the cruelties of the counter-revolution, they saw their own actions as a continuation of that previous struggle..."[228]

Central Leadership of the Revolution

The revolutionary forces needed competent and loyal leadership. On October 30 freedom-fighter representatives established the Revolutionary Council for Public Safety, which was immediately recognized by the prime minister as the central leadership organ of all the armed forces of the revolution. On October 31 a new Budapest Military Command was set up. On November 3 the staff of the commander in chief of the National Guard was established. Béla Király was in control of these institutions, as Lieutenant General Malashenko states in his sub-chapter below: "...in the early morning hours of November 4, after Imre Nagy had announced the start of the Soviet armed attack, Béla Király called the insurgent forces to arms."[229]

The name of Béla Király,[230] later the commander in chief of the National Guard, first came up not in insurgent circles but–typical of the period–at a session of the Hungarian Workers Party on October 26. There András Hegedűs, the ex-prime minister, analyzing the situation in Hungary and the possible outcome of the "negotiations" going on with the insurgents, said:

"If we go beyond the agreement [negotiations–authors], then there are two possible routes: either bourgeois restoration with several parties, or in a fascist form. Or a very forceful Soviet invasion, which would be very hard both for the Soviet government and for us.

"Extremely able officers are leading the military resistance. For example, Király at the Corvin. He was a general staff officer... we cannot fulfill his demands. There is a feeling that the armed fighters have gone a bit too far; they are now national freedom fighters. One must recognize that the leaders are bad elements. The great majority are military officers."[231]

Following the session on October 27, Chief of General Staff Lajos Tóth, who, unlike Hegedűs, knew that Béla Király was ill and was lying in the Military Hospital, called Colonel Dr. Zoltán Radó, the commander of the hospital, and asked him to find Béla Király and then to call Defense Minister István Bata. Dr. Radó called Király into his room, and when at last they got hold of Bata, "he said in a really friendly way to Király that they only wanted to know whether he really was in the hospital and whether he was leading the insurgents or not."[232]

Following the telephone conversation, Király decided that, if necessary, he would gladly go with Major General Tóth to Imre Nagy if his army knowledge and military experience were needed.

Radó–to whom Király disclosed his intentions–thought this was a good idea. "I persuaded him to carry out this plan. Partly because the increasing anarchy which the government could not control was very worrying, because I saw that the army leadership had completely collapsed and was incapable of restoring order, and partly because I believed in Béla Király's military experience and his whole personality. The statements he had made to me during his stay in the hospital had led me to trust him, and I was convinced that he would carry out the government's instructions properly.

"At the same time I thought that Béla Király would be able to establish a trust with the masses as well, that he would prevent them from taking things too far, even if only because he had just recently been released from prison and was about to be rehabilitated. Many people in the army knew him, and everybody with whom I spoke had a good opinion of him...,"[233] so Dr. Radó stated in his testimony following the suppression of the revolution.

At the October funeral of the executed generals, Király met Imre Nagy, whose parting words to him were: "I know that you are in hospital now. After you have recovered, get in touch with me! You are needed."[234]

Following this conversation Király decided that he would offer his services given the extraordinary situation. Emboldened by the conversation with Imre Nagy, he hurriedly wrote the following to his son-in-law Ferenc Jánosi, on October 29, 1956:

'I am overwhelmed with bitterness when I think that I should stay out of work like this, which is so close to my heart... Through you I offer my strength, my enthusiasm and my sympathy to Imre Nagy and his government. I believe you know that it is not the position or the glory that I crave but the task... I believe that my place is on the the Ministry of Defense Chiefs of General Staff..."[235]

The letter was entrusted to Colonel Dr. Zoltán Radó, but before it got to Jánosi, and through him to Nagy, Király had already taken over control of the National Guard at the invitation and request of Police Colonel Sándor Kopácsi, the leader of the Interior Ministry's Main Budapest Department.

It was Vilmos Oláh[236] who suggested that Kopácsi seek out Király. Radó went with Oláh to see Király. Kopácsi had put a car at his disposal and asked him to bring Király into the Budapest Police Department on Deák Square.

"When we arrived, Király was received very warmly by a delegation from the Ministry of Defense. The delegation consisted of Major General István Kovács, Major General Mihály Horváth, Major General Dániel Görgényi, and Major General Gyula Uszta, Colonel Szűcs, Major Rakos."[237]

Béla Király, in his already quoted work, writes about these events:

"...The freedom fighters led me into the big meeting room at the police station on Deák Square...Delegates from the Ministry of Defense, the chiefs of general staff, the state police, workers and youth and freedom-fighting groups were negotiating there. They elected me president with a great cheer...The objective was to establish a central leadership for these spontaneous freedom-fighting groups, which were formed and fought independently of each other.

"We saw the Committee's job as being to consolidate the armed freedom-fighting groups that were loyal to the revolution into the National Guard, and by doing so, to prevent Stalinist or other counter-revolutionary trends from influencing the armed forces in any way...

"The negotiations finished on the afternoon of October 30; we elected a delegation which I led to Prime Minister Imre Nagy. Before setting off I drafted a declaration. We wanted to ask Imre Nagy to sign this declaration and by doing so recognize on behalf of the government the Committee's right to operate... We believed that if our new revolutionary institution became an organic part of the government, then its influence through two sources–the revolution and the government–would be greater. In any case, we saw Imre Nagy as the embodiment of the revolution; we simply did not think of doing anything without his approval..."[238]

Imre Nagy accepted the proposal and recognized the formation of the Preparatory Committee. The declaration concerning this by the president of the Council of Ministers contained the following:

"...the Revolutionary Council for Public Safety should organize the units of the army and police who have taken part in revolutionary struggles, and a new public-safety force made up of workers' and young people's details. With their help it should restore order and internal calm in our country and carry out the duties expressed in the government programs of October 28 and 30..."[239]

In these government programs the announcement of the withdrawal of Soviet troops from the capital, beginning immediately, and the continuation of negotiations about the complete withdrawal of Soviet troops played an important part, as has already been mentioned.

The fulfillment of this demand of the revolution, and the carrying out of the part of the government program that dealt with this, was a central question at the meeting held in the Kilián Barracks by the Revolutionary Council for Public Safety on October 31.

About 100 came to the meeting called by the Temporary Revolutionary Council for Public Safety led by Béla Király, representatives of the insurgent groups, the army, the police and several industrial plants. Colonel Pál Maléter, as the host of the meeting, opened it as planned.

Maléter said that the first phase of the fight was over, that the revolution was victorious and that now the task was to defend the victories; for that an organization was needed. He thought that members of insurgent groups should be integrated into the army and police, while those under 18 should be sent to military schools. Anyone who did not agree with this solution should lay down their arms and return to their workplaces.

Following this Király spoke. First he said that the national democratic revolution had been won without any united central leadership. This victory could only be maintained if the participants in the revolution–the victorious young people, university students, young workers, military units factory guards then being formed, the united leadership of the army and police–protected the victories of the revolution from restoration attempts or attacks by reactionary elements.

'... The victories of the revolution are endangered by three elements:

'1. Restoration attempts

'2. Reactionary trouble-making, which we must fight against with arms

'3. Delays in the departure of Soviet troops from Budapest, which must be urged with all possible means.

'"We can only defend ourselves against these dangers if we organize the new public safety agency's supreme leadership–as designated in Imre Nagy's declaration on the 28th–quickly, unanimously and decisively, as the present situation conceals many dangers.

'"There are countless heroic freedom fighters who love their country, countless fighting sub-units. These disorganized fighting forces all want the same thing, but they are dispersed in small groups. Yet the victories of the revolution can only be preserved with a combined force and united leadership. ..."[240]

After sketching out the progressive traditions of the National Guard, Béla Király turned to the concrete tasks of the meeting.

He proposed that the session, as the general assembly of the Revolutionary Council for Public Safety, immediately form an Operational Committee to solve operative tasks. Its task would be to carry out the general assembly's decisions, to work out its measures and to forward them to the executive organs, to permit or reject recommendations concerning the operation of the National Guard formations, and to control the National Guard, army and police formations.

Concerning the National Guard Organizational Regulations, he said:
"The National Guard is a voluntary armed service established to defend the victories of the revolution against restoration and reactionary attempts. In other words, it is an armed formation which, controlled by the Revolutionary Council for Public Safety, along with the army and police, will restore and maintain internal calm in the country and provide public safety measures. Members of the National Guard will take an oath for armed service... Every National Guard unit will elect its own commander in democratic elections."[241]

"Revolution is Revolution"

Earlier, on the night of October 30, the army's leadership Revolutionary Military Council held a session in the Ministry of Defense. Those taking part included members of the council, military council delegates and commanders from the military units and institutions that were in Budapest or had been ordered there after October 23, as well as delegates from the police and armed groups.

Colonel László Zólomy testified about the session while in detention:

"On October 31, 1956, we held a Military Revolutionary Council session in the Ministry of Defense. I saw that the army leadership was in very weak hands, and so I proposed to the participants of the session that Major General Béla Király be nominated head of the Chiefs of General Staff. The insurgent delegates and officers agreed with my proposal; they sent a group to the building of the Main Police Department of Budapest to get Béla Király, He arrived at the Ministry of Defense at approximately 5 a.m. on October 31. I proposed Király because I thought that he alone was capable of controlling both the insurgents...and the army..."[242] During the session the insurgent delegates nominated Király for president.[243] Lieutenant Sándor Erdélyi, a member of the Tűzoltó Street rebel group, remembered the meeting thus:

"Somebody brought up Béla Király's name...Csongovai[244] called me over and ordered me to go for Béla Király... We found Király with Sándor Kopácsi and Major General Mihály Horváth in the Budapest Police Department; they were having some sort of debate. I informed Király of the Defense Committee's request and then, with Major General Mihály Horváth, we accompanied him to the Ministry of Defense.

"After we arrived, Major General Gyula Váradi objected to Béla Király; he said that he had been the people's judge during his trial and that he knew that he had been accused of spying and that his case had not been cleared."[245]

In his memoirs, Király records Váradi's statement: "'I was a member of the military tribunal that sentenced Béla Király to death.' ... 'It is true that during the Rákosi regime people were unjustifiably persecuted, but it was also true that real criminals stood before the courts. Béla Király confessed during the trial to being an American spy. The question is whether there is a place for an American spy in such an important institution as the Revolutionary Defense Committee?' Váradi finished and sat down."[246] Király replied to Gyula Váradi's question as follows:

"I believe it is beneath my dignity to defend myself from accusations that were made against me by the secret police terror organization. What I confessed to and what I did not has nothing to do with truth and justice. It would be laughable if, in the revolution against Stalinism, we spent our time defending the victims of Stalinism from the accusations made by Stalinism against them... I decline the call to defend myself against the essence of the accusation, but I will say to you, my compatriots, that I was not and am not an American spy."[247]

Following this, many spoke out and went over to Király. Király shook hands with Váradi, and they embraced. After this Király was unanimously elected as president of the Defense Committee.[248]

As Király's rehabilitation was still going on, one of the military judges, a colonel at the meeting, was entrusted with sorting it out.[249]

In the appeal put together by the participants in the meeting–preceding Király's arrival–the following demands can be found:

"1. We demand that after leaving Budapest, Soviet troops leave the country altogether. Members of the Committee recognize the necessity for diplomatic negotiations, but this does not mean that Soviet troops can remain in Hungary indefinitely.

"2. We demand that the government call together the member states of the Warsaw Pact and withdraw from it.

"3. Delegates of the Revolutionary Committee of Hungarian Youth and revolutionary delegates from the military formations demand that Soviet troops leave Hungarian territory by December 31, 1956. If this does not take place, we will rise up with arms for the country's freedom and the purity of the revolution, expressing our willingness to fight with our lives and blood so long as foreign arms endanger our country.

"4. We state that we will fight with arms against all external or internal enemies, who step onto our land to destroy our independence.

"5. We demand that the Hungarian People's Army, if necessary with the help of revolutionary forces, occupy all the uranium mines in Hungary within a week.

"6. Anyone who infringes the discipline of the revolutionary army or does not carry out orders from above damages the revolution and will therefore be brought before the revolutionary courts.

"7. Delegates of the revolutionary forces establish the Hungarian People's Army Revolutionary Committee as an elected revolutionary committee for the army, which is the highest command for the army.

"8. An agreement has been made that the revolutionary armed youth, in the interest of public safety, order and calm, will maintain order along with the police and the Revolutionary Defense Committee. They undertake to round up alien elements and trouble-makers and hand them over to the independent Hungarian courts.

"9. We support the dissolution of the ÁVH. At the same time we demand that members of the ÁVH not join any kind of armed or public safety formation..."[250]

In his book Béla Király wrote about this appeal:
"...When at the end of the session I read it, the passionate tone and the many maximalist demands worried me very much... I was afraid that we would not be able to consolidate order with such a declaration but only unnecessarily excite passions. But of course a revolution is a revolution. Without the force of passion, revolution dies after a time, but it can bring fatal misfortune too; it is a necessary curse."[251]

The Command of Budapest Public Safety Forces Is Formed

Revolutionary events followed in rapid succession. On the afternoon of October 31, 1956, the army higher leadership realized that Béla Király–once again major general–had been appointed commander of the Budapest Military Public Safety Forces by the government, and they decided that one of his tasks was to jointly control and lead the military, National Guard and police formations in Budapest.

Not long after his appointment, Major General Király appeared at General Staff Headquarters and requested information concerning the Budapest military formations from Colonel Miklós Szűcs. Szűcs complied.

Then Király told those present that the Budapest Public Safety Committee had been formed, within which a Budapest Military Public Safety Command staff had to be established to lead the military formations. Colonel László Zólomy and Lieutenant Colonel Takács proposed that this staff be formed out of the 4th Army staff–which at that time had no subordinates–but that its military operations department take on officers in the Operational Section who had, until then, dealt with the registration of Budapest military formations.

The staff, which Király commanded, was formed after a briefing held on November 1, 1956. He regarded its first and most important task as being to stop the shooting in Budapest immediately and create order by using military formations.[252]

The Budapest Public Safety Command staff had two staffs: one worked in the Ministry of Defense–this was the organ that controlled the army in Budapest–and the other operated at Budapest police headquarters and led the police and National Guard.

When large numbers of Soviet troops again crossed the Soviet–Hungarian border, Király drew up the "Defense Plan" with Colonel Zólomy, which contained the deployment of the National Guard groups and the military formations in Budapest and their tasks. The army staff, which was led by Colonel Zólomy, had kept in continuous contact with the commanders of the three military zones in Budapest–after the Soviet troop withdrawal–and with the National Guard Supreme Command.[253] The zone commanders were responsible for order, the creation of public safety, and the cessation of shootings in their zones of operation. They received the order to send out vehicles with 20–25 people as patrols and to act anywhere they encountered a disturbance. Furthermore, they were to arrest anyone who was armed and did not belong to the National Guard.[254]

The Soviet Embassy "Siege"

On November 2 Imre Nagy called Major General Király on the telephone. The prime minister informed the general that Andropov, the Soviet ambassador, had announced not long before that unknown armed hooligans were besieging the Embassy building and that, if the Hungarian government could not ensure the diplomatic immunity of the Soviet mission, then it would be guarded by Soviet troops.

"...Prime Minister, we are restoring order, and not one hair on the heads of the Soviet Embassy staff will be harmed," Major General Király announced to Imre Nagy and acted immediately.

He gave the order to Lieutenant Colonel Károly Csémy, the zone commander, to make battle-ready one mechanized rifle battalion and a tank battalion and to await his arrival. Following this, Király alerted a National Guard battalion and ordered them into their vehicles. The latter battalion was placed under the command of Lieutenant János Décsy, the leader of the operational section.

"Diplomatic immunity applies to the Soviet Embassy too. Anyone who tries to disturb their work must be seen off from there, whatever methods we have to use. You all know what the alternative is! If Soviet troops again enter Budapest to defend their Embassy, that is the end for us..."[255] Király evaluated the situation at a briefing for the National Guard sub-unit; then they departed. On the way to the Embassy, they stopped off at the Dózsa Barracks where, at the order, Lieutenant Colonel Károly Csémy's rifle and tank sub-units also fell into the column.

In his book Király recalls the "siege" of the Soviet Embassy and the meeting with the ambassador:

"When we got to Bajza Street, I stopped the column and looked over at the Soviet Embassy. There was total silence in the street. Not only was there no trace of any siege, but there were not even any people in the street. I took a freedom-fighter squad and hurried toward the Soviet

Embassy... I introduced myself and my interpreter to Yuri V. Andropov... Then the ambassador introduced his colleagues. Then I said:

'Mr. Ambassador! The president of the Council of Ministers, Imre Nagy, ordered me to come and defend the Soviet Embassy from besiegers. But where are the besiegers? I can't see anyone.'

'The prime minister, it seems, misunderstood me. Two old women came here to the Embassy,' said Andropov. 'They complained that their flats had been burned during the fighting, and they sought a place to stay. They looked around here but said that the rooms were too high and it would be hard to heat them, so the building did not suit them. Then they went away. Before they left we gave them tea in order to express the Soviet people's friendship towards the Hungarian people.'

Andropov lied without turning a hair, but at least he showed some humor. I have always valued humor, even gallows humor, but I did not take kindly to this bald-faced lying.

'Mr. Ambassador, even old women will not step over this threshold without your permission. I have set up a guard in front of the Embassy, and we will guard the building very carefully.'

'Let us not exaggerate,' said the ambassador. 'Let's forget this petty incident. There are much more important things at stake. Won't you come up to my office? I would like you to ring the president of the Council of Ministers from here and ask him something. Are you willing?"

'Naturally, I am at your service...'[256]

"We did not even sit down," Király writes later in the book.

Andropov pointed to one of the telephones on his table. It was plugged into the so-called 'K' system, the network which only members of the Political Committee, ministers and party and government leaders could use. It was typical of the colonial situation in Hungary that the Soviet ambassador was plugged into a system that was reserved exclusively for the domestic government.

'If you dial "1" Imre Nagy will answer,' said Andropov.

'I dialed '1.'

'I am calling from Ambassador Andropov's study. I am delighted to announce that there is, and was, no siege here. Before I leave I will even set up a double guard to protect the building. But this is not why I called. The ambassador asked me to ask you, Prime Minister, whether you have received the Soviet memorandum that the Soviet–Hungarian negotiations propose for the withdrawal of Soviet troops from Hungary.'

"'Yes, we have received it,' answered Imre Nagy, with evident satisfaction.

"'Please tell the ambassador that the Hungarian government accepts the Soviet proposal with pleasure and will be ready this afternoon to begin negotiating. We propose that negotiations begin in the Parliament building. In fact, you are also a member of the Hungarian delegation,[257] so please hurry over here. We will start discussing what the Hungarian delegation proposes. Give my greetings to the ambassador.'

"I told Andropov what I had heard and left...I left the freedom-fighter squad outside the Embassy gates with orders to stay there until I sent the relief guard, and not to allow anyone near the door unless the Embassy staff confirmed that that person had business in the Embassy.

"On Hősök Square I informed Lieutenant Colonel Csémy of the events and ordered him to take his troops back to barracks. I also ordered him to protect the building in which the Soviet Embassy resided with a double guard..."[258]

National Guard Supreme Command is Formed

The Revolutionary Council for Public Safety's general assembly held a meeting on November 3.[259] Major General Király decided that the most important objective of this meeting was to elect the organ that would direct the operations of the Revolutionary Council for Public Safety. In other words, the National Guard Supreme Command was to be established.

The major general spoke of how the Hungarian government had withdrawn from the Warsaw Pact and had asked the great powers to guarantee the neutrality that it had declared.

He announced that the Revolutionary Council for Public Safety had been made responsible by the government–until the holding of general secret elections–for maintaining order, and thus the National Guard had to be made into a disciplined, organized law-enforcement unit.

"The most important concern is to consolidate the organization of National Guard formations established up to now to the greatest possible extent and to execute to the letter the orders of the government,"[260] said Major General Király, who then summarized the tasks of the Revolutionary Council for Public Safety. First of all, a staff needed to be set up consisting of delegates from units who had taken part in the revolutionary fights, including representatives of the army, police, and the worker and youth armed forces.

This new staff would operate until a new government established through general elections and secret ballot came into being. The staff's most significant task was to consolidate and discipline the existing National Guard formations and to offer operative leadership that ensured law and order.[261]

The speakers stressed the importance of creating a united leadership.

Király was unanimously elected the commander in chief of the National Guard, with Police Colonel Kopácsi as his deputy. The staff was created of representatives of National Guard sub-units, units of the Corvin Cinema, Baross Square, Széna Square, Práter Street, the District IX armed groups, the Polytechnical University, representatives of the army and police.

A decree of the Revolutionary Council for Public Safety was accepted by the assembly unanimously. It stated, among other things, that the National Guard Supreme Command–in the interest of protecting the country's independence–would maintain law and order within the country until free, democratic elections were held. Since the strike endangered Hungary's defense readiness, the Council's general assembly–apart from total battle readiness–proposed returning to productive work.[262]

The newly elected Council continued its meeting after Király and Kopácsi departed.[263]

When they returned from Parliament, Király recalls the events thus:

'At the meeting there was a nasty episode. Numerous speakers demanded personnel changes in the highest army leadership in the interest of stricter controls in the Ministry of Defense. One of the speakers was Colonel [Lieutenant Colonel–authors] István Marián, who took part in the Council's work as the commander of the Polytechnical University National Guard brigade. Presumably out of opportunism, he made a long speech about the unreliability of the Ministry of Defense and proposed that the whole assembly march into Parliament and demand the appointment of Béla Király as minister of defense.

"The proposal infuriated me; I announced that if the assembly did not reject Marián's proposal, I would resign immediately and leave the assembly. In the present situation to make such a proposal was a crime, and I would not in any way accept the proposal even if the assembly unanimously voted for it. At this Marián withdrew his proposal and apologized..."[264]

Free Kossuth Radio announced at 14:25 that the Revolutionary Council for Public Safety had established the National Guard Supreme Command and that Major General Béla Király had been unanimously elected the National Guard commander in chief.

The Revolutionary Council for Public Safety general assembly issued the following, also put out on radio:

The Revolutionary Council for Public Safety "...stands firmly for the independence and neutrality of our country. It opposes all armed aggression against our independence and neutrality. Until free, democratic elections are held, we will use all our force to consolidate order and fulfill the government's orders to destroy restoration attempts and troublemakers.

"The strike is causing grave damage to our defense readiness, and that is why we propose the strike be ended and productive work begun so that the National Guard formations may be armed even while at work, so that in the event of aggression they can immediately be ready for battle and take up the fight against the aggressors.

"From today onwards only National Guard personnel can bear arms besides the members of the army or police. We will disarm anyone who is not a member of either the National Guard, police, or army in the interest of consolidating order.

"National Guardsmen! Long live our sacred country's independence and neutrality!

"Long live our victorious national democratic revolution! Preserve our national unity!"[265]

Lieutenant Colonel István Marián started to organize the operational section of the National Guard's Supreme Command. Later, while in detention, he summarized the events of November 3:

"At the meeting, Béla Király gave an account of the work done so far by the Operative Committee and announced the Committee's tasks. While doing so he said the situation was critical, that new Soviet troops were entering the country, but that there were negotiations going on and there was hope of an agreement, referring to the UN as well...

"He spoke with authority about the internal situation. He said that defense steps were being taken in case of another Soviet intervention...

"Béla Király and Kopácsi gave short accounts. They said that there had been changes in the government and that they had withdrawn from the Warsaw Pact. The situation was very critical, negotiations were going on, but judging from the further Soviet troop arrivals and deployments, another intervention was probable..."[266]

After the meeting Király held a command briefing where, following the voicing of general problems, the action to restore order planned for the next day–November 4–was discussed.

"We had to solve hundreds of urgent problems: regular provisions, coordination between groups and districts, control and inclusion of the freedom-fighter groups in the provinces in one united armed force; the arrangement of posts for soldiers and policemen; the control of the army and police sub-units who had joined along with their commanders; the coordination of the army, the police and the freedom-fighter units; the maintenance of order in the country, but especially in Budapest, all came under the National Guard Supreme Command..."[267] This work, which had started with such dynamism, was rendered impossible by the Soviet troop attack a few hours later.

Polish "No," Yugoslav "Yes"

The Soviet leadership began negotiations on the continuation of military operations–in accordance with the Soviet Central Committee's Presidium–on November 1 in Brest.

Leading up to the meetings, the Polish leadership, along with Gomulka, had supported Imre Nagy's consolidation ambitions and had condemned the first Soviet invasion. Therefore the Soviet and Polish leaders at Brest reached no agreement on the second military intervention.

In the Polish Central Committee's appeal of November 2, it was said that "the defense of socialism in Hungary must be ensured by the Hungarian people and not by external intervention."[268] Gomulka, upon hearing of the new turn of events in Hungary on November 4 at the Polish Central Committee's national party conference, apart from stressing the incorrectness of such intervention, announced that the "unity of the socialist bloc and internal calm comes above all." "With this Soviet attack Poland is faced with a fait accompli, and the Polish leadership must be realistic politically, it must continue its long-term policies, and the 'interest' of the country must not be sacrificed to sudden decisions made for momentary gain." Thus János Tischler summarized Gomulka's words on Hungary on the basis of documentary finds.[269]

On November 2 the Soviet leadership conducted talks in Bucharest with the Bulgarian, Romanian, and Czechoslovak leaders. Everyone supported a military operation. The Czechoslovaks and Romanians even offered to join in the operations against Hungary. This also came up in the meetings with Tito, where Khrushchev announced that "the Romanians are sending troops to Hungary." Tito thought this would be a mistake, and so "Khrushchev abandoned it."[270] Tito said that there was no necessity for such a move and that it would be better if the Soviet Union intervened alone and broke up the "counter-revolution."[271]

The Soviet leaders on the night of November 2–3, on Brioni Island, before the meeting with Tito, were afraid that the Yugoslav leadership would stick to its October 29 viewpoint. Tito sent a letter to the Hungarian Workers Party Central Leadership in the name of the Alliance of Yugoslav Communist Central Committees. In addition to warning them of the danger of "counter-revolution," he welcomed the new party leadership and the Hungarian government's October 28 declaration. "The essential elements of the new party and state leadership's political platform, such as... placing the relationship of socialist countries on the basis of equality and respect for sovereignty, its initiation of negotiations to withdraw Soviet troops from Hungary, etc., and the real analysis of Hungarian events contained in the government's declaration all prove that the policy of today's state and party leadership and the Hungarian working people's true, socialist and democratic ambitions converge..."[272] he writes.

V. Micunic, the Yugoslav ambassador to Moscow, who was present at the meetings and "took diary notes,"[273] noted some of Khrushchev's reasons for Soviet intervention. Khrushchev said that the Soviet Union "cannot by any means sit by idly" watching the events in Hungary–hangings of communists, Imre Nagy's appeal to the UN, the withdrawal from the Warsaw Pact–because if they did, "the capitalists will think that they are either weak or stupid, which can only lead to one thing. The capitalists will push their positions to the Soviet borders." Khrushchev announced that enough troops had been amassed and that they had decided to intervene in Hungarian events. "They will need only one or two days." Khrushchev told his host that Ferenc Münnich and János Kádár had "escaped from Budapest and now are on the plane to Moscow."

Khrushchev also gave as a reason for intervening the fact that in the Soviet Union 'there are, or would be, quite a few who would analyze the situation thus: while Stalin ruled, everybody shut up and there were no disturbances of any kind. Now that they (Khrushchev here used a very ugly word to describe the Soviet leadership) are in power, we have bloodshed and the breaking away of Hungary. And yet these same leaders condemn Stalin! According to Khrushchev the Soviet army would throw this in their faces first of all...Hungary as a Western ally has twice fought against Russia. Anti-Hungarian feeling is strong in the Soviet army: The Hungarians have now again joined up with the West and oppose Russia."[274]

The Yugoslav leaders noted that their viewpoint had been expressed in Tito's letter to the Hungarians. Then they announced: "We also see this clearly and are worried about this shift to the right, the counter-revolutionary turn of events, what kind of government can it be where communists are murdered and hung. If there is a counter-revolution in Hungary, then intervention is necessary, but it must not rely merely on Soviet weapons... Political preparations must also be made. We must save what we can and try to establish a revolutionary government with Hungarians, or at least announce its transformation, which can then turn to the people with some sort of program."

Reacting to the Yugoslav opinion and its proposal for government transformation, Khrushchev revealed that Ferenc Münnich, the former ambassador to Moscow, "had been entrusted with transforming the government," but there "is also Kádár."

Then the Yugoslav leaders–despite the fact that they did not know either of them 'well enough"–suggested that the "new revolutionary government be formed not by Münnich but by János Kádár."

"The Russians seemed to have decided on Münnich, but they did not oppose, in fact I could say that they accepted, our reasons," Micunovic wrote in his diary.

During the meetings the name of Mátyás Rákosi came up several times. Khrushchev said that Rákosi had announced in Moscow that "he would gladly help" in Budapest. But Khrushchev had only replied that "you can go there if you really want to, but the people will only string you up."

When the Soviet leadership asked what should be in the new Hungarian government's appeal, the Yugoslavs suggested "putting in a mention about the withdrawal of Soviet troops too."

Khrushchev agreed "with the promise to withdraw Soviet troops, although he obviously did not wish to especially emphasize it," noted Micunovic.

During supper Khrushchev again asked: Who should be in the government? Micunovic later remembered the conversation that followed like this:

"It seems that they cannot really stomach Kádár and that he is not really their candidate. Khrushchev again praised Münnich; he has only just realized that he was always against Rákosi. Münnich is an old communist, whom Khrushchev has known for 20 years. Sometime in the 1930s they both took part in a two-month Russian exercise as Soviet Army officers. They lived in the same tent. It looks as if the Russians have already put together the government, making Münnich prime minister. Then I (Micunovic) asked to speak. I said that I knew Münnich well, that we had often met in Moscow and that I had only good things to say of him. But if we had to choose between him and Kádár, we must take into account a vital political difference. Under Rákosi Münnich was ambassador to Moscow, while Kádár was a prisoner in Budapest. In the eyes of every Hungarian this will be a decisive factor in Kádár's favor. Khrushchev recognized the truth of what I said and did not argue any further."[275]

Later the Yugoslavs indicated as a possible solution in regard to Imre Nagy that Zoltán Szántó, along with Géza Losonczy, "might be willing to ask for refuge from possible persecution in the Yugoslav Embassy." Khrushchev and Malenkov announced several times that "everything done along these lines could be of decisive importance for the Nagy government." Weighing these ideas, Micunovic wrote the following in his diary:

"The Russians are not giving away the time the intervention will begin. We cannot ask them; they do not wish to speak about it. Because of this, it is not clear how much time and what possibilities we have–in order to reduce the numbers of victims and to avoid senseless bloodshed–to try to influence Imre Nagy, at least if this is what we have agreed.

Khrushchev, and chiefly Malenkov, invest this with huge significance and add that every attempt by the Yugoslavs in this direction is right and proper."[276]

On this basis the Yugoslavs promised to help Imre Nagy and those close to him step down from political life. The Yugoslav leadership saw as it as their primary objective to trick Imre Nagy into the Embassy on November 4, with the cooperation of Zoltán Szántó, and persuade him to make a declaration supporting the Kádár government. But the Yugoslav attempt was already outdated by November 4. The message from Soviet Ambassador to Belgrade N. P. Firyubin to Kardelj sent from Moscow on November 5 already states that the Soviet Central Committee's position on the declaration–on November 4–had changed. When Imre Nagy "was still prime minister, ... his declaration could have made the suppression of the counter-revolution easier. But they now thought that there was absolutely no necessity for a declaration from Imre Nagy."[277]

Despite this Imre Nagy prepared a declaration on November 5 in which, instead of his support for the Kádár government and his resignation, the following can be read:

"... The fact that Hungarian leading circles have requested the intervention of Soviet troops has made the situation and work of my government extraordinarily difficult. The workers have responded with a general strike, life is paralyzed and the armed struggle has escalated. I feel it is necessary to repeat to the country in this critical situation, as the responsible leader of the government, that I have always been led by communist conviction and conscience to be loyal to my people and country, a conviction that has influenced my activities for four decades and from which I will not be dissuaded, whatever the future holds."[278]

"This Government Should Not Be a Puppet Government"

Earlier, on November 3, an extended meeting of the Soviet Central Committee's Presidium was held with Kádár and Münnich participating (Serov and Konyev were not present because they were traveling to Hungary, and Zhukov was too busy planning military operations), where they again discussed the composition of the "counter-government" set up by the Soviet leadership.

It was then that Mikoyan, on the basis of the agreement with the Yugoslav leadership–despite the October 31 decision–proposed that János Kádár head the government and not Münnich.

Kádár then asked to speak and, despite the "shortage of time," asked several questions critical of the Soviet leadership. Malin's notes on Kádár's address shed light on Soviet-Hungarian relations after 1945.

"One thing: Why did they elect Gerő in the summer as first secretary?

"Soviet comrades have always helped, but they made one mistake ...they only trusted three or four Hungarian comrades completely: Rákosi, Gerő, and Farkas, even though there were many good people among the rest. Three or four people monopolized relations between Hungary and the Soviet Union. This was the source of many problems.

"Rákosi said: this is what the Soviet comrades think, and everybody was silent... It meant that to condemn Rákosi was to act against the Soviet comrades... The Soviet comrades were happy that Rákosi and Gerő were at the head for 12 years..."[279]

Analyzing Imre Nagy's "behavior," Kádár announced that the prime minister was concealing counter-revolutionaries who were killing communists[280] and that the "government has no strength to suppress them."[281]

Kádár asked rhetorically, "What is to be done?" and gave the following answer:

"A socialist country must not be allowed to suffer counter-revolution. We agree with you. The right measures–a revolutionary government–must be established."[282]

In his closing remarks Kádár stressed that the demonstrators "did not want to destroy the people's democratic system" and that the "withdrawal of Soviet troops was very important." If "we strengthen the military connection, we will weaken politically,"[283] he announced.

Kádár requested that the government, established according to Soviet leadership decisions and instructions, should not be a "puppet government" in that it "needs the support of the workers to act."[284] "Kádár should head the government,"[285] announced the Presidium unanimously.

Imre Horváth noted, in regard to the composition of the government, that "Prime Minister Kádár, Deputy, Interior and Defense Minister Münnich, with Apró, Rónai, Kiss, Marosán, Hidas, Berei, Andics, Kovács, Egri, Vég, and Dögei, are members."[286]

*

As we have seen, the Soviet leadership left nothing to chance. The government established by the Soviet leadership was formed on November 4. Its members were János Kádár, Ferenc Münnich, Imre Horváth, István Kossa, Antal Apró, Imre Dögei and Sándor Rónai.

The Hungarian Revolutionary Worker-Peasant Government program's 14th point read that "in the interest of our nation, working class and country, we have asked the Soviet army command to help our people suppress the dark forces of reaction and restore peace and order in our country."

The 15th point–taking into account the Yugoslav proposal–established the following: "After the restoration of law and order, the Hungarian government will start negotiations with the Soviet government and the other parties in the Warsaw Pact to withdraw Soviet troops from Hungarian territory."[287]

But Khrushchev and the Soviet military leadership were mistaken when they allowed only three days for the suppression of the revolutionary forces. Khrushchev and Malenkov, in their letter on November 5 to Tito, Rankovich and Kardelj, stated, despite the reality, that on November 4 at 12 o'clock Moscow time, the "counter-revolution" had been broken in Hungary and the enemy centers in the Corvin Cinema would be liquidated in the shortest possible time.

"Counter-revolutionary resistance has been strangled in all county and district centers too. Hungarian units have been disarmed, the weapons placed in warehouses and the soldiers returned to barracks."[288]

A flat contradiction of these claims was supplied by Malashenko and Kirov, relying on Soviet sources. Within the current work the authors–for reasons of space–have provided only a few glimpses of the resistance.[289]

The Revolution Turns Into a War

Béla Király, the president of the Revolutionary Council for Public Safety and the commander in chief of the National Guard, spoke to Imre Nagy several times during the night by phone about the advance of Soviet troops, and then their attack.

He later recalled one conversation between himself and the prime minister:

"Shortly after midnight, reports started to come in from Budapest's outer defense ring that Soviet troops were carrying out reconnaissance work on certain defense positions. I again called Prime Minister Imre Nagy and had the most dramatic conversation of my life.

"'Prime Minister! It is now certain that the Soviet Union has launched a war against us. The first Soviet waves are already attacking Budapest's outer defense ring. We do not have reliable contact with every defense position and zone. Until now we have ordered our troops not to shoot, so now many commanders may be very uncertain. It is possible that they will only act when it is too late, that Soviet troops will storm them. We have only one choice: either you, Prime Minister, or I must immediately make a radio broadcast. We must inform our troops that we are at war with the Soviet Union and that they must start their defensive struggle!'

"'This is a political affair. As a General Staff officer, you must know that such a declaration is a thing for the government, not for the military. I forbid you to make such an announcement!' Imre Nagy replied.

"'I am completely aware of this. That is why I proposed that you, as prime minister, make the declaration, or if you prefer I will do it with your consent,' I declared.

"'No. We will not issue such a declaration whatever the case,' said Imre Nagy. 'That would mean war and we don't want that, we cannot undertake war against the Soviet Union... Please continue to inform me of events!'"[290]

The National Guard commander in chief again rang Nagy when he saw a Soviet tank column winding its way towards Parliament.

"Prime Minister, Soviet troops have broken the defense ring in several places and have penetrated deep into the capital. One tank column is now advancing past our building and making for Parliament. I will count the tanks...,"[291] said Király to Nagy, who after a short pause said the following very decisively:

"I do not wish any more reports!"

Király could not figure out for a long time why, at a time of enemy aggression, the prime minister did not want further reports from the supreme commander of his armed forces. The general did not know that before Nagy's dramatic appeal over the radio, the prime minister, along with several others–accepting the proffered sanctuary–left Parliament for the Yugoslav Embassy. As we have already mentioned,

Lieutenant General Károly Janza, the ex-minister of defense, paced through the Defense Ministry offices giving the order that Hungarian troops should show absolutely no resistance and welcome the Soviet troops warmly. When Janza entered Colonel Zólomy's office, Zólomy rejected the lieutenant general's order, saying that he was only answerable to Imre Nagy's government. Janza repeated the order while the colonel called General Király and told him the orders had been given.

Then Janza requested the receiver from Colonel Zólomy and gave the same order to Király.

Király, like Zólomy, announced that Janza was not a member of the government and that he was only willing to serve Nagy's government, and that furthermore, he would not lay down his arms and would take up a battle position so that the Russians would not be able to capture him.[292]

Béla Király called the members of the Revolutionary Council for Public Safety and ordered them to follow him to the hills and continue organizing against the Soviet troops.[293]

"I met Béla Király at dawn on November 4, 1956; he called me over," remembers István Marián and then continues in his detention testimony:

"Several people were in Király's room: Béla Király, Sándor Kopácsi, József Lantos, and Vilmos Oláh. When I entered, a sharp debate was going on. Király said that the Soviet troop attack against Budapest had started from all directions. Imre Nagy had called on the groups to resist and had turned to the UN for help.

"Then I went out of the room, and without Király's knowledge I gave the order over the phone for the formations at the university not to take up the fight but to leave the university and that only a guard–provided by the fire service–should stay behind.

"When I went back into the room, Király was saying that from here the situation could not be assessed, that we had to relocate in fighting position. He asked me how many university students could be counted on. I told him that I thought 3000–4000.

'Király announced that we were leaving; I got into a car with him and Vilmos Oláh. First we went up to the castle, where I gave Király's order for the liaison officers to come out to the 56 tram stop. From there we went to Zugliget... From here we went to the border guard barracks in Fácános, where, at Király's command, I organized the security blockade.'"[294]

The commander of the National Guard unit made up of university students, General Dániel Görgényi, called Király at the barracks and told him that, at a meeting held in the Political Officers Academy, it had been decided that "truce bearers must be sent to the Soviet command and offer a ceasefire. The condition of the Hungarian ceasefire would be that no criminal proceedings should be initiated against anyone and that the Soviet command especially guarantee the personal safety of Generals Maléter and Király."

"Béla, I ask you to come down here and sign this decree before we give it to the Soviet command. Please tell the Supreme Command to come down with you," finished Major General Görgényi."[295]

General Király thought this plan naive. He believed that if the Imre Nagy government existed and was capable of making some sort of agreement with the Soviet leadership, then it would do so unconditionally.

"If I had known that the Imre Nagy government did not exist, then I would have advised the freedom fighters to cease the hopeless fight and save what lives and public property we could. But then I thought that the Imre Nagy government would somehow come to the surface and give some sort of sign,"[296] writes Király in his book. Following Görgényi's call, Király and the members of his staff debated further.[297]

Lieutenant Colonel Marián proposed that the command go one by one to the Academy, but Király and the majority of the National Guard were for staying put.

"At this point everybody must listen to their own conscience. If somebody tries to save something that is salvageable, that is laudable. If someone wants to fight, he should. If someone decides to take a road that leads straight to the West, that is also acceptable. I now ask all those who want to join General Görgényi to leave immediately. Let us not stand on ceremony or be emotional. Those who want to go should go, but right away,"[298] Király concluded. Lieutenant Colonel Marián and a few others left immediately.

Later the general said about his aim to continue resisting:

"Even if it does not sound heroic, I have to say that I did not keep the Supreme Command together in order to organize a guerilla war, or to prolong Hungarian suffering with stubborn warfare. My only aim was that if Imre Nagy did make some sort of acceptable compromise, that there be some sort of organization on which he could rely. That is why I strengthened the defense of Szabadság Hill, and that is why I was willing to fight on to keep the Supreme Command alive until such a moment arrived..."²⁹⁹

A Mosaic of the Resistance

The Soviet troops started the attack at dawn on November 4. They began Operation "Whirlwind."

Ferenc Münnich, the minister of the armed forces in the Kádár government, ordered that the Hungarian army not open fire on arriving Soviet troops, but send truce bearers ahead of them.

Lieutenant General Károly Janza, who was in the Ministry of Defense along with Major Generals Gyula Uszta, Gyula Váradi and Imre Kovács, forbade resistance. The Ministry of Defense main sections, sub-sections and directorate, as well as the National Air Defense Command, passed the order on to their subordinates.

At 5:20 Imre Nagy's appeal went out on radio: "Imre Nagy speaking, the president of the Council of Ministers of the Hungarian People's Republic. Today at dawn Soviet troops attacked our capital with the obvious intention of overthrowing the legitimate Hungarian democratic government. Our troops are fighting. The government is at its post. I announce this to the people of the country and of the world."

Major General Király decided to continue resistance.

In Budapest, near the Petőfi Barracks, five to 10 minutes of firing took place between Soviets marching into the city and the troops in the barracks. Following this the Soviet forces fired at the barracks for an hour and a half. The 8th mechanized regiment in the barracks became afraid. The commander of the Esztergom tank regiment led eight tanks against the Soviets, but instead of fighting they set off back to Esztergom.

The forces of the Hungarian army organized their resistance in Budapest near the Juta Hill, where a medium air defense artillery company subordinate to the 51st air defense artillery unit (under the command of Pál Rémiás), a light air defense artillery unit led by Lieutenant János Kicska, and an air defense cannon were in firing positions. Some of these forces opened fire on a Soviet military column on November 4 at 10 o'clock; it lost two tanks, two rocket launchers and a vehicle as a result. Of the Soviet soldiers and the security officers in the vans more than 16–11 Soviets and three Hungarians–died, 10 were wounded and the others fled. Of the state security officers that were captured, two were shot in the head by soldiers. In the afternoon these same cannons were already opening fire from other positions. They shot at a motorcycle and sidecar. They also caught the fuel tank of one of the Soviet tanks on fire, but those inside managed to escape from the burning vehicle.

Sixteen soldiers from the Hungarian Army's 2960 Air Defense Regiment took up firing positions on Jászberényi Road, Kőbányai Road, the corner of Éles, on Zalka Máté Square and in Csajkovszkij Park with the rebels and six cannons. At 13 hours they opened fire on four Soviet tanks approaching the Éles corner. Three tanks caught fire and the rebels attacked the burning tanks. Until November 8 they continued to fight Soviet tanks and even fired at a helicopter as well.

It was typical of the cruelty of Soviet troops that Soviet tanks fired at unarmed soldiers from the 19th air defense artillery unit in Záhony when they surrounded their barracks. Five died, eight were wounded, and 60 soldiers were captured and transported to the Soviet Union.

In Budapest, rebels in the Hungarian Railways Directorate building on Kerepesi Road fired several rounds at Soviet troops who were grouping near Keleti Station, who then left by the back entrance. Following this the Soviet sub-unit that checked out the building seized two officers from the No. 1 Railway Directorate Military Transport Section and executed them very shortly afterwards.

In Budapest Soviet tanks attacked and crushed the Jászberény 50th artillery regiment's column. Many vehicles were burned, and the ammunition in them exploded.

In Budapest many of the Ráday Street rebels fought Soviet troops from the house at Ferenc Boulevard 18, while the majority of those in Tompa Street fought from the Electricity Board building on the corner of Ferenc Boulevard and Tompa Street. Members of the Tűzoltó Street and the Ferenc Square group resisted near the Perpetual Adoration Church, by Nagyvárad Square, in Viola Street, Mester Street and near the church on Hámán Kató Road. There was fierce fighting in and around Üllői Road, Práter Street and Kisfaludy Street, where both rebels and Soviet troops suffered serious losses. Some of the Vajdahunyad Street group also continued to resist. The sub-unit of the National Guard in the District VIII Police Station also fought against Soviet forces.

On November 5 and 6, the Thököly Road fighters–reinforced by János Fulós's group–delivered a serious blow to the Soviets. Rebels also fought against Soviet forces in the areas around Lehel Road and Fóti Road.

On November 7 the Steiner group at Baross Square fought with Soviet troops. Some of the Vajda Street group and the rebels around the Royal Hotel organized an attack against a Soviet truck.

On November 9 Soviet troops and Hungarian law enforcement agencies attacked a group of Corvin rebels near Tarján as they were retreating towards the Austrian border, during which many rebels died or were wounded.

On November 11 the rebels in Pesterzsébet gave up resistance. Soviet troops had suffered significant losses in this district.

Between November 20 and December 5, Zoltán Kovács and his group twice organized attacks in Obuda near Filatorigát against the Soviet formations stationed there.

Twenty soldiers from the 6th battery of the Hungarian People's Army 93518 air defense formation took up firing positions with rebels on Imre Square in Csepel and prepared to start fighting the Soviets.

The soldiers and rebels blasted at a Soviet armored transport and a tank in the afternoon. In return Soviet armored troops fired on the center of Csepel. A small group of Csepel National Guardsmen blew up an ammunition vehicle in the fight against the Soviets in the Királyerdő. The next day a rocket launcher fired on Tököl Airport from the vicinity of the Csepel Suburban Railway Station. On November 6 air defense guns on Imre Square shot down an IL-28 Soviet airplane, and a Soviet tank was destroyed near Kikötő Street. In the early hours of November 7, in order to obstruct the entry of Soviet troops, the rebels blew up the road on Vámmentesi Road and Kikötő Street. On November 8 National Guardsmen and soldiers pushed a railway coach in front of the Soviet troop column arriving in Csepel and blew up a tank. In the afternoon Soviet artillery fired on the area around Imre Square. In Csepel Soviet troops only managed to break the resistance in Csepel on the 10th, according to other sources on the 11th.

In Szolnok at 4:15 Soviet troops begin to invade the barracks of the garrison. As guards at the non-commissioned officers' training school fired, the Soviets returned fire with tank cannons, killing one trainee and wounding another. One soldier from the 27th air defense artillery regiment died, and two were wounded. Two of the 56th mortar artillery regiment were wounded. The Hungarian units were disarmed.

In Békéscsaba shots were fired on the Soviet troops occupying the town from the revolutionary council building, as a result of which two to four Soviet soldiers, two policemen and a civilian lost their lives. Soviet tanks, armored vehicles and infantry then opened fire. Outside the recruitment center building a Hungarian officer was shot in the stomach and later died of his wounds in hospital. Soviet troops disarmed the National Guard and army formations.

In Dunaföldvár the Soviets shot up the technical station of the air defense artillery regiment, then fired on the barracks with tanks and artillery.

Most of Székesfehérvár was occupied by Soviet troops after 4 o'clock. During the fight many shots were fired at the Army Corps command, the officers' mess, the town council, county council and post office buildings. When the airport barracks was captured, the Soviets shot down a surrendering soldier. Near the Cartridge Factory a wounded soldier and a surrendering soldier were shot in the head by Soviets. A third was wounded. Three died from the 75th signal corps battalion, and two were wounded.

The Tab 89th independent anti-tank artillery regiment's 1st and 2nd battalion took up firing positions, but the soldiers did not shoot. The cannons captured by civilian rebels were crushed by Soviet tanks.

In Sárbogád Soviet troops fired a salvo on the secondary school and the station building at 3:30. In the latter four were killed and three wounded. In the evening a Soviet soldier opened fire on a patrol from the 2nd Vehicle Driving School; two soldiers died and an officer was wounded.

In Szombathely, during a battle that began at 4 in the morning, Soviet troops captured the important public buildings. In the fight about 10 Hungarians lost their lives, mostly National Guardsmen, police and railway workers. The Soviet military command and the former Hungarian state security officers who came with them arrested members of the National Committee.

In Kaposvár Soviet troops occupied the prison and the party committee headquarters with around 35 tanks. Seven Hungarians lost their lives in the fray.

In Kecskemét occupying Soviet forces shot down an officer from the recruitment center; three were wounded.

In Miskolc a guard fired warning shots at Soviet troops as they occupied the university; the Soviets then fired on the building. Some of the National Guard in the student colleges took up the fight. Two university students died in the crossfire and three were wounded. There were no Soviet casualties. Soviet troops opened fire without warning on the 2nd air defense artillery battery, which had not shown any resistance at all; a Hungarian soldier was killed.

On November 6 at 18 hours, Russian and Hungarian truce bearers from the Soviet armored division at Dunaföldvár arrived in Dunapentele and ordered the National Committee to lay down their arms. The National Committee members announced that they would not do so and that if Soviet troops attacked the town they would defend it. On November 7 the Soviets started to fight at 24:30, and after 25 minutes of fire eight MIG 17s attacked the cannons which had fired on the planes. The Soviets surrounded the town with tanks and fired on it with heavy mortar and 122 mm howitzers. At 16:30 the defense of Dunapentele collapsed. In the fight eight people died and 35 were wounded. Forty-one medium and light air defense guns were put out of action.

National Guardsmen–both civilians and soldiers–gathered near the Óbuda Schmidt Castle to fight against the Soviets. They organized themselves into officers and officer trainee squads and companies and prepared for the defense.

Members of the group blew up the nearby radio jamming station that day. The next day the group fought Soviet troops. After the rebels inflicted significant losses on the Soviet troops, the commander disbanded the group on November 7. On November 8 the freedom fighters around the Schmidt Castle gave up the fight.

In the morning of November 4 the Széna Square group started to fight the attacking Soviet forces; then some of the rebels withdrew in the direction of the Buda Hills.

Later a group concealed near Széna Square started to fight Soviet forces, but they were forced to retreat. A part of the group came into conflict with Soviet troops on November 13 in the Solymár area. Seventeen rebels fell; the leader of the group, János Szabó, then disbanded it.

As far as we know, what happened in Izsák on November 4 is unique in the history of the revolution. Soviet armored troops arriving in Izsák opened fire at 3 in the morning on the 7th army ammunition depot's law enforcement detail, during which an officer was wounded. Later the infantry approached the depot under cover of fire. The commander of the Soviet sub-unit, Captain Dolgopolov, demanded that arms be surrendered, but when the Hungarian commander was not willing to undertake this "shameful act," he went twice to his superior divisional commander, then a third time to the Army Corps commander to get the order to lay down arms rescinded. Two or three days later the depot was given permission to keep its arms by the Soviet Army Corps commander, and they continued to guard the depot.

According to Soviet forces Hungarian resistance was finally broken, and the army disarmed at the end of November. Following this Soviet troops carried out the tasks of the military administration–patrols and sentry duty within the town commands throughout the country. But Soviet state security organs (the KGB) continued to arrest rebels and resistance fighters and collect weapons from the population.

During the revolution, from the effectives of the Hungarian People's Army 185 soldiers lost their lives and 1347 were wounded (these are not final figures).

Operation "Whirlwind" had come to an end. One of the most important demands of the revolution–the withdrawal of Soviet troops from Hungary–was not realized for long decades.

Marshal Konyev announced in a meeting held on November 24, 1956, in Hungary that the Soviet government had issued a decree to establish a Southern Army Command from the majority of formations sent to Hungary.

After November 4, the great Western powers relied on the tactics they had employed after the first intervention on October 24. Strongly worded declarations were made, but support, even from the UN, faded into humanitarian aid and the acceptance of Hungarian refugees.

"We felt for the Hungarians with all our hearts," Eisenhower, the recently re-elected American president, announced on November 14, "and we will do everything to assist those who suffer. But the government of the United States does not suggest, and indeed never can suggest, that a defenseless population start an open revolution against a power which it is not capable of defeating."

Notes

Report of V. I. Fomin, who was on the staff of the 2nd division's political section in 1949. Published in *Magyarország* (Hungary)–weekly paper p. 4, No. 42, 1990.

Proper minutes were not taken of the Soviet Party Presidium's sessions, but Vladimir Nikoforvich Malin, the section leader of the Central Committee, took notes on the proceedings. These notes–17 in all–and some of the documents pertaining to them were published in János M. Rainer's *"Decision in the Kremlin, 1956–An attempt to analyze notes"* study in March 1996 for the 1956 Institute. *Decision in the Kremlin, 1956* is extraordinarily interesting and high-quality work, and we recommend it to readers.

Decision in the Kremlin, 1956–The Soviet Party Presidium's Debates on Hungary, edited by the 1956 Institute: Vyacheslav Sereda and János M. Rainer. The introduction was written by Sereda and the accompanying study by Rainer. (Hereafter: *Decision in the Kremlin...*), p. 26.

Ibid.
Ibid.
Ibid.
Ibid., p. 27.
Ibid.

On June 28, 1956, around 5000 workers marched into the streets of Poznan in Poland demanding bread and free elections. The security forces broke up the protest by force. Fifty people died as a result, 300 were wounded and more than 300 were arrested. On October 8 and 12, 1956, several participants in the Poznan "disturbances" were sentenced to prison.

Decision in the Kremlin... p. 22.
Ibid., p. 24.
Ibid., p. 22.

Missing pages from the history of 1956. Documents from the former Soviet Communist Party's Central Committee archives. Selected and introduction and notes written by Vyacheslav Sereda and Alexander Stikalin. Móra Ferenc Publishing House 1993 (hereafter: *Missing pages...*) pp. 99–100.

[14] In September Gerő was on holiday in the Crimea, but Hegedűs was not with him. From October 15 to 23 Ernő Gerő headed a delegation taking part in negotiations in Belgrade, probably at Soviet instigation. Tibor Hajdú: "The Meeting in Moscow on October 27, 1956". Source Publication. *Yearbook 1992*. Budapest: The 1956 Institute, p. 153.

[15] Ibid.
[16] Ibid.
[17] Ibid.
[18] Ibid.
[19] Ibid.
[20] Ibid., p. 154.
[21] Ibid., pp. 154–155.
[22] Ibid., p. 155.
[23] Ibid.
[24] Ibid.
[25] János M. Rainer, "From Parliament to Fő Street. Imre Nagy's train of thought November 4, 1956–April 14, 1957." *Yearbook 1992*, 1956 Institute (Hereafter: János M. Rainer, *Institute Study*) p. 125.
[26] Ibid., p. 125.
[27] *I was Colonel Miklós Szűcs in 1956 with the General Staff*. Budapest. Szabad Tér Publishing House–1989, pp. 60–62.
[28] Ibid.
[29] See Malashenko's memoirs, p. 222.
[30] *The "Yeltsin Dossier": Soviet documents on 1956*. Századvég Publishing House–1956 Institute, Budapest, 1993 (Hereafter: *Yeltsin Dossier...*) pp. 47–49.
[31] Mikoyan and Suslov, coming in from Veszprém, first of all sought out the Ministry of Defense, where they continued their conversations with members of the HWP Central Leadership's Military Committee and the leadership of the Special Corps working out of the Ministry of Defense.
[32] This concerns the forces of the Piliscsaba regiment sent to the radio station.
[33] There was no such division. We believe that this refers to the Interior Ministry's Main Section, which used arms against protesters in Debrecen on October 23 [the authors].
[34] *Yeltsin dossier...* pp. 47–49.
[35] Military History Archive (hereafter: MH.) 1956 collection. 1. Preservation Unit (hereafter p.u.) pp. 406–407.
[36] Ibid. 7. p.u. pp. 362–363.

³⁷ Interior Ministry (hereafter: IM.) Historical Archive (hereafter: HA) Review Documents (hereafter: R) 150005/7. pp. 330–335.
³⁸ HA. 56 collection 7. p.u. p. 368.
³⁹ IM. HA. R–150005/4 p. 80.
⁴⁰ Ibid.
⁴¹ Ibid., pp. 308–309.
⁴² MA. 56 collection 7. p.u. pp. 362–363.
⁴³ Ibid., p. 501.
⁴⁴ IM. HA. R–150005/5 p. 165.
⁴⁵ Ibid. R–150005/7 pp. 219–220, 285–286.
⁴⁶ *Missing pages...* pp. 99–100.
⁴⁷ Ibid., p. 100.
⁴⁸ On June 17–18, 1953, a workers' uprising broke out in East Berlin and other towns in the GDR in order to prevent the introduction of certain measures announced on June 9 in the "new period" (such as adjustment of norms). The movements came to an end with a show of force by Soviet armored formations.
⁴⁹ See Kirov's study pp. 138, 144, 183.
⁵⁰ See Malashenko's memoirs p. 223.
⁵¹ The Council of Ministers 1071/1956 decree. Hungarian National Archives, *András Hegedűs Writings* XIX-A-2, p. 1048.
⁵² MA. 102/05/168.
⁵³ Hungarian People's Army maxim concerning the maintenance of state and social order, and in case of natural disaster the organization of the security/law enforcement services. MA. *Hungarian People's Army Headquarters Operations Staff Writings,* 1954/T. Box 8, batch 1.
⁵⁴ Ibid.
⁵⁵ The committee established by the HWP Central Leadership for armed struggle coordination. Its members were Antal Apró, Lajos Czinege, Lajos Fehér, László Földes, István Kovács, Imre Mező, László Piros (interior minister) and István Bata (defense minister). The Military Committee started its work in the Ministry of Defense.
⁵⁶ *Decision in the Kremlin...* p. 75.
⁵⁷ A small place west of Madrid where Franco's residence and the royal family's hunting lodge were located at the time.
⁵⁸ The memoirs are in the possession of Jenő Györkei. Excerpts have appeared in the weekly magazine *Köztársaság* (Republic) 1992, Nos. 32–33.
⁵⁹ Csaba Békés, *The 1956 Hungarian Revolution in World Politics*, Budapest 1956 Institute, 1996, p. 55.
⁶⁰ Ibid., p. 120.
⁶¹ Ibid., p. 121.
⁶² Ibid., p. 61.

63 Ibid.
64 The main reason for France and Great Britain's "reluctance" was that between October 22 and 24 the secret English–French–Israel negotiations held in Sevres, France, decided to attack Egypt on October 29.
65 MA. 56 collection, 3 p.u. p. 356.
66 Ibid., p. 435.
67 The Voice of the Revolution. *Századvég Notes 3*. Századvég Publishing House and Nyilvánosság Klub joint publication, Budapest, 1989, p. 29.
68 Ibid., p. 30.
69 Ibid.
70 Ibid., pp. 31–32.
71 MA. 56 collection, 8, batch pp. 131, 134, 144, 145, 150.
72 Y. I. Malashenko, "Osobi Korpus v. ognye Budapesta." *Vojeno-istorichesky zhurnal* part 2 1993, p. 30.
73 Ibid., pp. 44, 46.
74 MA. 56 collection, 8. p.u. pp. 131, 134., 144., 145., 150
75 *The Voice of the Revolution* pp. 61–62.
76 Ibid., pp. 66–67.
77 MA. 56 collection, 8 p.u. p. 154.
78 *Yeltsin dossier...* pp. 50–51.
79 Ibid., p. 50.
80 *Decision in the Kremlin...* p. 43.
81 The authors are grateful to András Kő and J. Lambert Nagy, who so willingly helped them with some of their research findings, and recommend to readers their soon-to-be published book–"*Kossuth Square–1956.*"
82 *Secret Reports–October 23–November 4, 1956*. Taboo series, Hírlapkiadó Vállalat, 1989. Sándor Geréb selected the documents, series editor Ferenc Várnai (hereafter: Secret Reports...) p. 45.
83 Ibid. John MacCormac, a New York Times reporter, reported on the telex message as an eyewitness.
84 Ibid., pp. 45–46.
85 *TOP SECRET–Hungarian–Yugoslav relations–1956* (Hereafter: *Hungarian–Yugoslav relations–1956*) documents–Budapest 1995. The papers were collected, selected, edited and introductory study written by József Kiss–Zoltán Ripp–István Vida. p. 132.
86 MA. 56 collection, 1. p.u. pp. 208–225.
87 *Yeltsin dossier...* pp. 50–51.
88 Ibid., p. 51.
89 Ibid.
90 *The Voice of the Revolution*. p. 71.
91 Ibid., pp. 71–72.

⁹² Ibid., p. 72.
⁹³ Ibid.
⁹⁴ Ibid.
⁹⁵ Ibid.
⁹⁶ *Decision in the Kremlin...* p. 33.
⁹⁷ *The Voice of the Revolution.* pp. 71–72.
⁹⁸ Ibid., p. 72.
⁹⁹ MA. 56 collection, 3 p.u. pp. 138–167.
¹⁰⁰ The minutes can be found in the papers on the trial of "Imre Nagy and his colleagues." National Archive Examination XX–5h. box 23. volume 7. Published by Ferenc Glatz, *História*, No. 4–5. 1989.
¹⁰¹ This concerns forces who joined the uprising after the shooting outside Parliament.
¹⁰² *Missing pages...* pp. 106–107.
¹⁰³ Ibid., p. 108.
¹⁰⁴ Ibid.
¹⁰⁵ Ibid., p. 106.
¹⁰⁶ Ibid., p. 111.
¹⁰⁷ Ibid., pp 111–112.
¹⁰⁸ Ibid., p. 112.
¹⁰⁹ Ibid.
¹¹⁰ Ibid.
¹¹¹ Ibid., p. 110.
¹¹² Ibid.
¹¹³ Ibid., p. 111.
¹¹⁴ Ibid., p. 112.
¹¹⁵ *The Voice of the Revolution* p. 83.
¹¹⁶ Ibid.
¹¹⁷ Ibid.
¹¹⁸ *Missing pages...* pp. 114–116.
¹¹⁹ Ibid., p. 115.
¹²⁰ Ibid.
¹²¹ Ibid., p. 116.
¹²² *The Voice of the Revolution* p. 103.
¹²³ Ibid., p. 111.
¹²⁴ IM. HA. R. 150005/3. István Kovács's notebook.
¹²⁵ Ibid. István Kovács's confession.
¹²⁶ Ibid., p. 136. Zoltán Tóth's confession.
¹²⁷ IM. HA. R. 150005/3 p. 104. Miklós Szűcs's confession.
¹²⁸ Ibid., p. 326. Zoltán Tóth's confession.
¹²⁹ Ibid., p. 331. Zoltán Tóth's confession.

[130] Ibid., p. 194. Miklós Szűcs's confession.
[131] Ibid.
[132] Ibid.
[133] Zoltán Tóth's personal statement.
[134] IM. HA. R. 150005/3 p. 309 Károly Janza's confession.
[135] *Yeltsin dossier...* pp. 54–55.
[136] Ibid., p. 54.
[137] Ibid., p. 55.
[138] Ibid.
[139] *Decision in the Kremlin...* p. 35.
[140] Ibid., p. 36.
[141] Ibid.
[142] Ibid.
[143] See pp. 49, 50, 54.
[144] *Decision in the Kremlin...* pp. 37–38.
[145] Ibid., pp. 38–39.
[146] Ibid., pp. 40–41.
[147] Ibid. The Military Command issued a statement in which it stated that the Soviet troops would put a stop to the firing and following this would only use their weapons in self-defense.
[148] Ibid., p. 41.
[149] Ibid., p. 42.
[150] Ibid.
[151] The minutes can be found in the papers on the trial of "Imre Nagy and his colleagues." National Archive Examination XX–5h, box 23, volume 7. Published by Ferenc Glatz, *História*, No. 4–5, 1989.
[152] Imre Nagy proposed the commencement of negotiations on withdrawal.
[153] Mikoyan and Suslov.
[154] Soviet and Hungarian troops attacked in order to liquidate groups around Corvin Alley.
[155] *The Voice of Revolution* pp. 131–132.
[156] *Decision in the Kremlin...* pp. 43–44.
[157] At first they thought of Béla Király and then of Pál Maléter. The Corvin Alley group's activities were directed and coordinated by László Iván Kovács until November 1–according to some sources, until November 2. According to the papers, in the first days of the revolution there really was in the Corvin Alley a colonel or lieutenant colonel who had served in the army before 1945, whom the rebels arrested on the night of October 29 and who was imprisoned in Kilián Barracks at the intervention of Pál Maléter.
[158] *Decision in the Kremlin...* p. 44.
[159] Ibid., pp. 43–44.

¹⁵⁰ The "Revolutionary Military Committee," according to the members of the Presidium, meant the formation of a counter-government.
¹⁵¹ *Decision in the Kremlin...* pp. 44–45.
¹⁵² Ibid., p. 45.
¹⁵³ Ibid.
¹⁵⁴ Ibid., pp. 45–46.
¹⁵⁵ *Yeltsin dossier...* pp. 62–63.
¹⁵⁶ *Missing pages...* pp. 125–126.
¹⁵⁷ *Yeltsin dossier...* p. 62.
¹⁵⁸ Ibid., p. 63.
¹⁵⁹ *Missing pages...* pp. 125–126.
¹⁶⁰ Ibid., p. 126.
¹⁶¹ Ibid.
¹⁶² Ibid., p. 126.
¹⁶³ These vehicles were used to transport aid to Hungary and not for military purposes.
¹⁶⁴ *Decision in the Kremlin...* p. 51.
¹⁶⁵ Ibid.
¹⁶⁶ Ibid., p. 52.
¹⁶⁷ Ibid., pp. 52–53.
¹⁶⁸ Ibid., p. 53.
¹⁶⁹ Ibid.
¹⁷⁰ Ibid., p. 55.
¹⁷¹ Ibid., p. 56.
¹⁷² Ibid., p. 57.
¹⁷³ Ibid., p. 55.
¹⁷⁴ Ibid.
¹⁷⁵ Ibid., p. 57.
¹⁷⁶ Ibid., p. 57.
¹⁷⁷ Ibid., p. 62.
¹⁷⁸ The "question" was not solved on the basis of Khrushchev's recommendation. The members of the negotiating delegation–Erdei, Maléter, Kovács and Szűcs–were indeed arrested at Tököl during negotiations, but the removal of the government took place with Yugoslavia's cooperation.
¹⁷⁹ *Decision in the Kremlin...* pp. 62–63.
¹⁸⁰ Imre Horváth, the foreign minister, left for New York, but his plane was diverted by the Soviets. The plane landed in Moscow. Personal statement by Nikolai Dzuba.
¹⁸¹ *Decision in the Kremlin...* p. 64.
¹⁸² Memorai Nikita Sergeyevicha Khrushcheva, *Voprosi Istorii*, No. 5, 1994, p. 80. Published in *Decision in the Kremlin...* p. 73.

[193] *Decision in the Kremlin...* p. 69.
[194] Ibid.
[195] Ibid., p. 70.
[196] Ibid.
[197] Ibid.
[198] Ibid., p. 71.
[199] Ibid.
[200] Ibid., p. 72.
[201] Mikoyan perhaps hoped that the idea of reconciliation underway with leaders of the socialist countries–chiefly Yugoslavia and Poland–would modify the Soviet decision. He was to be disappointed. *Decision in the Kremlin...* p. 72.
[202] Ibid., pp. 71, 73.
[203] *Missing pages...* pp. 127–128. Andropov was called into the Foreign Ministry at midnight on October 30 because of the second entry of Soviet troops, at which point Foreign Minister Imre Horváth asked for an explanation. Andropov managed to avoid giving an answer by declaring that he was not informed. Returning to the Embassy, Andropov was informed over the telephone that the news of Soviet troops was not true. *Yeltsin dossier...* pp. 67–68.
[204] *Missing pages...* p. 127.
[205] Ibid., pp. 127–128.
[206] Ibid., p. 128.
[207] *The Voice of Revolution.* p. 371.
[208] *Decision in the Kremlin...* p. 75.
[209] Ibid.
[210] Ibid.
[211] Ibid., pp. 75–76.
[212] Ibid., p. 76.
[213] Ibid.
[214] Ibid.
[215] Ibid., p. 77.
[216] Ibid., p. 78.
[217] Ibid., pp. 78–79.
[218] Ibid., p. 79.
[219] Ibid., p. 80.
[220] Ibid.
[221] Ibid., p. 81.
[222] Ibid., p. 77.
[223] Ibid., p. 81.
[224] Ibid., pp. 82–83.
[225] See Kirov's study, pp. 155, 174, 186.
[226] See Malashenko's memoirs, p. 237.

²²⁷ Further details: Witness Speaks. *Új Magyarország* (New Hungary), January 9, 1993, p. 8.
²²⁸ See Malashenko's memoirs, p. 279.
²²⁹ p. 259.
²³⁰ Béla Király (April 14, 1912–, Kaposvár). During the revolution the commander in chief of the National Guard, and chairman of the Revolutionary Council for Public Safety. After November 4, he personally organized and led the battle against the Soviet troops in the area around Nagykovácsi. At the end of November 1956 he emigrated to Austria and then at the end of December to the United States.
²³¹ Record of evidence found among the "Imre Nagy and his Colleagues" trial papers. MOL. detention documents XX–5 h. Box 23, volume 7. Published by Ferenc Glatz: *Historia* No. 4–5, 1989.
²³² Dr Zoltán Radó's testimony, MOL detention papers XX–5 h. 2 26/42., 50–55.
²³³ Ibid.
²³⁴ Béla Király's statement to the authors.
²³⁵ Béla Király "From the Hungarian Army to People's Army"–Budapest. Publisher: CO–Nexus Print-ter Kft. p. 243.
²³⁶ Vilmos Oláh, an arrested insurgent, and several of his compatriots were taken to the Army Hospital from the Ministry of Defense–where they were in custody–in order to collect the Soviet and Hungarian bodies there. One of the hospital doctors, with approval from the commander, did not allow them to carry out this task and sent the soldiers guarding them away, saying that the government had issued a general amnesty. In order to protect them from being arrested again, they were taken in as patients.
²³⁷ Vilmos Oláh's testimony MOL, XX–5 h. detention papers 26/67–70.
²³⁸ Béla Király op. cit. p. 251.
²³⁹ Miklós Horváth "*Pál Maléter*"–Budapest 1956 Institute–Osiris–Századvég, p. 131.
²⁴⁰ MOL Imre Nagy and Colleagues XX–5 h. Operative papers. Box 2, volume 6, pp. 30–38.
²⁴¹ Ibid.
²⁴² László Zólomy's testimony MOL. XX–5h. detention papers 26/87, 88.
²⁴³ Gyula Váradi's testimony MOL. XX–5h. detention papers 26/134, 135.
²⁴⁴ Per Olaf Csongovai, member of the Tűzoltó Street rebel group.
²⁴⁵ Sándor Erdélyi's testimony MOL. XX–5h detention papers 27/17.
²⁴⁶ Béla Király op. cit. p. 255.
²⁴⁷ Ibid pp., 255–256.
²⁴⁸ Sándor Erdélyi's testimony MOL. XX–5h. detention papers 27/17.
²⁴⁹ Gyula Váradi's testimony MOL. XX–5h. detention papers 26/135, 136.

[250] For the complete text of the appeal, see Kirov study pp. 149–150.
[251] Béla Király op. cit. pp. 256–257.
[252] László Zólomy's testimony MOL. XX–5h. detention papers 26/95–99, 100.
[253] László Zólomy's testimony Interior Ministry. TI. V-150005/4 p. 164.
[254] Ibid, p. 167.
[255] Béla Király op. cit. p. 264.
[256] Ibid., pp. 265–266.
[257] Since the Soviets were determined to conduct negotiations at a ministerial level and since one of the leaders thought the Soviets would consider it a provocation to include Király, who had only been released from prison a month before, on the committee, Imre Nagy decided not to include him in the Hungarian negotiating delegation.
[258] Béla Király op. cit. pp. 266–267.
[259] István Kovács and colleagues Interior Ministry TI. V–150005/21. pp. 74–77.
[260] Ibid.
[261] Ibid.
[262] Ibid.
[263] Ibid., pp. 78–83.
[264] Béla Király op. cit. pp. 269–270.
[265] *The Voice of the Revolution*–Hungarian Radio Broadcasts October 23–November 9, 1956–Századvég notebooks. Joint publication by Századvég Publishers and the Nyilvánosság Klub Budapest 1989, p. 458.
[266] Ibid.
[267] Béla Király op. cit. p. 272.
[268] János Tischler, "Polish Party Leadership and the 1956 Revolution," 1956 Institute, *Yearbook 1994*, p. 190.
[269] Ibid., p. 194.
[270] *Hungarian–Yugoslav Relations 1956* p. 155.
[271] Notes by the party and state delegation of the Polish People's Republic on the negotiations with the Soviet state and party leadership conducted in Moscow on May 24–25, 1957. Copy of János Tischler's manuscript belonging to the authors.
[272] Press opinion on *Szabad Ifjúság* (Free Youth), October 30, 1956. Kossuth Könyvkiadó–1989, p. 151.
[273] *Hungarian–Yugoslav Relations 1956* pp. 151–156.
[274] Ibid., p. 152.
[275] Ibid., pp. 153–154.
[276] Ibid., p. 155.
[277] Ibid., p. 165.

²⁷⁸ Ibid., p. 68.
²⁷⁹ *Decision in the Kremlin...* pp. 88–89.
²⁸⁰ According to Imre Horváth's notes, Kádár said the following: "It looks as if the Imre Nagy government is covering up the slaughter of communists, but that is just how it seems. The government is powerless..." Hungarian National Archives XIX-J-1-k (Foreign Ministry, Foreign Minister Imre Horváth's documents, Box 55. Published by László Varga: "Khrushchev's and Kádár's secret negotiations, November 3, 1956." *Magyar Hírlap*, October 22, 1992. The document appeared, with László Varga's permission, in *Decision in the Kremlin...* p. 94.
²⁸¹ *Decision in the Kremlin...* p. 89.
²⁸² Ibid.
²⁸³ Ibid.
²⁸⁴ Ibid., p. 90.
²⁸⁵ Ibid.
²⁸⁶ Ibid. Published in *Decision in the Kremlin...* p. 93.
²⁸⁷ *1956 Placards and Leaflets*, Zrínyi Kiadó–1991. Collected and edited by Lajos Izsák, József Szabó and Róbert Szabó, pp. 274, 276–277.
²⁸⁸ *Hungarian–Yugoslav Relations 1956*, pp. 165–166.
²⁸⁹ The authors took some of the data concerning the insurgents' resistance from László Eörsi's work. Eörsi knows the subject well. The authors recommend his book–*The Tűzoltó Street armed group in the revolution* (Századvég Kiadó–1956 Institute, Budapest, 1993)–and his other studies on the subject.
²⁹⁰ Béla Király op. cit. pp. 279–280.
²⁹¹ Ibid., p. 280.
²⁹² MOL. Imre Nagy and his Colleagues V/26/130. Károly Janza's testimony.
²⁹³ MOL. Imre Nagy and his Colleagues V/26/175. Károly Janza's testimony.
²⁹⁴ MOL. Imre Nagy and his Colleagues V/26/211.212. István Marián's testimony.
²⁹⁵ Béla Király op. cit. pp. 283–284.
²⁹⁶ Ibid., p. 284.
²⁹⁷ MOL. Imre Nagy and his Colleagues V/26/75. Vilmos Oláh's testimony.
²⁹⁸ Béla Király op. cit. p. 284.
²⁹⁹ Ibid., p. 285.

SOVIET MILITARY INTERVENTION IN HUNGARY, 1956

Alexandr M. Kirov

Questions Are Increasingly Being Raised

The whole world was moved by the tragic events in Hungary in the autumn of 1956. Forty years has gone by since then, but the peoples of Russia still do not know what really happened in Hungary. Except for the relatives of those who died–wives, parents and children–who, defending Stalinist–Rákosi "socialism," gave their lives in this bloody conflict in the name of "internationalism."

For them the Hungarian events are still a mystery, although several people in the territory that was in alliance with the Soviet Union have revealed the secrets and mysteries.

People in Russia and Hungary are entitled to an objective and unbiased explanation. But it is not easy to answer the legitimate questions about this period increasingly raised. Russian researchers are barred from most of the military archives, for reasons that are unclear.

Eventually, I believe, we will be allowed access to the documents in the Historical Archives and in the Russian Federation Armed Forces Central Military Archive.

Despite these difficulties the first steps have been taken. Articles about 1956 have appeared in the Russian press. Archival sources have shed new light on the unknown chapters of the Soviet–Hungarian war.

The author attempts to present the truth on the basis of archive documents, reports, notes and studies on the Soviet troops deployed in Hungary. He will try to present the unknown bloody pages of 1956 Soviet–Hungarian relations. The author completed a part of his studies from material he found in the archives, but his notes were destroyed.[1]

The Hungarian Workers Party Proves Unable to Lead Society

In the mid-1950s, the Stalinist–Rákosi regime in Hungary was in a blind alley. The policy that the Hungarian Workers Party followed in order to build socialism provoked dissatisfaction and protest from most of the population.

The reform wing of the Hungarian Workers Party realized that changes were necessary. But any attempt at change met strong resistance from the party's conservative forces, who enjoyed the support of the Soviet Central Committee's leadership.

Nevertheless, in this period the most radical reformers were able to formulate their vision of the country's future. They produced a program for the democratic renewal and transformation of the Hungarian society which provoked great interest from society, a program that posed an alternative to the Moscow-controlled hard-line dictatorship.

The outlines for a democratic society in Hungary relied in part on the work of Imre Nagy. One of his more notable works is his two-volume work *One Decade,* published in 1954,[2] and "Morals and Ethics," "Five Basic Principles of International Relations," "Some Pertinent Questions" and other writings he wrote at the end of 1955 and the beginning of 1956.

In these works Nagy, the president of the Hungarian People's Republic Council of Ministers, expressed a theory of a unique Hungarian way, which could be pursued without "dictatorship of the proletariat." Nagy also supported the re-establishment of a multi-party system, free elections, press freedom, national independence and withdrawal from the Warsaw Pact. The reformers, apart from formulating their own opinions and visions, started enlightening and winning over the people, which was just as important. Imre Nagy and his supporters attached great significance to winning over the intellectuals.

In 1955, within the framework of the Hungarian Youth Organization, the Democratic Youth Alliance, the Petőfi Circle was formed in order to debate questions surrounding Hungary's situation and to propagate political and economic knowledge. On June 27, 1956, it organized a debate on press and information issues. In October 1956 Imre Nagy's supporters–Géza Losonczy, Ferenc Donáth, József Szilágyi and others–criticized the HWP's activities. In lectures given all over the country, they called for the creation of a multi-party system and the holding of free elections. As a result of their work, the HWP's ideological struggle was paralyzed in 1956, and its activity as the vanguard became untenable. During this period about 70 periodicals were published in the country.

In such circumstances the HWP became incapable of uniting Hungarian society. Party workers, by grossly violating the law, came into conflict with the people and the workers' movement as a whole. An expression of protest against the HWP's policy emerged from the solemn reburials of László Rajk, György Pálffy, Tibor Szőnyi and András Szalai, who had been executed after show trials in 1949. Thousands of Budapest inhabitants attended the reburials on October 6, 1956; many thought they were burying not just the martyrs but a cruel chapter in the country's past. This silent protest against the Rákosi system was, as later events prove, unforgettable for Ernő Gerő.

The burial of the show trial victims made a great impression on the Budapest population, who, as later events show, were prepared to fight, if necessary with weapons, for the country's democratic renewal.

The possibilities for transformation and reform were complicated by the fact that the HWP, even when it was bankrupt, could rely on Moscow and on support from Soviet troops stationed in Hungary. These troops were stationed in the country because of the treaty of unconditional surrender signed by Nazi Germany and the 1947 Paris Peace Treaty. In 1955, following the signing of the Austrian State Treaty, they were to leave Hungary But one day before this was signed, on May 14, 1955, the Soviet Union concluded a treaty of friendship, cooperation and mutual aid with its Eastern European allies, including Hungary. This treaty, the Warsaw Pact, created an international legal basis for Soviet troops to remain in Hungary.

The Hungarians were disappointed that the Soviet troops would be staying. They understood that Soviet troops in Hungary meant the preservation of the rotten Stalinist system and continued oppression. Thus Hungary's democratic ambitions were bound to conflict with the stationing of Soviet troops in Hungary. The reformers, headed by Imre Nagy, therefore demanded the withdrawal of Soviet troops and the country's withdrawal from the Warsaw Pact.

The "Wave," a Plan for Armed Intervention

For the Soviet leadership these demands clearly meant that they would have to give up their right to preserve the Eastern European alliance. Thus they considered all possibilities, including armed intervention, in order to prevent any such developments.

In mid-July 1956 General A.I. Antonov, first deputy of the Soviet Armed Forces' chief of staff, arrived in Budapest at the head of a review committee to inspect the preparedness of the Special Army Corps troops. Following this the Army Corps staff worked out a top secret plan at the behest of the Moscow leadership and with its help. This plan was titled "The Special Army Corps's Participation in the Restoration of Order on Hungarian Territory." In the plan the operation was code-named "Volna" ("Wave"), and it was to be carried out when the password "Compass" was given. The plan was approved by P.N. Lashchenko, commander of the Special Corps, on July 20, 1956. The plan also included a supplement of special instructions. In them those objectives, which if necessary Soviet troops would occupy and guard, were designated. They also included the use of weapons and the system of cooperation between the troops and the local state security organs and the Hungarian People's Army command, ammunition for tanks, artillery and guns and the amount of military equipment that could be employed.[3]

Following the formulation and approval of the plan, the commanders of the higher units and units received detailed instructions on their duties for carrying out operations. Between October 6 and 19, 1956, the Soviet ambassador to Hungary, Yuri V. Andropov, met the corps' leading staff several times. Commanders of the higher units and units were also invited to these meetings, where Andropov analyzed the Hungarian political situation and demanded that preparations be stepped up.[4]

On October 21 the corps leadership inspected how well the units were prepared for carrying out the duties issued by the corps command after the password "Compass" was given.

At the same time security measures were taken on Soviet territory in case events in Hungary got out of hand. Already by October 19 the 108th parachute guard regiment belonging to the 7th air mobile division was in a state of complete battle readiness and ready to depart from the airports at Kaunas and Vilnius on October 20 on 54 LI-2 and 45 Il-12 planes.[5]

How It Began

During this period the events in Budapest had developed fast and did not bode well for party and government leaders, who were working for Soviet interests. Social and political life in Budapest, and in the larger towns, was in ferment. Students in the universities and colleges were activated, as well as writers and young people.

On October 22 the lecturers and students at the Budapest Polytechnical University decided to hold a protest the next day. The leadership was uncertain how to respond. On October 23 about 50,000 protesters gathered at the monument to General Josef Bem, Polish hero of the 1848–1849 Hungarian Revolution. The protesters expressed their solidarity with the demands of Polish youth. Anti-party and -government slogans were voiced; then the protesters marched towards Parliament. In the evening, an estimated 200,000 people gathered there, both civilians and soldiers.[6]

The protesters demanded, among other things, the return of Imre Nagy to the leadership, the retraction of the HWP Central Leadership decree denouncing "revisionists," the removal of Rákosi's circle from power, and the rehabilitation of those unjustly punished.

At 19 hours Ernő Gerő called Andropov and Moscow several times in a panic and asked that Moscow order Soviet troops stationed in Hungary to liquidate the opposition movements. At 20 hours a speech by HWP leader Ernő Gerő was broadcast on the radio. Its message only offended the people's national feelings and whipped up the atmosphere in the crowd. After this one group of protesters went from Parliament to the Radio building, while another marched to the Stalin statue. There at 21 15 the statue of "the greatest leader of all time" was toppled.

The first group of protesters wanted to hand their demands to Gerő, who they thought was in the Radio building, and to broadcast the demands they had formulated the day before. The radio leaders would not allow this.

Fistfights broke out between Radio guards and protesters, and later the conflict developed into an armed battle. It is still not known who fired the first shots, but it seems likely that the state security guards could not restrain themselves and that they fired from the building.

The great majority of the inhabitants in Budapest and other towns supported the protesters' demands and agreed with them. During the assembly in the Construction and Transport Polytechnical University on October 22, the following decision was issued:

"We join the proposal of the Szeged students and have formed the Construction and Transport Polytechnical University MEFESZ Organization. Students from the Technical University and the Horticultural College have also joined. The task of this new MEFESZ will be to publicize the opinions of the students on weighty political questions and to help solve the currently unsolvable problems of the university students (concerning defense training, canteen, dorms, train fare reductions, exams, and foreign trips). MEFESZ was established during a spontaneous meeting of university students in which 4000–5000 people took part.

"1. An immediate convening of the HWP congress, a leadership elected from below, the establishment of a new Central Leadership.

"2. The government to be headed by Imre Nagy.

"3. The establishment of Hungarian–Soviet and Hungarian–Yugoslav friendship based on complete political and economic equality and non-interference in each other's affairs.

"4. The total withdrawal of all Soviet troops from Hungary in accordance with the Hungarian peace treaty.

"5. General, equal, and secret ballots, with multi-party participation, and the election of a new National Assembly.

"6. The reorganization of Hungarian economic life, the introduction of experts and the Hungarian use of Hungarian uranium ore. Foreign trade agreements to be made public and an inspection of the plan-based Hungarian economic life.

"7. The introduction of immediate norms based on minimum wages for all industrial work and the introduction of workers' autonomy into the factories.

"8. A review of the quota system and support for individual working peasants.

"9. Review of all political and economic trials, a complete amnesty for innocent political prisoners and rehabilitation for those who were persecuted.

"10. A public hearing in the Mihály Farkas affair and an examination of Rákosi's role. The return home of Hungarians wrongly imprisoned in Russia.

"11. The return of the old Kossuth coat of arms instead of the foreign one. March 15 and October 6* (March 15, the anniversary of the 1848 revolution, and October 6 that of the execution of thirteen generals by the Habsburg oppressors. The editors.) should become public and national holidays. A new uniform for the army.

"12. The establishment of complete freedom of opinion, press and radio, and a separate daily paper for the new MEFESZ. A cessation of the old cadre propaganda.

"13. The immediate dismantling of the symbol of dictatorship and tyranny, the Stalin statue.

"14. We undertake complete responsibility for each other.

"The university students express their unanimous solidarity for the Warsaw workers and youth, for the Polish independence movement.

> "The Construction and Transport
> Technical University
> Assembly October 22, 1956
> MEFESZ"[7]

The protesters announced that their demands were formulated on the basis of Marxist–Leninist ideology and that they were publicizing them in the interest of renewing and developing democracy.

At the same time, on October 23, the destruction and defilement of liberation monuments and graves of Soviet soldiers began. This took place in Hajdú–Bihar County, for example, in Biharkereszt, Berettyóújfalu and Dunaföldvár.[8]

The Plan Is Set in Motion

On October 23 at 20 hours, V. D. Sokolovsky, marshal of the Soviet Union and Chief of General Staff of the Soviet Armed Forces, ordered the higher units and units of the Special Corps to introduce complete battle readiness and to depart to their assembly points.[9]

On October 23 at 22 hours, the Special Corps troops received the order to march into Budapest "in the interest of maintaining order."[10]

On the same day at 19:45, the commander of the troops stationed in the Carpathian Military Zone, General P. I. Batov, issued the alert to the 128th infantry, and the 39th mechanized guard divisions that belonged to the 3rd infantry corps, which was part of the 38th field army. He ordered them to cross the Soviet border at Chop–Beregovo–Vinogradov and to march within the zone lined with Chop–Miskolc–Hatvan on their right, and Vylok–Debrecen–Szolnok on their left. Then the 128th infantry guard division was to assemble in the Hatvan–Jászberény zone and the 39th mechanized guard division in the Szolnok–Abony zone.[11]

The 315th infantry guard regiment, subordinate to the 128th infantry guard division, received the order, as the advance detail, to fight their way across the border if necessary and secure the route of the main forces through Hungary.

On October 24 at 00:15 until 7 in the morning, the troops crossed the border unopposed and assembled in the designated zones. The 315th regiment was sent onto Budapest, where they began fighting.

On the night of October 23–24, the HWP Central Leadership worked out and accepted an action program, which they thought necessary to follow step by step in order to wipe out the mass movement.

The Central Leadership started with the premise that anyone who attacked a state institution with weapons was a counter-revolutionary and therefore had to be destroyed with weapons. The Central Leadership thought it had to unite all the forces, arm the workers, and deploy the army and state security troops. It decided that, if necessary, it would ask for military assistance from the Soviet Union.

During the night of October 23–24 the 195th fighter air guard division stationed in Hungary and the 177th bomber guard division, who had been awarded the Cherkas Red Flag and Suvorov Award, were ordered to battle readiness.[12]

At 20:10 the 17th mechanized guard division stationed in Szombathely, Kőszeg, Győr and Hajmáskér was ordered to battle readiness by General P.N. Lashchenko, and those under the division marched out of the barracks and onto the designated zones. The commanders of the 83rd tank regiment and the 1043rd artillery regiment received orders to march immediately to Budapest. The commander of the 90th artillery regiment received the order to seal off the Austrian–Hungarian border.[13]

On the night of October 24, the rebels started their armed struggle. József Dudás and his squad occupied the headquarters of the newspaper

Szabad Nép (Free People) and placed his own staff in it.¹⁴ Troops came from Miskolc, Sztalinváros (today Dunaújváros), Pápa and Vác to reinforce Budapest. The rebels disarmed some of the Hungarian People's Army and were able to get hold of weapons from army depots as well.

On the same night the units of the 7th mechanized division of the Hungarian army arrived in Budapest from Esztergom. They cooperated with Soviet troops.

The 8th and 27th infantry and the 5th mechanized divisions belonging to the 3rd infantry corps led by Major General Lajos Gyurkó did not support the rebels.¹⁵ These forces broke up and destroyed a group of 30 rebels in Kecskemét between October 24 and 26 on orders from the corps commander. In Szabadszállás the activity of these Hungarian troops caused the deaths of about seven rebels and wounded 40.

Soviet Troops in Budapest

On October 24 at 00:00, Lieutenant General P. N. Lashchenko, commander of the Special Corps, arrived in Budapest with his staff's operative group from Székesfehérvár; the permanent garrison of the corps took up operational headquarters in the Ministry of Defense.¹⁶

At dawn the Soviet 2nd mechanized guard division formations under Major General Lebedev started to march into Budapest. First the 37th tank regiment took up defense positions around the Ministry of Defense building. The main forces of the division arrived in the capital, where the units carried out the following tasks:

' The 4th mechanized regiment occupied the rebel leadership headquarters, the Astoria Hotel and the Kossuth Radio building,¹⁷ the National Museum and the area immediately surrounding these buildings.

' The 6th mechanized regiment occupied the Parliament, Party Headquarters, the National Bank, the main post office and the Nyugati Railway Station; it also provided defense for the Soviet Embassy and the Soviet military hospital.

' The 5th mechanized and 37th tank regiments defended the Ministry of Defense and the Csepel factories.

' The 87 heavy tank–assault gun regiment fought to take Keleti Railway Station and the Corvin Cinema and its environs.'"¹⁸

Soviet troops found themselves faced with well-organized and strong rebel resistance, e.g. on Gorkij Alley, Sztálin, Rákóczi, Üllői, Markusovszky and Soroksári Roads and on the Hungaria and Lenin Boulevards. In the Astoria Hotel there were more than 500 rebels, while in the Kossuth Radio building there were more than 1500.

On October 23 at 22:35 the Herzen 33rd mechanized guard division, who had been awarded the Red Flag and Suvorov Orders, and who were stationed on Romanian territory (in Timisoara), were ordered to battle readiness and were made to march 300 kilometers to their assembly point 15 kilometers south of Budapest. Later they were to take part in smothering the "counter-revolutionary uprising." After the march, between 9 and 11 in the morning, the units and independent sub-units of the 104th and 105th, 106th mechanized guard regiments, the 100th artillery regiment, the 1093rd air defense artillery regiment, the 71st tank regiment, the 133rd heavy tank-assault gun guard regiment, the 61st howitzer battalion, the engineering battalion, the signal corps battalion, the transport battalion and the independent chemical warfare company assembled in their designated zones with weapons and equipment. Their staff and logistical service sub-units totalled 75,000 effectives.

The weapons of the division consisted of 182 T-34 tanks, 6 amphibious tanks, 18 ISZ-3 tanks, 26 SZU-100 self-propelling cannons, 76 BTR-50 armored transport vehicles, 845 vehicles, 21 SZU-152 self-propelling cannons, 36 122mm howitzers, 12 81mm cannons, 11 57mm cannons, 12 82mm non-recoil cannons, 12 160mm trench mortars, 12 BM-113 rocket launchers, 12 85mm air defense guns, and 32 31mm air defense guns.[19]

Subsequently, the 104th mechanized guard regiment arrived in the capital after a short march. It fought its way to Parliament and the Ministry of Defense, where it fought alongside the units of the 2nd mechanized guard division.

On October 24 Soviet troops drove the rebels out of the *Szabad Nép* editorial building, the railroad stations, the munitions factory and the ammunition depots.

The sub-units of the 8th mechanized regiment of the Hungarian People's Army that were stationed in Budapest, the construction and air defense units and the officers of the Zrínyi Academy and the cadets of military schools went over to the rebels.[20]

After midnight on the same day at 00:15 the Poltav 39th mechanized guard division which was subordinate to the 38th army unit and had been awarded the Lenin, Red Flag, Kutuzov and Suvorov Orders, crossed the Hungarian border and assembled in the Szolnok zone at 22 hours. The division stayed there for three days. [21]

At the same time on the 24th, the commander of the Special Corps ordered the 56th mechanized guard regiment and a reconnaissance company that belonged to the 17th mechanized guard division to Budapest. The company was to undertake reconnaissance and to defend the Soviet leaders who had arrived in Hungary.[22]

The 56th mechanized guard regiment arrived in the capital at 10 o'clock, where it was ordered to prevent armed rebels from crossing from Pest into Buda and occupying the government's radio transmitter and the special communications system. At the same time it was to defend Kelenföld Railway Station, the Budaörs Airport and the artillery depots in Törökbálint.[23]

On the same day the 177th bomber–guard division's planes made 84 reconnaissance flights and shows of force above Budapest and other towns.[24]

On October 24 TASS reported on the HWP Central Leadership's evening session. Entitled "Failure of the Anti-Democratic Adventure in Budapest," the article stressed that the Central Leadership had been newly elected and that Ernő Gerő had been confirmed in the post of first secretary. The HWP's Politburo proposed to the Presidential Council that Imre Nagy be appointed prime minister with András Hegedűs as his deputy.[25]

On the same day the government issued a decree introducing a state of emergency and martial law.

On October 24 in the areas of Szolnok, Vác, Sztálinváros (today Dunaújváros) and Dunaegyháza, the monuments and graves of the Soviet soldiers who had fallen in World War II were destroyed and desecrated.

On the night of the 24th–25th, in Várpalota, three officers of the 17th mechanized guard division were murdered–Major Fedorov, logistic services deputy to the commander of the 56th tank training school battalion; First Lieutenant Pronkin, technical deputy to the commander of the 83rd tank regiment's transport company; and one of this regiment's platoon commanders, Lieutenant Mikhno. Along with these officers 10 soldiers from the regiment fell. A few soldiers and officers suffered broken arms and legs, five people had their heads cut off and–according to surviving documents–one Soviet soldier was impaled.[26]

"A Friendly Message to the Workers of the Hungarian People's Republic"

On October 25 the insurgents gathered in small groups and shot at Soviet troops from cellars, roofs and windows. The rebels managed to seize two tanks of the Hungarian People's Army and three armored transport vans. They organized a strong resistance around the Corvin Cinema. In Districts I, VIII, IX and XIII the rebels regained independent objectives.

At 14 hours the 54th pontoon regiment, which belonged to the Carpathian Military District, built a pontoon bridge across the Tisza River close to the Szolnok railway bridge, for heavy tanks.

On October 25 the main Soviet newspapers published the Soviet Central Committee slogans on the 39th anniversary of the October Socialist Revolution. The 10th slogan read:

"A friendly greeting to the workers of the Hungarian People's Republic, who are fighting a self-sacrificing battle for the further development of economy and culture, for a permanent rise in the people's living standards, for peace and for the construction of communism. Long live cooperation and everlasting friendship between the Soviet and Hungarian peoples!"[27]

In the morning units from the 128th infantry guard division assembled in the Jászberény and Hatvan zones.

The 2nd mechanized guard division's subordinates–with the exception of the 104th mechanized guard regiment–received the order to clear the southeast of the capital, from the Felső Kőbánya Railway Station–Keleti Railway Station to the Danube, of rebels.

During the day Imre Nagy retracted the government decree forbidding public assemblies, mass assemblies and demonstrations.

The following day, October 26, the papers *Izvestia* and *Krasnaya Zvezda*, in articles entitled "Failure of the Anti-Democratic Adventure in Budapest," quoted the following from the Budapest radio report given by the Council of Ministers of the Hungarian People's Republic on October 25:

"At the orders of the Council of Ministers of the Hungarian People's Republic, the army, with the help of the state security forces, armed workers' brigades and Soviet troops, liquidated the counter-revolutionary putsch attempt on the evening of the 25th. The counter-revolutionary forces were broken up. Only a few small armed groups are still operating here and there, and in a few places there are isolated shootings... János Kádár has replaced Ernő Gerő as first secretary of the HWP. Imre Nagy, president of the Council of Ministers, announced in his radio speech that... shortly after the rule of law has been restored, the National Assembly will be convened. At this assembly I will present an across-the-board and well-founded reform program, which will embrace all the important issues of national life."[28]

On October 25 Soviet military monuments were destroyed in Mezőkereszt and Hatvan.

On October 26 at the HWP Central Leadership session, Ferenc Donáth condemned the accepted official version of events–according to which a counter-revolution was underway–saying that the events in Hungary were a broad-based, mass democratic movement, seeking to repair socialism and put a stop to the distorted construction of socialism.

Donáth's address was sharply criticized by the 'older' members of the Central Leadership, especially by András Hegedűs.* Kádár did not support Donáth's point of view either, although in his address he recognized that the party leadership had certainly come into conflict with broad strata of the population. The Central Leadership rejected Donáth's remarks.

On the same day TASS issued another report on the "failure of the anti-democratic adventure in Budapest."

On the night of October 26–27, the 27th mechanized division subordinate to the Carpathian Military District received the order for battle readiness and was ordered to the assembly point west of Szolnok by October 28 going through Beregovo, Nyíregyháza–Debrecen–Szolnok.[29]

The 70th infantry-guard division, belonging to the Carpathian Military District, was also made ready for combat on this day. The division received the order to fill up its effectives and occupy the assembly areas in the territory of Debrecen–Miskolc–Nyíregyháza after a march of 500

* Editor's note: Hegedűs was 33 years old.

kilometers over the Carpathian passes on motor vehicles and troop carriers within two days.[30]

The 104th assault gun regiment, belonging to the division, had already been transported by rail from Rava-Russkaya to Beregovo, then on October 26 at 10 o'clock they occupied the assembly point in the Nyíregyháza area. In the morning the 33rd mechanized guard division units also marched into Budapest and there took part in the bitter struggle until October 29.[31]

At the same time the 2nd mechanized guard division units fought against the rebels from the objectives which had been designated to them.[32]

In response the population of Nyíregyháza, Abony, Eger, Gyöngyös, Füzesabony, Miskolc, Besenyőtelek, Tiszanána, and Dombrád desecrated and destroyed the graves and monuments honoring Soviet soldiers who fell in World War II.

On October 27 TASS issued a report on the new composition of the Hungarian government. According to the report, the members of the government confirmed by the Patriotic People's Front National Council and the Hungarian People's Republic Presidential Council were Prime Minister Imre Nagy, Deputy Prime Ministers Antal Apró, József Bognár, and Ferenc Erdei, Minister of State Zoltán Tildy, Foreign Minister Imre Horváth, Minister of the Interior Ferenc Münnich, Minister of Defense Lieutenant General Károly Janza, and others.[33]

On the morning of October 27 at 8 o'clock, the 27th mechanized guard division also crossed the border and reached its assembly point near Szolnok.

On the same day the rebels again started fighting in Buda, and on the Pest side they continued to guard the capital's southeastern districts, holding the Corvin Cinema and the surrounding houses. The leader of this 700–800-strong resistance group was László Kovács Iván. The 1221st, 1222nd and 1226th construction battalions, stationed at the Kilián Barracks under the command of Colonel Pál Maléter, also went over to the rebels.[34]

The mass movement strengthened and spread to most of the provincial towns, including Debrecen, Miskolc, Székesfehérvár, Pécs, and Tatabánya.[35]

Troops from the Special Corps attacked the Hungarian army's Red Star Printing Works, where they confiscated about 200,000 anti-Soviet leaflets. To collect information about the rebels' intentions and clarify the situation, the Army Corps commander sent about 200 reliable Hungarian communists among the rebels, posing as volunteers.

That day, the commander of the Soviet troops sent an ultimatum to the defenders of Corvin Cinema to surrender.[36]

The 1st Warsaw railway guard brigade, who had been awarded the Kutuzov medal, were put on the alert on October 27 and ordered to march to the railway station at Chop and set the disrupted railways running once more.[37]

The 39th mechanized guard division that was subordinate to the 3rd infantry corps, which had been at its assembly point in the Szolnok–Abony area since 7 o'clock on the 24th, received the order to occupy the assembly point in the Támasi zone by nightfall, marching through Szolnok–Cegléd–Nagykőrös–Kecskemét–Dunaföldvár and Cece–Pincehely–Nagykónyi–Kalocsa–Dombóvár.[38]

On the night of October 27–28 the commander of the Carpathian Military District, General of the Army Batov, ordered the 32nd and 11th mechanized guard divisions, belonging to the 8th mechanized army units, two regiments of the 60th air defense artillery battalion, and the units directly subordinate to the army to ready themselves for combat. The higher units and units belonging to them were given the command to reach Hungary's eastern counties as soon as possible from their garrisons—Berdichev, Novograd–Volinsky, Zhitomir, Chmel'nickij, Zhmerinka—by rail and road.[39]

Soviet monuments were destroyed in Jászberény, Mezőtúr and Salgótarján.

Re-evaluation of the Situation

On October 28 the 70th infantry guard division crossed the state border at 5 o'clock after marching from its permanent base in Stanislav to Beregovo, and on October 28 at 23 hours it arrived at its assembly point near Debrecen.

On the same day *Izvestia,* under the headline "The Organizers of the Counter-Revolutionary Putsch in Hungary Have Miscalculated," published the following: "In the liquidation of the Hungarian counter-revolution the main role is being played by the Hungarian nation itself, the

Hungarian People's Army and the state security forces. Soviet military formations stationed in Hungary as part of the Warsaw Pact also helped. In the restoration of order, they rushed to help Hungarian People's Republic troops after the Hungarian government turned to the Soviet government for aid." [No comment–Kirov]

During this period large numbers of rebels had around 100–120 blocks in southeast Budapest under their control. The battle raged in Buda as well. The Corvin Alley fighters did not accept the ultimatum to surrender, and their fire prevented the Soviet sub-units from engaging in reconnaissance.

The Hungarian People's Army units did not carry out the orders from Imre Nagy's government to liquidate the rebels; they did not receive orders to continue active fighting. Soldiers from some units, for instance the 37th regiment and the 46th air defense artillery battalion, went over to the rebels and gave the rebels their weapons.[40]

The 128th infantry guard division units, who had been in the Jászberény and Hatvan zone since 7 a.m. on the 24th, marched into Budapest.[41]

The units of the 33rd mechanized guard division were also fighting. The rebels renewed their resistance in the 2nd mechanized guard division's zone.

The 27th mechanized division arrived at the designated zone west of Szolnok.

On October 27 at 23 hours the 32nd mechanized guard division, belonging to the Carpathian Military District, started its nearly 700-kilometer march from Mukachevo.

On the same day in Budapest, Generals Béla Király, Lőrinc Kána and István Kovács, Colonel Pál Maléter and five others formed the Hungarian People's Army Revolutionary Military Council.[42]

On October 27–28 the HWP Political Committee accepted Ferenc Donáth's platform which he had proposed on October 26, which had not been opposed by A. Mikoyan and M. Suslov, who were present.

On October 28 Imre Nagy announced on the radio: "...the government condemns those views that say that the present mass people's movement is a counter-revolution." In his evening declaration, Nagy also talked about how, because of the relevations of the mistakes made in the previous period, "the events of the last few weeks have developed with tragic speed." Nagy announced that the government would try in the future to rectify the mistakes made and would fulfill the will of the people.

Hungarian workers were satisfied with the announcement of the formation of workers' councils, the strengthening of democracy and the dissolution of the state security forces, and the government declaration on pay raises, Soviet withdrawal and a ceasefire.[43]

The UN Security Council placed a debate on the Hungarian situation on the agenda.

On October 28 at 10 o'clock, the 114th and 381st paratroop regiments, which belonged to the 31st air mobile guard division, were put on alert and ordered to march by road to Lvov and Chmel'nickij airports with individual and freight parachutes, and then to go onto Veszprém Airport by air and there prepare for combat.

At 18 hours, after they had made the necessary preparations for the jump, the 114th paratroop regiment set on the march to their designated departure point, through Novograd–Volinsky–Lvov, and Novograd–Volinsky–Chmel'nickij. On the 28th at 23 hours, the 70th infantry guard division completed its march, and its troops assembled in the Debrecen area.

On October 29 at 2 o'clock, the 381st paratroop regiment arrived at its departure point by following the course designated for the 114th regiment.

At 20 hours Soviet troops in Budapest received the order to cease fire.[44] The 2nd and 33rd mechanized guard divisions' units stopped fighting in accordance with the order. At the same time the rebels continued to occupy the southeastern areas of the capital with significant forces.[45]

On the same day the independent road and railway construction battalion, arrived in Szolnok after marching 237 kilometers by motor vehicle through Chop–Záhony–Szolnok. There it was to defend and guard the train station and the railway bridge. But later General of the Army Malinyin, reckoning on the negative reaction of the local railway workers, ordered the battalion to withdraw from the railway. That is why, until November 2, the battalion was in the Nyíregyháza area, where it continued military and political training in order to fulfill its duties.[46]

Between October 29 and November 1, the Hungarian People's Army Military Council announced that it had gone over to the rebels.

Hungarian troops received the order to form military councils, to liquidate the institution of political deputies, to change their stripes, to pin the national colors to their caps and to support the workers' councils.[47]

Command to Cease Fire

On October 30 the Soviet government made a declaration on the "basic principles for further strengthening and developing cooperation and friendship between the Soviet Union and the other socialist states." In this declaration it emphasized that "the mutual relations of the socialist nations, who all belong to a great community, can only be built on the principles of complete equality, respect for territorial integrity, state independence and sovereignty and non-interference in each other's internal affairs."

The formulators of the declaration also showed that, at the request of the Hungarian government, the Soviet government had agreed to withdraw the Soviet units from Budapest who had helped restore order along with the Hungarian People's Army and the Hungarian state security forces.[48]

At 15:30 the Imre Nagy government demanded that Soviet troops immediately withdraw from the capital.[49]

The Revolutionary Military Council announced in its appeal that if Soviet troops did not withdraw, the Hungarian People's Army would launch a war against them.

The Soviet military units could not remain in Budapest after this as the situation would have worsened otherwise. Thus the Soviet government gave the order to withdraw.

In the capital the rebels, taking advantage of the cease-fire, renewed their attempts to occupy important party and state objectives.

At 18:30 the Hungarian People's Army 3rd infantry corps formed a Revolutionary Military Council, which issued the following decree:

"Fellow Hungarians! Fellow fighters!
"Working people of Bács–Kiskun County, inhabitants of Kecskemét!

"1. The corps, in the name of all its soldiers, warrant officers and officers, has joined the decrees and demands of the workers', young people's and intellectuals' revolutionary councils and embraces them. The corps defends the victories of our heroic revolution.

2. We agree with the declaration made by the government on Kossuth Radio.

3. We have disarmed the state security organs and arrested those among them who were against the revolution.

4. We agree and support your demand for the Soviet troops to start withdrawing immediately from Hungarian territory. We have sent this demand to the national government.

5. We appeal to you to establish revolutionary worker-peasant councils in your workplaces and factories.

6. We ask Bács–Kiskun County and the inhabitants of Kecskemét to cooperate with the revolutionary military councils and to support the work of the newly formed National Guard in its consolidation of order and discipline.

> "3rd Army Corps Command's
> Revolutionary Military Council"[50]

On orders from the Soviet government, Soviet troops started to withdraw from Budapest. A warning was broadcast on the radio that the Soviet command would respond forcefully if Soviet troops were fired upon and would not be responsible for the consequences.[51]

The 38th army's higher units and units started to work out their plans for Operation "Storm" or "Whirlwind." On the same day in Budapest, after several hours of fighting, armed rebel groups occupied the Budapest Party Committee building on Köztársaság Square. Numerous party committee workers and guards died. Later that night the armed rebels freed Cardinal József Mindszenty from his prison.[52]

On October 30 at 10:30–contrary to the declaration of the Soviet government–the 114th parachute regiment of the 31st air mobile guard division arriving from Lvov and other airports landed at the airport of Veszprém. The effectives of the regiment consisted of 1120 solidiers, 12 82mm trench mortars, 18 non-recoil cannons, six air defense guns, and 13 motor vehicles of Gaz-69 and Gaz-67 types. Major General Ryabov, commander of the air mobile guard division, together with his operatical detail settled at the combat headquarters of the 1st fighter air division of the Hungarian People's Army at Veszprém airport. At 20 hours the 381st parachute regiment landed at Veszprém also. The logistical base of the air mobile formations was established near the Mukachevo military airport.[53]

Refugees and Hosts

Soviet troop withdrawal from Budapest was completed by October 31. The command and political section of the Special Corps took up quarters in Tököl Airport. But before the withdrawal started, Soviet troops tried to get some of the state and party functionaries and those working in the defunct state security forces out of the city. A group of ÁVH officers later took part in Operation "Whirlwind" on the night of November 3.

Some of the HWP's highest leaders and their families arrived at Tököl, including Béla Végh, secretary to the HWP Central Committee, along with his wife and three children; Gyula Egri, secretary to the HWP Central Committee; István Hidas, member of the Politburo, deputy president of the Council of Ministers, with his wife and three children; Andor Berei, president of the Planning Office; Erzsébet Andics, member of the HWP Central Committee, leader of the scientific and cultural section; Erdélyi, deputy to the Hungarian ambassador to Moscow; Antal Apró, member of the HWP Politburo, minister of trade and works, with his wife and two children; Sándor Nógrádi, the section leader of the HWP Central Committee; László Piros, minister of the interior, Károly Kiss, György Marosán, both members of the Politburo; and Ede Virág, the leader of the international section of the Hungarian People's Army. The Special Corps command provided food, warm clothing and shoes for them all.[54]

Krasnaya Zvezda wrote that "plants in Budapest are not operating. The workers' councils established in factories and plants have announced that the workers will not start working until their demands have been met."[55]

Following the withdrawal of Soviet troops, only small sub-units remained in the capital to defend Soviet military objects and the city command.

Izvestia wrote a detailed report on October 31 about the imperialist conspiracy against the Arab countries and the Israeli aggression against Egypt.

On the night of October 31, the 31st tank division which had been decorated with the Red Flag, Suvorov and Kutuzov Orders, and belonged to the Carpathian Military District prepared for combat and, taking a course through Chmel'nickij–Beregovo, arrived at 18 hours at its assembly point in the Beregovo area.[56] It contained 5625 soldiers, 279 T-54 tanks, 15 PT-76 amphibious tanks, 25 ISZ-2 tanks, 15 self-propelling guns, 8 BTR-50 armored transport carriers, 1 tank traction engine, 734 motor vehicles, 135 armored transport carriers, 80 cannons and trench mortars, 38 air defense guns, and 12 air defense automatic guns.

At 18:45 the 35th mechanized guard division belonging to the Odessa Military Zone and decorated with the Red Flag, Suvorov and Kutuzov Orders received the order to load up into railway wagons after 11 hours of preparation for combat.[57]

Prime Minister Imre Nagy announced on that day that negotiations were starting on Hungary's withdrawal from the Warsaw Pact. The newly formed government appointed Zoltán Tildy, János Kádár, and Géza Losonczy ministers of state and Colonel Pál Maléter minister of defense. The majority of the smaller political groupings re-formed as well as the old coalition parties: the National Smallholders Party, the Social Democrats, and the National Peasant Party (under the name the Petőfi Party).

Two hundred fifty representatives of the army, the border guards, revolutionary youth and the police elected the 21-member Revolutionary Defense Committee. The Committee decided to establish new armed forces that would consist of 50% National Guard, 25% army and 25% police staff. Béla Király was elected commander of all the armed rebel forces in Budapest–about 13,000 people belonged to the staff of the National Guard.[58]

The rebels and the delegates of the Army's Revolutionary Military Council appealed to the country with the following:

"The Revolutionary Forces' delegates and the elected representatives of Revolutionary Councils of the Units of the People's Army decree the following:

"1. We demand that after leaving Budapest, Soviet troops leave the country altogether. Members of the Committee recognize the necessity for diplomatic negotiations, but this does not mean that Soviet troops can remain in Hungary indefinitely.

"2. We demand that the government call together all the member states of the Warsaw Pact and withdraw from it.

"3. Delegates of the Revolutionary Committee of Hungarian Youth and revolutionary delegates from the military formations demand that Soviet troops leave Hungarian territory by December 31, 1956. If this does not take place we will rise up with arms for the country's freedom and the purity of the revolution expressing our willingness to fight with our lives and blood so long as foreign arms endanger our country.

"4. We state that we will fight with arms against all external or internal enemies who step onto our land to destroy our independence.

"5. We demand that the Hungarian People's Army, if necessary with the help of revolutionary forces, occupy all the uranium mines in Hungary within a week.

"6. Anyone who infringes the discipline of the revolutionary army or does not carry out orders from above damages the revolution and will therefore be brought before the revolutionary courts.

"7. Delegates of the revolutionary forces establish the Hungarian People's Army Revolutionary Committee as an elected revolutionary committee for the army, which is the highest command for the army.

"8. An agreement has been made that the revolutionary armed youth, in the interest of public safety, order and calm, will maintain order along with the police and the Revolutionary Defense Committee . They undertake to round up alien elements and trouble-makers and hand them over to the independent Hungarian courts.

"9. We support the dissolution of the ÁVH. At the same time we demand that members of the ÁVH not join any kind of armed or public-safety formation."[59]

The uprising spread to all corners of the country. Various segments of the population supported the revolution. This is proved by the Cegléd Revolutionary Committee's appeal in which the following can be read:

"1. Until all Soviet troops have been withdrawn, we will not begin work.

"2. We demand that the compulsory teaching of Russian be removed from the curriculum."[60]

Troop Invasion Continues

On November 1 the Soviet government issued a declaration entitled "Armed Aggression against Egypt" which said: "Egypt has become the victim of aggression. Israeli troops have invaded its territory, and there is a danger that England and France will intervene. We condemn this aggression and appeal to the UN Security Council to take immediate measures necessary to stop it."[61]

Prime Minister Imre Nagy announced Hungary's neutrality and its withdrawal from the Warsaw Pact and in a message to the UN secretary general requested that the Hungarian question be put on the agenda for the UN Assembly.

Higher units and units from the 8th mechanized army led by Lieutenant General A. H. Babadjanyan crossed the border in order to reach the assembly points in Debrecen, Szolnok, Kecskemét, Gyöngyös and other places in eastern Hungary by the end of November 2 and to be ready to suppress the uprising.[62] When the army arrived at its designated areas, the 70th infantry and the 35th mechanized divisions were subordinated to it.

On orders from the Odessa Military District's command, the 35th mechanized guard division started to load up into wagons in the stations at Reni in the Soviet Union and at Gelati in Romania. The division was given the task of approaching the Hungarian border by rail across Romanian territory and unloading north and northwest of Timisoara, then marching to Békéscsaba and relieving the mechanized regiment of the 32nd mechanized division there.[63]

The 177th bomber division started to evacuate the families of soldiers. Between November 1 and 3, more than 600 families were evacuated from the country.[64]

At 11 o'clock the 108th parachute guards regiment, belonging to the 7th air mobile guard division, had finished loading up. It contained 1046 soldiers, 12 82mm trench mortars, 18 82mm non-recoil cannons, 6 air defense guns, 891 sub-machine guns, 81 machine guns, 54 armor piercing hand-operated missile launchers, and 10 Gaz-69 and 4 Gaz-63 motor vehicles.[65]

At 19 hours the 31st paratroop guard division's command received the following order: The division must defend Veszprém Airport with the 114th and 381st paratroop regiments. The effectives were to prepare for combat.[66]

On November 1 from 11 o'clock to 3rd 12 noon the 108th parachute guard regiment was transported by rail from the city of Kaunas to its deployment area. This operation was completed by midnight.

From 15 hours on November 1 until 23 hours on November 2, the 1st and 2nd battalions of the 80th parachute regiment reached Beregovo from Gajzhunaj and south from Mukachevo.[67]

In the morning about 3000 soldiers from the Veszprém garrison went over to the rebels. The entire party political apparatus and the commands of the units in the garrisons were dismissed from their posts and arrested. The rebel soldiers did not recognize the existing government and received their orders from the leading rebel center. In the morning more than 200 sub-machine guns and carbines were issued from the military units. The Soviet command received information about an attempt to establish a Transdanubian Army based in Veszprém.[68]

The newspaper *Soviet Hungary* wrote on November 1, 1956:

"1. After lunch on Wednesday, a great crowd assembled in Budapest on Kossuth Square. Imre Nagy, president of the Council of Ministers, went out to the Kossuth monument and made a speech. Speaking of his own role, he stressed that he had not asked for help from Soviet troops and that they had come without any request being made. He announced: "At the same time as we renounce the Warsaw Pact, we also request that Soviet troops be withdrawn." Following the speech the prime minister stood around for a long time talking to small groups in the crowd and said that he was dissatisfied with his interior minister, Ferenc Münnich.

"2. 'It is strange that the Soviet Union does not understand that troops must leave the country immediately,' said Imre Nagy.

"An unofficial report from Debrecen says that yesterday evening Soviet troops built two pontoon bridges in the Záhony area and crossed the River Tisza. Two divisions have arrived in Hungary. This morning, between 6 and 7 o'clock local time, 70–80 tanks sped toward Nagykálló from Nyíregyháza–probably to suppress the disturbances that broke out in Transylvania. There are Soviet troops in Nyíregyháza. Many armored sub-units have gathered on the main roads in the town. Around Beregsurány, near the border, there are a significant number of Soviet tank sub-units.

'3. Social Democratic Party representatives Anna Kéthly, Gyula Kelemen and József Kőműves requested that the party's old building and the editorial offices of the newspaper *Népszava* at Conti Street 4, along with its printing works, be returned to their party. These persons announced that they will reply to the prime minister's request that representatives from the Social Democratic Party join the coalition after they have conferred with Social Democratic Party leaders.

'4. The Chief Public Prosecutor's Revolutionary Committee sent military and civilian detectives to review the cases of those imprisoned for taking part in the revolution, and the material for their offense, along with the local revolutionary organs. The demands of the revolutionaries for the release of political prisoners also resulted in the release of those who had defended the Rákosi regime, who had taken part in suppressing the revolution and who the people wanted condemned. The Chief Public Prosecutor's Revolutionary Committee took steps to release those who had been imprisoned for opposing the Rákosi regime, centralization and collectivization. It asked all revolutionary organs to help them with their work by all possible means. The Chief Prosecutor's Revolutionary Committee started to review the laws that infringed the rights of the people, after which the Prosecutor's Office wishes to propose ways of modifying them and introducing new laws.

'5. Cardinal József Mindszenty, who was released by the victorious revolution on Tuesday, arrived at his Budapest residence on Wednesday morning at 8:55."[69]

Preparations for a New Military Operation

On November 2 editorials appeared in the major Soviet newspapers with headlines like "Aggressors Must Be Stopped" and "The People Demand That the Aggressors Be Stopped." The Council of Ministers of the Russian Soviet Federated Socialist Republic and those of the Kazakh, Azerbaijani and Uzbek Socialist Republics issued a report about "The Treacherous Attack on Egypt," but they also covered the strikes by factory, transport and state workers in Budapest, Miskolc, Győr, Debrecen and other towns in Hungary and the closure of schools, theaters, museums and stadiums.[70]

"Hundreds of Planes are Heading for Hungary" was the headline of an article in *Izvestia* which stated that "hundreds of planes from Austrian airports are heading straight to Budapest. This is not about medicine and first-aid kits as the official reports would have us believe; a whole continent could be provided with medicine with this number of planes. Observers are convinced that hundreds of Hungarian soldiers and officers who served in Horthy's and Hitler's armies are heading to Hungary from the West."[71]

On November 2 the 1st railway guard brigade began their march to Hungary in two railway wagons, and by November 3 every unit had already completed a considerable part of the journey.

During this period the 21st independent mechanized battalion was at Záhony Station, the 12th transport battalion, the 15th signal battalion and the 13th independent engineering company were at Debrecen Station, the 20th independent mechanized battalion was at Szolnok Station, the 11th independent transport battalion was at Püspökladány and the 27th independent transport battalion was at Cegléd Station.[72]

By the end of the day, units from the 27th mechanized division stationed west of Szolnok regrouped near Győr, Komárom and Mosonmagyaróvár. The higher units and units of the Special Corps led by Lieutenant General Lashchenko, the 8th mechanized army led by Lieutenant General A.H. Babadjanyan, the 38th field army led by H.D. Mamsurov were made ready for active combat.

The rebels defending Veszprém received more than 1000 weapons from the garrison's units. Units from the 31st paratroop guard division guarded Veszprém Airport and carried out other defense duties. Soviet troops found leaflets in their assembly areas which said things such as: "Soviet soldiers!

"Do not shoot at the Hungarian people! You would not tolerate it if foreign troops were stationed on Russian soil! Go home! The Hungarian people wish to live in friendship with the Soviet people! Don't let Soviet or Hungarian blood be spilled! You are the soldiers of a great state, but we are a small people. But our slogan is: rather a bayonet plunged in our hearts than the stamp of ignominy. Soviet soldiers, go back to your homes!"[73]

From November 2 to 4 more groups of Special Corps families were evacuated from Veszprém, directly out of Tököl, from Komárom and Győr through Czechoslovakia to Soviet territory. The families who were in Kecskemét or in the eastern parts of the country left the country by car through Chop. Family members of the 407th artillery regiment's officers in the south were taken home through Romania. Patients in the Soviet military hospital were also evacuated at this time.

On November 3 *Izvestia* published an editorial entitled "Fraternal Cooperation and Mutual Aid according to Leninist Principles" in which it published the Soviet Peace Council's declaration on aggression against Egypt and reported on the Hungarian situation as well. The newspaper, citing a TASS report, wrote: "In Budapest an official radio report announced that the government formed on October 27 has relieved the following ministers of their posts: Foreign Minister Imre Horváth, Interior Minister Ferenc Münnich, Defense Minister Károly Janza, Finance Minister István Kossa, Justice Minister Erik Molnár, Metal and Engineering Minister János Csergő and ministers Sándor Czottner, Gergély Szabó, Mrs. József Nagy, Ferenc Nezvál, Miklós Ribnyánszki, József Bognár, János Tausz, Rezső Nyers, Antal Gyenes, Antal Apró, Lajos Bebrits, György Lukács, Albert Kónya and Árpád Kiss. The new government is composed of Prime Minister and Foreign Minister Imre Nagy, Ministers of State Zoltán Tildy, Béla Kovács, István B. Szabó, István Bibó, Ferenc Farkas, János Kádár, Géza Losonczy, József Fischer, Gyula Kelemen and Anna Kéthly, and Minister of Defense Pál Maléter."[74]

Reports from Yugoslavia stressed that the violent wave of reaction had not ceased in Budapest. Many communists had been brutally murdered.[75]

A TASS reporter in New York wrote: "Yesterday at the demand of the United States, England and France, the UN Security Council had a special plenary session to debate 'the Hungarian situation.' At this session A.A. Sobolyev, the Soviet delegate to the UN, announced: the hastily taken up Hungarian question in the Security Council by the Western states is nothing more than a maneuver to divert attention from the Anglo–French aggression in Egypt. The debate on the Hungarian question is a mere smokescreen to cover up this intervention."[76]

The evacuation of the families of the 17th mechanized guard division continued from November 3 to 7. The infantry division of the Hungarian People's Army stationed in Pápa worked out a plan to destroy the forces of the 195th Soviet fighter guard division. The command of the Hungarian infantry division stationed in Veszprém occupied the airport with more than 100 cannons and trench mortars.

On November 3 Cardinal Mindszenty's declaration went out over the radio.

On the same day, at 5 o'clock, the 31st tank division received the order to depart from Beregovo and start crossing the border at 8 o'clock and then to march forward through Nyíregyháza–Hajdúnánás–Mezőkövesd–Füzesabony–Gyöngyös–Hatvan.[77]

At 8 o'clock Lieutenant General A.H. Babadjanyan ordered the higher units and units belonging to the 8th mechanized army to disarm the Hungarian military units on their operational territories and to occupy important objectives, such as post offices, telephone exchanges, revolutionary committee buildings, electricity boards, and railway stations (18 in all). On the night of November 3 the order reached all the troops.[78]

On the same night Lieutenant Colonel Vladimir Ivanovich Petrov, political deputy to one of the regiment commanders of the 32nd mechanized guard divisions, got drunk. As a result it was proposed that he be removed from the armed forces.

On November 3 at 19 hours, a Soviet soldier of Hungarian origin, Matvey Janovich Lukács, in the regiment subordinated to the 32nd mechanized guard divisions stationed west of Békéscsaba, fled. On November 6 he came back without boots or coat, in Hungarian People's Army trousers. He had dropped his carbine and 10 rounds of ammunition in a well. He was therefore expelled from the Komsomol and handed over to the military courts.

According to the order issued to the commander of the 17th mechanized guard division, the division was to be ready for combat at 22 hours and was to start to fight alongside other troops at the appointed time.[79]

All the effectives of the 108th parachute regiment of the 7th air mobile guard division were ready for action at the Tököl Airport on November 3 at 17:30. After landing the regiment's commander received the following order from General of the Army Malinyin, deputy chief of staff of the Soviet Armed Forces:

1. On November 4 at 4 o'clock, the main forces of the regiment were to capture and disarm the six air defense artillery batteries which were part of the air defense system for Budapest and were in firing positions in the Tököl Airport zone. At the same time they were to organize the defense of the airport and prevent rebels from getting in. Later they were to prevent foreign planes from landing and sending down para-

troops, and they were to ensure the smooth operation of Tököl Airport for their own troops and defend General of the Army Malinyin's staff.

2. To form two details of 100 men each and hand them over to the command of the 2nd and 33rd mechanized divisions at 3 o'clock on November 4. The details were to capture the Ministry of Defense building, the Kilián Barracks and the Corvin Cinema, where the rebel leadership was based. The regiment's commander determined how to carry out the order.

At 18 hours the 80th parachute regiment's column started its march through Mukachevo–Szolnok–Budapest. Preceding this, at 14 hours, the railway wagon of the 107th air mobile guard division arrived at Mukachevo Station. After unloading, the division took up its assembly point in a woods five kilometers south of Mukachevo Airport.

The Beginning of Operation "Whirlwind"

On the morning of November 4, the evacuation of families of soldiers belonging to the 195th fighter air guard division began.

At dawn on November 4, following the signal to attack, higher units of the Special Army Corps–the 2nd and 33rd mechanized guard divisions and the 1128th infantry division–marched into Budapest, where they started to fight.

They captured the bridges and major administration and public works establishments. They seized Parliament, the HWP Central Leadership, the General Staff building, railroad stations and radio stations and disarmed People's Army formations in the center and suburbs of Budapest. The corps troops disarmed three Hungarian tank regiments, a tank trainee regiment, two artillery regiments, two air defense regiments, 12 air defense artillery battalions, one 57mm anti-tank artillery battery and a military school. During this process they captured 105 tanks and assault guns, 140 motor vehicles, 30 airplanes, 216 guns of various caliber, 25 trench mortars, 95 machine guns, 30,000 rifles, 8 military depots and two armories. Of the higher units in the Hungarian People's Army, the 7th mechanized and the 27th infantry divisions, the Zrínyi Miklós Military Academy and the Kossuth Artillery Officers School did not put up any resistance.

On November 4 the 80th parachute regiment near Szolnok, in Törökszentmiklós, encountered resistance. The regiment's column came under fire from well-constructed hiding places. Soviet troops liquidated the attack after about 15 minutes of fighting. One soldier in the regiment died and five were wounded.[80]

The effectives of the 31st paratroop guard division, at 2 in the morning, took the oath to carry out the division's duties. At 4:15 the fight began to capture objectives in Veszprém and its surroundings. At 8 o'clock the division's forces captured a barracks 1 kilometer north of Veszprém and another 4 kilometers south of Veszprém, as well as the gunpowder factory, and continued the fight in the center of the town. By 13 hours the paratroops had captured the entire town. The Soviets suffered 10 dead and 25 wounded.[81]

The 108th parachute regiment of the 7th air mobile division started the attack at 4:30. Six task forces of 20–25 men each were formed in order to seize and disarm the Hungarian air defense artillery batteries, which by capturing the Hungarian batteries enabled Tököl Airport to operate unhindered and the back-up planes to land. During this operation the regiment seized 56 85mm air defense cannons, a huge amount of ammunition, grenades and handguns and captured 350 soldiers.

On November 3 the first separate task force of 162 men from the 108th air mobile guard division led by Guard Major L. A. Donchenko, the deputy commander of the 3rd parachute battalion, came under the command of the 2nd mechanized division's 37th tank regiment which was fighting in Budapest. This task force consisted of the fittest soldiers and non-commissioned officers. Before the force set off an assembly was held at the airport in which the battalion commander, Lieutenant Colonel Kovalenko, wished them every success. At 3:30 in the morning the commander of the detail was given the task of seizing the Ministry of Defense building along with the tank regiment and disarming the soldiers in it. At 6:30 the paratroopers captured the building without a shot being fired: here they disarmed 13 generals and 300 officers, and the leaders were taken to General of the Army Malinyin in Tököl.[82]

The regiment's second task force of 171 men under Guards Major A. V. Saluhin, deputy commander of the 1st parachute battalion, came under the command of the 33rd mechanized division on the morning of November 4. This division's task was to capture the Corvin Cinema, one of the biggest rebel centers, and the barracks of the 20th engineering batalion, the Kilián Barracks and the surrounding apartment blocks. A defense had been prepared for the Kilián Barracks and the cinema, yet the detail successfully completed its mission, during which it took 450 prisoners and more than 200 machine guns, 600 sub-machine guns, several dozen grenades and a great amount of war materiel. They inflicted casualties of 500 on the rebels.[83]

On November 4 at 7 in the morning, the 104th and 105th air mobile guard divisions were made ready for action and transported to the Hungarian border in railway wagons. On that date at 15 hours the 107th air mobile guard division completed its assembly in the area around Mukachevo.[84]

The 8th army captured and disarmed 32 military garrisons in eastern Hungary between November 4 and 6. The forces taking part disarmed a total of 1115 officers and 14,745 non-commissioned officers and seized 31 T-34 tanks, 5 assault guns, 74 airplanes, 72 152mm howitzers, 177 122mm howitzers, 152 air defense guns, 434 guns of various caliber, and 837 motor vehicles. Of the Hungarian formations in 32 garrisons, six put up resistance: Debrecen, Miskolc, Mezőkövesd, Szolnok, Kecskemét and Békéscsaba.[85]

The soldiers of the Gyöngyös and Eger garrisons, the 4th tank division (which had 150 tanks), did not support the rebels, and when the units from the 31st Soviet tank division arrived there, the Hungarian division went over to the Soviet side in complete battle readiness.[86]

The forward detail from the 31st tank division and the division staff's operative task force arrived in Mezőkövesd on November 4 at 10 o'clock, where it received Marshal I. S. Konyev's Order No. 1 and joined the fight.[87]

On the morning of November 4, the first transport of the 35th mechanized guard division arrived in the Timisoara area. Since the division had very little time to prepare for action, the troops entered the battle in units as they arrived.

The higher units of the 38th army, the 17th, 39th, and 27th mechanized divisions, the 31st air mobile guard division and the 61st air defense artillery division and its units started Operation "Whirlwind" on the same day at 4:15. By November 7, 219 members of revolutionary councils in the seized garrisons had been arrested; they were taken to prison in Uzhgorod.

The units seized 6776 handguns, 7834 motor vehicles, 601 machine guns, 552 cannons and trench mortars, and 58,500 grenades on their operational territories and seized 13 artillery and food stores.[88]

The 27th mechanized division was given the task of encircling and disarming Hungarian People's Army formations and seizing the important targets, settlements and institutions and railway junctions on the night of November 3–4. They were also to liquidate the rebel groups and to guard a 30-kilometer zone of the Austrian border and the towns of Győr, Komárom, Eszterháza, Esztergom, Tatabánya and other settlements–a more than 200-kilometer border zone covering two counties.[89]

The 39th mechanized guard division stationed in the Tamási zone received its task from Lieutenant General H. D. Mamsurov, commander of the 38th army, on November 4 at 4:15 and had already completed it by 6 o'clock. At the same time the 17th mechanized guard division started to invade their "Whirlwind" objectives at 4:15.

The 57th mechanized regiment along with the 1043rd artillery regiment, short of one artillery battalion, attacked Pápa; the 90th artillery regiment, with the exception of two artillery battalions, attacked Kőszeg; the 56th mechanized guards regiment with the 27th heavy assault gun regiment, the 110th independent reconnaisance battalion and the 163 independent signal battalion attacked Szombathely, while the 58th mechanized guards regiment with an artillery battalion from the 90th artillery regiment, the 21st independent trench mortar guards battalion and a tank battalion from the 83rd tank regiment occupied Zalaegerszeg and Lenti.

The 57th mechanized guards regiment, after completing its task in Pápa, arrived in Budapest and entered the reserves of the 38th army command.

The 61st air defense artillery division provided the anti-aircraft defense for the army staff and troops assembled in the Székesfehérvár zone, and took part in rounding up weapons. The division's units, meanwhile, arrested 40 "suspicious persons" and handed them over to the state security organs.

The 195th fighter air guard division disarmed a Hungarian division on November 4. The 1st railway guard brigade also took part in disarming the rebels.

On that day at 6:30 the 11th mechanized guard division received the order to capture Szolnok and Cegléd where some resistance had arisen.

In Jászberény there was resistance, so the town was taken by assault on the morning of November 5.[90]

The 419th air defense artillery regiment of the 60th air defense artillery division, subordinate to the 11th mechanized division, secured the roads leading out of Szolnok. The 479th air defense artillery regiment, subordinate to the 60th air defense artillery division, defended Debrecen Airport. Some of the effectives of this air defense artillery division received the order to isolate and disarm rebels and "release communists."

Second Lieutenant Usakov's company, consisting of three batteries from the 419th air defense artillery regiment, subordinate to the 60th air defense artillery division, accompanied members of the Revolutionary Worker-Peasant Government led by János Kádár from Szolnok to Budapest on November 7.[91]

In the evening the following was read out on Budapest radio: "Appeal to the Hungarian People!," "The Appeal of the Revolutionary Worker-Peasant Government," "Announcement to the Hungarian People!," "Hungary's Four Politicians' Letter to the Hungarian Working People!" The latter was signed by Antal Apró, János Kádár, István Kossa and Ferenc Münnich–"The Hungarian Revolutionary Worker-Peasant Government's appeal to the governments of fraternal socialist countries."

On November 4 the new revolutionary government appealed to the Soviet Union to help suppress the uprising and restore law and order in the country.

UN General Assembly Decision

On November 5, in the latter part of the day, the extraordinary plenum of the UN General Assembly began in which the situation in Hungary was debated. A. A. Sobolyev, the Soviet Union's UN delegate, protested against this issue appearing on the agenda. In his address he stressed:

"On November 4 some of the democratic figures in Hungary demanded the removal of the Imre Nagy cabinet from power and decided to take power into their own hands by forming the Revolutionary Worker-Peasant Government. The new legitimate government [legitimate or not?–Kirov], in accord with the Warsaw Pact, turned to Soviet troops with the request that they help stop counter-revolutionary elements."

"Hungary's workers continue to support the removal of Imre Nagy's government and the formation of a new revolutionary workers' government." TASS reported at the same time that "at the proposal of the Taiwanese delegation, the U.S. resolution was put to a vote, and the majority of the voters approved it."

The Polish, Czechoslovak, Romanian, Bulgarian and Albanian delegations voted against the proposal, while delegates from Yugoslavia, India, Indonesia, Egypt, Iraq, Finland, Afghanistan, Burma, Ceylon, Jordan, Libya, Nepal, Saudi Arabia, Syria and Yemen abstained.[92] The extraordinary plenum of the UN General Assembly accepted the following resolution–with 50 "for," eight "against" and 15 abstentions):

"The UN General Assembly:

"1. Appeals to the government of the Soviet Union to cease armed attacks immediately.

"2. It appeals to the Soviet Union not to send more troops to Hungary and to withdraw its troops immediately.

"3. It reinforces the Hungarian people's right to freely elect their government and way of life.

"4. It requests the secretary general of the UN to review the foreign intervention, to study the Hungarian situation, to report to the UN and designate the ways and methods to put a stop to Hungary's unfortunate conditions.

"5. The Assembly appeals to the Hungarian and Soviet governments to allow observers into Hungarian territory.

"6. All members of the UN are asked to cooperate with the secretary general.

"7. The UN Assembly requests the secretary general to ascertain what, primarily, the Hungarian people are in need of (food, medicine, etc.) and report to the Security Council.

"8. It asks all members of the UN and all the charitable organizations to aid Hungary."[93]

On the same day in Budapest, at 13 hours, the 3rd battery from the 975th air defense regiment, which was subordinate to the 128th Soviet infantry division, fired on the Egyptian delegation for no reason. After the firing had ceased a few soldiers entered the building, which they looted, and fired automatic pistols. At 16 hours Soviet soldiers again entered the building. They stole several personal effects from the delegation's staff Zade, Egypt's extraordinary envoy and minister plenipotentiary, protested. Although some of the stolen goods–including a traveling bag, a fur coat, two women's outfits, and a radio–were found at the 3rd battery, the perpetrators were not apprehended. The goods were then returned to the Egyptian envoy.[94]

In clashes on November 4 and 5, 54 men from the 38th army–3 officers, 51 non-commissioned officers and privates–died, and 177 men–12 officers, 165 warrant officers and privates–were wounded.[95]

The Transdanubian Army Supreme Command made the following appeal:

"Hungarian mothers, Hungarian fathers, Hungarian young people and Hungarian children!

"The Russian army violates the Geneva Convention and the most basic human rights by attacking our country. It destroys and massacres innocent children, old people, mothers and young girls, wounded soldiers, and Red Cross institutions with its tanks and bullets.

"The Russians declare peace, but they want to thoroughly destroy us. They appeal to us to lay down our arms so that they can withdraw peacefully. Hungarians! Do not believe them, they have been lying to us for 12 years. Do not lay down your arms!

"Destroy the Russians with all the means and force available! Bury food! Don't give them accomodation or gasoline, or any kind of technical assistance! Poison the spirits and the water they demand from you!

"Destroy with all means the Russian oppressors! Don't give them a minute's peace! Let every tree, every bush, every blade of grass, every living thing be their enemy! Think of our ancestors who fought with death-defying bravery against the Turks! All the nations of the world, apart from the satellite states, are with us. Rise, Hungarians, against the Russians in total war!

"Comply with the Transdanubian Military Supreme Command!"[96]

On November 6 the Soviet press published the telegram sent to UN Secretary General Dag Hammarskjöld by Prime Minister János Kádár and Foreign Minister Imre Horváth on behalf of the Worker-Peasant Government, which contained the following:

"The Hungarian Revolutionary Worker-Peasant Government announces that Imre Nagy's appeal to the UN in which he requests the UN to review the Hungarian question is not legitimate, and the UN cannot regard this as an official request from the Hungarian state. The Revolutionary Worker-Peasant Government categorically protests against this issue being debated, whether in the Security Council or by the General Assembly, as this question belongs exclusively to the sphere of competence of the Hungarian People's Republic."[97]

In Moscow, at the special session of the Moscow Council on the anniversary of the October Revolution, M. A. Suslov, a member of the Central Committee Presidium, said:

"Soviet peoples, workers of the socialist countries, all the progressive forces in the world, who were anxious about Hungarian events, are overjoyed at the victory of the Hungarian workers [i.e. Soviet soldiers–Kirov] over the counter-revolution. Hungary was, is and will remain a member of the family of socialist countries as a free, independent and equal state."[98]

Special Army Corps troops received and heard Suslov's speech and the special order given by Minister of Defense G. K. Zhukov on the 39th anniversary of the October Revolution.

At the same time the 128th infantry and the 33rd and 2nd mechanized guard divisions were fighting a bitter struggle in Budapest in order to wipe out the rebels.[99]

In eastern Hungary the 8th army continued liquidating rebels. Between November 4 and 6, 17 in this army (3 officers, 14 soldiers and non-commissioned officers) lost their lives and 27 (5 officers, 22 soldiers and warrant officers) were wounded. The losses by division were as follows: 31st tank division: 7 dead and 19 wounded; 70th infantry division: 3 dead and 16 wounded; 32nd mechanized guard division: 4 dead and 8 wounded; 11th mechanized guard division: 2 dead and 3 wounded.[100]

The higher units and units of the army during this time had captured 78 rebel organizers and imprisoned them. During the fight 450 people were "destroyed" from the Hungarian army and the local population.[101]

Special Corps higher units and units active in Budapest were reinforced by the 100th tank regiment and the 98th independent reconnaissance battalion which belonged to the 31st tank division. These units were ordered to resolutely crush the rebels in Budapest.

An armored transport vehicle driven by Lieutenant Borisenko and three soldiers was shot. Borisenko and the soldiers died. The rebels poured gasoline over their bodies and set fire to them. [102]

The 80th parachute regiment, which was subordinate to the 7th air mobile guard division, fulfilled its duty to "clear" certain residential areas of Budapest of rebels and went on to defend Marshal S. Konyev's staff, which was stationed near Kerepesi Road.

"Who Represents the Will of the People?"

On November 7, at the celebrations on Moscow's Red Square for the 39th anniversary of the October 1917 revolution, Minister of Defense G. K. Zhukov announced: "...the patriots of people's Hungary, hand in hand with the units of the Soviet army, who were asked for assistance by the Revolutionary Worker-Peasant Government, have decisively blocked the path of fascism and reaction in Hungary."

On behalf of the Soviet leadership, Zhukov summoned the UN to "stop the aggression of England, France and Israel against Egypt... As for the Soviet Union, we are prepared to take part in stopping the aggressor on the basis of the UN resolution."[103]

At the same time the paratroopers buried their compatriots, who had fallen while fulfilling the order to take Veszprém, in a common grave.[104]

At the same time the rebels shot down a plane above Budapest from the 880th regiment, which belonged to the 177th bomber guard division, with an air defense cannon. The pilots—Captain Alexander Andreyevich Bobrosky, commander of the company, born in 1922 and Captain Dimitri Dimitreyevich Karmisi, navigator, and Lieutenant Vladimir Yegoroivich Yartsev, the chief signal officer of the air force company—lost their lives.

In District XVI of Budapest, the Soviet troops established their first city command.

The 128th infantry, the 33rd and 2nd mechanized guard division continued fighting in the Hungarian capital. Special Corps troops "celebrated" the 39th anniversary of the October Revolution with losses (See Appendix 1).

Units and higher units from the 8th mechanized army continued to fight against armed rebel positions. While carrying out orders the No. 33 military helicopter crashed into a hill and burned because of a faulty altimeter. Three officers died in the crash, and two were wounded.

Troops from the 17th mechanized guard division were not able to complete their duties in the given time and so continued Operation "Whirlwind."

The 142nd Hungarian air defense regiment stationed in Dunapentele did not allow itself to be disarmed and resisted Soviet troops. Before occupying the town, the Soviet army sent one of its units to parley with the Dunapentele National Committee. The Soviet command appealed for a laying down of arms by promising to allow the rebels and soldiers to withdraw. Otherwise Soviet troops would besiege the town, disarm the garrison and treat anyone found there as a prisoner of war.

The commander of the garrison and the president of the Dunapentele National Committee sent the following answer to the Soviet troop command's ultimatum:

"1. Dunapentele is the first socialist town in Hungary; workers are in the majority here and the whole town is under worker's guard.

"2. The entire population of the town is armed and will defend itself; it does not agree to disarmament. The people are ready to defend their socialist town, their homes, factories, and the whole town which they built for themselves with their last drop of blood.

"3. We promise that we will not turn our guns on Soviet troops if they do not come closer than 10 kilometers to our town.

"4. We would like to continue to live in friendship with the Soviet people, but on the condition that they do not interfere in our domestic affairs. Law is upheld in our town by the revolutionary workers; there are no counter-revolutionaries or fascists among them.

"5. If the Soviet command does not want bloodshed and accepts our conditions, we request that he send a delegate to a neutral zone to negotiate. On the basis of a workers' resolution, we will not lay down our arms, as they could be used against the peaceful population."[106]

After reading the reply, the Soviet command decided to take the town by force.

On November 7, units from the 35th mechanized guard division occupied Cegléd, Kistelek and Békéscsaba and put them under guard. The Soviet division seized 10,942 rifles, 6880 carbines, 11,687 submachine guns, 4684 TT pistols, 1174 PRD-type machine guns, 347 SZG-43 grenades, 333 26mm flare pistol, 213 82mm trench mortars, 455

120mm trench mortars, 187 57mm cannons, 107 76mm cannons, 65 37mm air defense guns, 6 85mm air defense guns and 4 radio locator stations.

In their common appeal issued on November 7, the Hungarian Armed Forces Command, the Writer's Association and the University Students Revolutionary Committee demanded an immediate cease-fire and the prompt withdrawal of Soviet troops and urged negotiations, first with the country's internal forces and then between the Soviet Union and the UN. "We have questions to debate, but we will solve those later on. Our attitudes are unchanged. With great efforts we have established the organizational and technical bases for a National Guard that has started to restore order. Our demands can only be realized in this way, but a significant part of the Soviet army is still weighing us down.

"Why? Because the Soviet Union and the people's democracies are not told the truth. Because the groups that have broken off from the masses still do not recognize the point of the revolution. They do not fulfill the will of our entire people, they do not trust our people and rely on Soviet troops rather than the people...

"Who represents the people's will? We trust Imre Nagy. We support members of the Hungarian Workers Party's Central Leadership who represent the people's interests... Out with Soviet troops....we want to create our own fair system for ourselves!..."[107]

The Organization of the Soviet City Commands

In Moscow on November 8, in the Sports Palace of the Lenin Central Stadium, the Komsomol was awarded the Order of Lenin during an assembly organized for young Muscovites. Khrushchev, in his address, also touched on the Hungarian events and warmly greeted the suppression of the Hungarian counter-revolution on behalf of the workers of socialist countries and the progressive thinkers in the world.[108]

Special Corps troops, under the command of Lieutenant General Lashchenko, continued fighting the rebels. At the end of the day, the 128th infantry guard division broke the resistance of the rebels in their zones of operation. The division seized 60 tanks, 32 planes, 160 guns of various caliber, 400 motor vehicles, more than 300 air defense guns, 14 trench mortars, 15 122mm howitzers and more than 800 handguns.[109]

Units from the 33rd and 2nd mechanized guard divisions continued to fight. On November 8 and 9 a Soviet military city command was established in every district in Budapest.

The activities of these commands were regulated by special rules in which objectives and duties were laid down:

"To carry out, alongside the local state security organs, the order to clear the towns and other settlements of counter-revolutionary elements; to search for weapons and confiscate them; to ensure the safety of Soviet people and the local population; to help the local authorities maintain order; not to allow any group of the population to hold gatherings, protests or mass assemblies; to keep places suitable for assembly, such as cinemas and clubs, closed; within the state and local trade network, to ensure the provision of food to the workers and transports of food to the villages; to immediately resume operation of local public works and health institutions; to defend property, state enterprises, radio stations, the radio and telephone network, printing works and other cultural institutions; not to allow leaflets and other printed materials to appear without permission from the city commands; to take steps to restore Soviet army monuments and Soviet graves desecrated during the counter-revolution; to study the atmosphere within different strata of the population; to continue providing information to the population; to take steps to restore the authority of local state and party organs."[110]

Formations from the 8th army, led by Lieutenant General Babadjanyan, continued to fight against the still-resisting rebel centers and started to set up military city commands.

Between November 8 and 11 the 17th mechanized guard division combed the area around Bicske northeast of Budapest.

The workers' councils set up around the country voiced not only economic but political demands. For example, on November 8 the leadership and workers' council of the Hajdú–Bihar County factories issued the following manifestos, most of which contained the basic demands of the revolution:

"1. We demand that the terror cease against those who legitimately took part in the revolutionary movement...

"7. We will support the new party and state leaders if they recognize the people's rightful demands and will fight for them.

"8. Free the apartments of Soviet families and give them back to their rightful owners..."[111]

In Debrecen the majority of the workers did not work during this period.

On November 8 the parachute regiments took part in supervising and guarding and other commando tasks; they kept an eye on law and order and helped local state security forces return life to normal.

The 177th bomber guard air division had made 20 reconnaissance missions since the beginning of the uprising in Hungary, during which they took aerial photographs. Between November 4 and 8 they dropped 14.5 million leaflets in (about 27 tons worth). The LI-2 planes made 28 takeoffs in various directions. Taking off from Debrecen and Tököl airports, they transported away 560 responsible Hungarian party and military leaders.[112]

The End of the Suppression of the Uprising

On November 9 TASS issued a report concerning the destruction and outrages wrought by the counter-revolutionaries in Budapest and about the normalization of life. *Izvestia* reported on the "Hungarian white terror frenzy." On that day the 33rd mechanized guard division troops fought a bitter struggle in the southeastern parts of the town in order to wipe out the rebels.

Higher units and units from the 8th mechanized army continued to liquidate the rebel strongholds. Thirty-two city commands were set up in the army's zone of operations on November 9. During Operation "Whirlwind" the army forces disarmed 52 Hungarian garrisons consisting of 12,133 soldiers and civilians. Of these, 22 people were sent to the Soviet Union and imprisoned in Uzhgorod and Stry, and 16 people were handed over to special division in the zone, 21 various warehouses were seized, 10 airports were occupied, and during the disarming of the military formations 30 T-34 tanks, 8 self-propelling guns, 1639 guns and trench mortars, 37,876 rifles, carbines and sub-machine guns, 4712 pistols, 500 chests of ammunition, 19,072 grenades, 153 airplanes, and 50 artillery traction engines were seized. Of the army effectives 33 men–11 officers, 6 non-commissioned officers and 16 privates–died, 49 men–6 officers, 9 non-commissioned officers and 34 privates–were wounded and 6 men–1 officer and 5 soldiers–disappeared by November 8.[113]

Late on November 9 the paratroopers who had been killed were buried in Alsónémedi, 24 kilometers southeast of Budapest.

Between November 10 and 12, the 33rd mechanized guard division, which belonged to the Special Corps, continued fighting to liquidate isolated rebel positions. The Corps' military city commands distributed about 150,000 leaflets and more than 300,000 copies of the newspaper *Szabad Nép*. In the leaflets issued by the Hungarian Socialist Workers Party's Central Committee, the news of Hungarians being arrested and sent to the Soviet Union was denied.[114]

One of the regiments of the 17th mechanized guard division received the order to march 120 kilometers from Budapest to the Zirc zone and to close the retreat routes between Veszprémvarsány and Zirc used by westward-bound rebels. Seventy-two Hungarian-speaking officers were made available to the commander of the 38th field army, Lieutenant General H. D. Mamsurov, while 73 such officers were provided to the commander of the Special Corps, Lieutenant General P. N. Lashchenko, who interpreted for the population.[115]

On November 10 the soldiers from the 381st parachute regiment and the 128th infantry guard division were buried at the monument to fallen truce-bearer Captain Ostapenko in Budapest.

TASS reported on the return of calm to Budapest.

On November 11 *Izvestia* published an editorial entitled "The Flag of Peace, Socialism and People's Friendship" in which it said that the socialist forces in people's Hungary had beaten back the forces of reaction and had not allowed the counter-revolution to destroy the achievements of socialism. On Budapest Radio, Prime Minister János Kádár announced the new program of the Hungarian Revolutionary Worker-Peasant Government. Kádár declared that in Budapest and the provinces, the uprising had been completely crushed and that people had gone back to work everywhere.

At the same time *Izvestia* published a TASS report stating: "The leading circles in the Soviet Union have expressed their satisfaction at the declaration of the governments of England, France and Israel that they will abandon their fight against Egypt."[116]

During this period units from the 33rd mechanized guard division, which belonged to the Special Corps, continued fighting to crush the still-active rebel positions. The 8th army command continued to establish military city commands. Its formations patrolled 44 towns in their zone of operations. From the beginning of their operations, the army published and distributed 12 different leaflets (13 million copies in all). Three of the leaflets were written by the political section of the army, and nine of them by higher political organs.[117]

Rearguard Actions

On November 12 the Revolutionary Council published and distributed the following appeal:

"Soviet Comrades!

"Do not fight against the Hungarian people! In Hungary it is not fascists who are fighting but millions of workers who do not wish to live in the Stalinist–Rákosi system.

"We are fighting for the freedom of our people. Show us that the Soviet people do not interfere in the internal affairs of other countries, that they want peace and not mass murder! You are responsible for the whole world!

"You know that there will be no peace in Hungary while foreign troops remain on her soil!

"Soviet soldiers! At the UN the Soviet delegation states that there are no Soviet troops in Hungary. So which country are you in?

"The Hungarian people wish to live in friendship with the Soviet people. It is our belief that you also want this and that it is just your leaders who want to oppose us."[118]

A leaflet issued by the Szolnok County Youth Resistance Movement stated:

"Hungarians! The Soviet system wants to destroy you all. The number of murdered Hungarians amounts to thousands."[119]

On the appeal issued in Jászberény is the following: "Down with the Soviet stooges, the traitorous Kádár government! Russians go home! The Hungarian people want free elections!... Many people doubt the legitimacy of the Kádár government. But does this clique, which conceals Soviet interests, exist or not? The Soviet government sent its own nearly 300,000-strong army and 1000 tanks not to defend the powers of the Hungarian people but to preserve its own colonial system and to gain and keep Hungary as a source of raw materials, bauxite, uranium and other commodities of our land...Hungary is a strategic part of the

Soviet Union's defense zone. We don't want to be a Soviet colony! If on 'bloody Sunday' the Soviet stab in the back had not taken place, then the whole nation could have continued its work by Monday... But the Kádár government does not want to restore order and begin work peacefully. Its aim was to strengthen the Soviet Union...

"We demand basic guarantees for the realization of our national program. These are:

"1. Soviet troops must withdraw from our country immediately!
"2. Leadership must be handed over to Imre Nagy and his government until the next elections!

"Until this happens we will strike!"[120]

Miskolc and other towns also supported the demands of the Szolnok workers. One of their leaflets reads:

"Long live the strike spreading nationwide to defend workers' rights!
"Death to Kádár and his band–traitors!
"Soviet soldiers! We demand that you go home. Don't hurt Hungarian workers, who are fighting for an independent, democratic Hungary and against their own traitorous rulers. Believe us that without you, and only without you, is it possible to defend our beloved country from careerist capitalists!"[121]

At the 11th session of the UN General Assembly, delegates from Hungary, the Soviet Union and Czechoslovakia protested against debating the Hungarian question.

The Soviet UN delegate, V. V. Kuznyesov, announced: "Putting the Hungarian situation on the agenda today, when democratic forces in Hungary have just managed to crush the fascist putsch organized by anti-democratic and counter-revolutionary elements, who were supported by certain foreign circles, can only be detrimental to the Hungarian people." Then he pointed out: "The review of this question merely serves to cover up the aggression perpetrated against Egypt."

On November 12 the assembly voted by 62 votes–with nine against and eight abstentions–to put the "Hungarian question" on the agenda.

Most factories in Budapest were not operating. Higher units and units from the Special Corps had stopped fighting but were patrolling the towns. A few university students who were distributing leaflets were arrested. There was a sudden decrease in the number of people going to work.

While about 600 employees had gone to Keleti Railway Station until November 11, by November 13 only 96 turned up, and they had dispersed by noon.[122]

The people of Budapest demanded the release of Imre Nagy and the withdrawal of Soviet troops. The students started to agitate among the Soviet troops.

Between November 14 and 19, the troops patrolled the city. On the 14th, apart from some sporadic fire, there was calm in Budapest. On November 15 the workers went into the factories, but they did not start work.

Sub-units from the Special Corps arrested 49 suspicious persons on November 15 and started proceedings against them.

Between November 12 and 14, sub-units from the 128th infantry guard division collected 292 air defense guns, 14 trench mortars, 15 122mm howitzers and 8000 hand guns.[123] The officers, non-commissioned officers and privates in the Corps had already thought about the reasons for their stay in Hungary and announced that the Soviet press had thrown a false and subjective light on Hungarian events, especially concerning the Soviet troops' role in events and the operation of industrial plants.

On November 13 a leaflet confiscated (along with a duplicator) from the Petőfi mining settlement contained the following demands from the workers in the five Borsod heavy industrial factories, the Duna Iron Works, the Gyöngyös Engineering Works, the Diósgyőr factories, the Miskolc industrial plants, the Borsod Coal Mines Trust, the Tiszapalkonya Power Station and the workers of Gyöngyös: "3. In the interest of order and calm, we demand that (the government) take immediate steps to put a stop to the Soviet action and for the prompt withdrawal of troops. 4. The government must request the immediate release of those arrested by Soviet soldiers and units during the revolution–civilians, workers, university students–by putting their cases before an independent Hungarian court who will decide if they are guilty or not. ... 8. We demand that UN delegates be allowed into the country and that their freedom of movement be ensured. The government should allow the delegates into our county as well.... 14. We demand that young people studying in the Soviet Union and prisoners of war there be returned home immediately."[124]

On November 17, 111 Soviet soldiers were exhumed from a common grave in Kerepesi Cemetery. Among them was the body of Sergei

Yevdokimovich Sviridov, the commander of the 104th mechanized regiment's anti-air defense machine gun and artillery battalion, which was part of the 33rd mechanized guard division, and had been decorated with the Red Flag and Suvorov orders. It was ascertained that Sviridov had been brutally murdered. The left side of his torso and his left shoulder were pierced by 15 bullets, and his right arm had been broken at the elbow. The right side of his body had been hit twice, and his legs had been hit several times. There were several other broken bodies in the grave that could not be identified.

The bodies of five Soviet soldiers who had escaped into the reeds around Soroksár were dug up. One of them was found covered with earth in a yard.[125]

The 8th mechanized army continued carrying out Marshal Konyev's orders to wipe out the remnants of the counter-revolutionary bands between November 13 and 26. Until November 16 the rebels were in control in Ózd. On November 17 the 31st tank division captured Ózd and Salgótarján. Units from the 8th army operated in northern and northeastern Budapest and around Tokaj and Miskolc. Fifty activists were captured and imprisoned.[126]

Between November 3 and 16, the 38th army combed the woods and collected weapons and military equipment. The army forces arrested 362 members of revolutionary councils and other organizations in the garrisons under their control, who were then transported to Uzhgorod prison.[127] While carrying out orders they seized 25,609 sub-machine guns, 45,663 rifles and carbines, 2502 machine guns and 363 tanks and assault guns and 941 guns of various calibers.[128]

On November 15 the 31st air mobile division's commander, Major General P. Ryabov, reported to Moscow:

"The political situation in Hungary remains confused. Party organs and people's authorities are uncertain and are not active enough. Most of the plants are not operating. A significant number of workers are not going to work. Isolating and discovering rebels is hard because of the breakup of the state security forces. The mass of the people believe in the Kádár government program and are loyal to it, but they are held in check by fear of enemy agitation and the activities of provocateurs. Some of the population are guided by UN decisions, but they are afraid that a war will break out in Hungary. Delegations of workers have arrived in Veszprém at the County Party Committee and at other institutions. Professors and lecturers at Veszprém University do not recognize the authorities. Russian-speaking groups of university students agitate among the soldiers serving in the town. The rebels have become activated. The local state security organs are not taking decisive steps to isolate the local leaders of the resistance movement in the factories, institutions and schools."[129]

On November 15 *Izvestia* published a TASS report from New York, according to which, on November 14, the UN Secretariat made public the telegram sent by István Sebes, the Hungarian foreign minister's delegate, to the secretary general of the UN. In the telegram he evaluated the events of recent weeks, cleared up the reasons for the Soviet troops' presence in Hungary, and informed him of the outcome of elections. He said that he did not think that sending delegates from the UN secretariat to Hungary would be useful.

On the same day the Hungarian Independent Democratic Movement started to distribute its "10 Points for the Rebirth of Hungary," which stated the following:

 1. The legitimate government recognized by the Hungarian people is the government of Imre Nagy.

 2. Foreign troops cannot be permitted to remain on Hungarian soil against the will of the people and the legitimate government.

 3. The Hungarian people do not recognize the government of János Kádár and other traitors and use strikes, boycotts and resistance and all possible means to express this, and they will never agree to Soviet occupation.

If the Soviet Union fulfills the above conditions, then the Imre Nagy government must take power into its own hands and start negotiations with the Soviet authorities.

Earlier conditions:

 1. Complete cease-fire

 2. Soviet troops must return immediately to the bases named in the Warsaw Pact.

 3. Arrested members of government Maléter, Kovács and Erdei should be released, along with imprisoned soldiers, police, youth and workers.

"4. Before negotiations start, Imre Nagy's government must hear the opinions of the Budapest and provincial delegates of the workers' councils, peasants and intellectuals.

"5. The Hungarian government should demand at the negotiations that the occupation troops begin withdrawing within a month.

"6. The Soviet Union must recognize Hungary's independence.

"7. Imre Nagy's government, following the takeover of power, must employ democratic armed forces, which must consist of the best rebel groups, police and soldiers who have proved themselves loyal to the nation and armed workers. The government, relying on this armed force, will be capable of putting an end to all lawlessness and disorder. Every counter-revolutionary aspiration shown by the fascists and Stalinists must be crushed.

"8. The government must rely on the revolutionary councils and the advice of the workers who have chosen the democratic path. They unconditionally guarantee that, in the new Hungary, land will belong to the peasants, the plants and mines to the workers and that everybody will have the right to study.

"9. The government must give every democratic party complete freedom to act.

"10. Three months after the Soviet withdrawal, free elections must be held in which every democratic party can take part."[130]

Between October 24 and November 24, the 195th fighter air guard division had taken part in 570 actions–including guarding 23 airports, 38 active combat operations, 15 captures, and 96 patrol flights, 140 reconnaissance flights, 143 flights to secure ground troops, 16 escort flights, and 99 flights to other airports.[131]

"Sepilov Lied"

On November 18 a TASS report was put out on the formation of new armed forces in Hungary. The Soviet Union's main newspapers published the Soviet government's declaration on the measures taken to reduce international tension.

Hungarian youth turned to the Soviet troops with the following appeal:

"Russian friends!

"Do not shoot! You have been misinformed! You are not fighting reactionaries but revolutionaries.

"We fighting Hungarians want an independent, democratic, free Hungary.

"You have no idea against whom you are fighting.

"You are not shooting at fascists but at workers, peasants and students.

"Stop the fighting!"¹³²

On November 19, at the plenary session of the UN Assembly, the Soviet Union's foreign minister, D. T. Sepilov, spoke out against UN attempts to interfere in Hungarian domestic affairs, evaluated the events and criticized all those who had not taken the Soviet Union's standpoint into account and who proposed a debate on the Hungarian question. Responding to a speech about Hungarians being deported to the Soviet Union, the foreign minister announced that no such thing had happened. [Sepilov lied–Kirov]

At the 11th session of the UN General Assembly, on November 20 Imre Horváth, Hungary's foreign minister, announced: "The question of Hungary's situation is Hungary's internal affair." On November 21 the Foreign Ministry of the Hungarian People's Republic, in its telegram to the UN secretary general, called the news of Hungarians being transported to the Soviet Union tendentious. In fact, the Hungarian foreign minister said, not a single imprisoned person had been taken off Hungarian territory. [No comment necessary–Kirov]

On November 21 Sepilov heaped criticism on the Cuban delegation and the U.S. delegate who had introduced a "slanderous" proposal concerning the mass transport of Hungarians by Soviet commanders.

The leaflets of the Hungarian Revolutionary Committee stated:

"János Kádár!

"You hide behind the Soviets in vain. It makes no difference what you say to the Hungarian nation. Twenty infantry divisions entered our country in vain. The Hungarian people are defending their own national flag and will fight for Hungary's independence. Down with the puppet Kádár government!

"Workers, railway workers!!

"Do not allow the deportation of women and children to the Soviet Union!"¹³³

Sepilov demanded in his address at the plenary sitting of the UN General Assembly on November 22 that the UN block the path of the aggressors and reactionary forces [What forces?–Kirov], and announced that it was unforgivable to use the Hungarian question to increase international tension.

On the same day appeals and leaflets were issued in Balassagyarmat, Pásztó and Salgótarján and distributed in various towns and settlements. In Balassagyarmat, for example, the following appeal was sent out to the population:

"Residents of Balassagyarmat!

"Do not make friends with the murderers of our people! Let silent resistance be our weapon. Anyone who speaks to the Russians is a traitor. Do not allow the murderers of the nation into your homes!

"Children!

"Do not approach the Russian tanks! Do not make friends with the Russians who killed hundreds of thousands of loyal Hungarians!"[134]

On the leaflet addressed to the workers of Pásztó appeared the following:

"...Workers, peasants, intellectuals, young people!

"We will fight until they meet our demands:

"1. The immediate withdrawal of Soviet troops.
"2. Establishment of Imre Nagy's government.
"3. General secret ballots with all the basic parties.
"4. Free trade.
"5. The creation of an independent, neutral Hungary."[135]

On November 24 in Salgótarján, the following appeal was handed to the Soviet unit guarding the bank:

"Soviet soldiers, non-commissioned officers and officers!

"Your bravery during World War II amazed us. You crushed Hitler's fascism and now you are fighting against freedom-loving Hungarians.

"Our factories and plants are in the hands of workers, half of whom are members of the HWP.

"We don't want to believe that you are fighting against the Hungarian people.

"For us COUNTRY and FREEDOM are sacred!

'We want a democratic and free life! And you really want to take this away from us?

'Don't shoot Hungarians! They are your friends.

'Freedom is our common cause."[136]

"There Have Been, and Will Be, Arrests"

I.S. Konyev, marshal of the Soviet Union, ordered all the commanders of the military garrisons to Budapest on November 24 for a briefing. The commander-in-chief of the Warsaw Pact forces evaluated the political and military situation in Hungary, then gave orders to the commanders: "Help the factory party committees to establish and direct party organs and help party organs with the mass political work among workers and employees, influence the workers' councils, help party workers to clear party organizations of enemy elements, supervise the work of the police through the local state security organs, search for and confiscate weapons, ensure the precise provision of patrols and sentries and increase the standard of the city commands' work."[137]

General of the Army I. Serov, president of the KGB, also spoke at this meeting. He said:

'There have been, and will be, arrests, but you must know whom to arrest. The following persons must be arrested at all costs:

'organizers of armed resistance;

'organizers of strikes and sabotages;

'organizers of anti-government assemblies, provocateurs and Horthy officers;

'leaders of anti-government organizations."[138]

To conceal the fact that this was a KGB operation, President Serov thought it necessary that Hungarians make Hungarian arrests in the future.

During the meeting Marshal Konyev announced the Soviet government's decree by which the majority of the higher units stationed in Hungary should become part of the Southern Army Group Forces when the Special Corps ceased to exist.

On November 26 a TASS report announced that life had started to return to normal in Hungary and that 80% of the workers and employees in Budapest had gone back to work. At the beginning of December, the Presidential Council of the Hungarian People's Republic issued a general amnesty for those who had gone abroad after October 23 if they returned before March 31, 1957.

On December 2 a several-day session of the Hungarian Socialist Workers Party Temporary Central Committee started.

The population did not work; it was on strike, demanding the return of the Imre Nagy government and a multi-party system as well as the liquidation of concentration camps, an end to deportations, the release of those imprisoned and under arrest, the recognition of the total innocence of those who had taken part in the national revolution and the strikes, withdrawal of Soviet troops, permission for foreign consignments of aid to enter Hungary unhindered, and the distribution of the aid through the International and Hungarian Red Cross.

"We protest that anyone or any type of government calls the freedom fight, which was fought heroically by workers and young people, and which the Hungarian people enthusiastically supports, a fascist counter-revolution, and that the thousands of people who died a heroic death for freedom and our indisputable democratic rights be branded as fascists."[139]

The women's movement also joined the protest against the Soviet occupation. One of the leaflets distributed throughout the whole country says the following:

"Hungarian women, girls and mothers!

"The government slanders our true revolution as fascism and counter-revolution. They besmirch our sons, husbands, and fathers and humiliate the memory of our dead.

"We protest against these slanders instead of our husbands. On December 4, a month after the second treacherous Soviet attack, we will go out onto the streets at 11 in the morning. We will march to Hősök Square silently and with dignity and will decorate the heroes' monument with our wreaths.

"Only women can take part in the protest, which will last from 11 until 12 o'clock!

"Do not allow any provocation; do not allow men into our ranks! We will not give them reason to disperse us with weapons or break up our march!

"Hungarian women, Csepel and Újpest working women, women of Budapest!

"The revolution now depends on our unity, our discipline and our self-awareness.

"We will all be there!"¹⁴⁰

On December 6 the leadership of the rebel armed forces, the Hungarian Revolutionary Alliance and the staff of the Bükk partisan forces informed the Hungarian population of the formation of the armed national movement. The Hungarian Revolutionary Alliance (HRA) issued the following appeal:

"People of Hungary! Workers, peasant, intellectuals, university students... Comrades-in-arms!

"The leadership of the HRA condemns in the strongest terms the unparalleled provocation of the Soviet Union, which is aimed against order and the people's authority in the Hungarian People's Republic.

"Our nation and our state have not suffered such a bloody attack for 10 years.

"Numerous Soviet divisions bombed and destroyed our country's capital and other towns.

"Tens of thousands of workers died or fled, including innocent passersby and the brave freedom fighters who resisted. We want to inform the Hungarian people that, by this unparalleled provocation, the Soviet Union wants to make Hungary its colony forever.

"We declare in the strongest terms that we do not willingly allow them to turn us from the path to democracy, that the Soviet Union or other enemy forces should destroy our people's state and distort the sacred will of the people.

"We have requested the UN to appeal to the Soviet Union to withdraw its troops in Hungary and declare Hungary a neutral state.

"The Hungarian people, in the spirit of the UN resolution–on the basis of independence and equality–wish to live in peace with its neighbors and with all the countries of the world.

"The Hungarian people–without belonging to any kind of state formation–want to strengthen and in the future further develop the achievements of the revolution.

"A 100-year-old dream of the Hungarian people will thus be realized. The revolutionary struggle for which our ancestors fought in the past and for which they fight now results in a victory for freedom and independence. For our people this heroic fight allows for the realization of our basic national interest, the declaration of neutrality in international relations.

"We turn to our neighbors, to near and distant states to respect this and help the Hungarian people's irrevocable will and decision.

"People of Hungary!

"We appeal to the Hungarian people to heroically and systematically defend the 10-year-old achievements of people's democracy. Help and fight for total victory!!!!

"We will fight with strikes and weapons against the treacherous Rákosi–Gerő–Kádár puppet government and the Soviet army.

"Long live Hungary! Long live the heroic Hungarian people!"[141]

On December 9 the government dissolved and outlawed the workers' councils, including the Central Workers' Council. To protest the government's decision, an appeal was published for a general nation-wide 48-hour strike.

And What Happened Afterwards

On December 18, as part of a decree by the Presidium of the Supreme Council of the Soviet Union, more than 10,000 Soviet officers and soldiers received medals for their participation in the military operations in Hungary "for bravery and heroism displayed while carrying out orders." Twenty-six of them received the "Hero of the Soviet Union" medal–14 posthumously–for valor and for remaining at their posts while fulfilling their internationalist and military obligations.

On the same day the Soviet Central Committee Presidium debated the "unworthy activities" of Soviet troops residing in Hungary.[142]

In November–December 1956 about 200,000 Hungarians left the country.

On March 15, 1957, the Soviet Union's defense minister, Marshal of the Soviet Union G. K. Zhukov, in his address at a briefing for the leading officers of the Soviet Army Group deployed in Germany, analyzed the October–November 1956 events in Hungary as follows:

"At the beginning two of our divisions were stationed in Hungary. The first covered the Austrian border; the second marched into Budapest and there 'was absorbed.' Hungarian army units started to go over to the counter-revolution. It became necessary to withdraw our division formations from Budapest. We withdrew the division.

"After this we secretly ordered 12 divisions to Hungary, some of which, setting off from the Military Districts in the Carpathians, Romania and Odessa, moved 400 kilometers a day. On the night of November 4 we ordered our tank companies to the airports.

"Our tanks captured the runways, pointed their cannons at airplanes and opened fire on those who tried to take off.

" We occupied every radio station and telegraph center; we seized all state and international communications. We surrounded the generals' apartments, all military staff and the 'heads' of the Ministry of Defense well in advance. Then at midnight–so as not to give them an opportunity to organize any resistance–we took them prisoner.

"The Hungarian troops, the air defense artillery, tanks and others were surrounded by our troops on all sides and blockaded along with government institutions.

"The Hungarian army was strong: it consisted of 120,000 men, approximately 700 tanks, 5000 cannons, and a few air force divisions and regiments. The Hungarians are not bad fighters, as we know from our experiences in the two world wars. This army ceased to exist in precisely five minutes."[143]

The Hungarian October and the Present

My view on the events of 1956 taking into consideration also the report issued by a special committee of the Hungarian Socialist Workers Party in 1989[144] could be summarized as follows:

After the Soviet Communist Party's Twentieth Congress, by the summer of 1956 the Rákosi–Gerő group had no chance of staying in power. On October 23, 1956, a people's uprising broke out in order to put a stop to Hungarian Stalinism and to renew socialism.

On October 31, 1956, the Hungarian Socialist Workers Party (HSWP) led by János Kádár and Imre Nagy declared its intention to fulfill the people's fair demands, for which the renewal of democratic socialism was one of the essential conditions. They planned to shape the HSWP's policy on a declaration of national independence and sovereignty, putting an end to the monopoly of the party, and the recognition of workers' councils and a multi-party system.

But the Soviet government, contradicting its October 30 declaration, decided on a military intervention and the suppression of the uprising.

In November, seeing the danger of the restoration of the Rákosi–Gerő wing, the HSWP wing, led by János Kádár, took it upon itself to carry out the task of consolidation. The new leadership, disregarding its initial isolation, strove for fundamental changes. But this historical situation gave rise to a terrible human tragedy and grave contradictions.

This applies to both the founders of the HSWP. After November 4 Imre Nagy was unwilling to make any concessions; instead he chose a martyr's death.

János Kádár was forced to make difficult compromises. The international communist movement and the leaders of the domestic conservative groups demanded a cruel settlement, the deaths of Imre Nagy and his associates.

Although at the end of 1956, Kádár himself recognized the multi-party system, he was forced to accept the construction of a monolithic political system and central planning. Apart from this, he was also temporarily forced to renounce the reforms drafted before November 4. But Kádár–remembering all this–tried with the help of his careful, gradual, partial changes, with the change in style of his politics, to realize all of the 1956 HSWP's plans, which were not possible at the time because of the Soviet intervention.

On May 2, 1990, the Hungarian Parliament passed a resolution declaring that in October 1956 a revolution had broken out in Hungary, and a war of independence had developed, in which the masses took an armed stand against Stalinist tyranny, and that this revolution was crushed with the help of Soviet troops.

On October 24, 1991, *Izvestia* reported that Grachov, the leader of the press service of the Soviet Union's Supreme Council's presidium, categorically condemned the Soviet troop intervention into the 1956 events in Hungary and thought it infringed international rights.

Other analyses showing opposing viewpoints in regard to Soviet "aid" also came up. The following leaflet gives quite a different analysis of the Soviet leadership and the activities of Soviet troops who entered Hungary:

"Why did you come to Hungary? Is it possible that you did not know who you are fighting against? You are fighting against the Hungarian people. Didn't you know that the Hungarian people hate the Soviet army? Have you not seen murderous looks aimed at you? Did they tell you that there are lots of fascists in Hungary, or that there are military exercises? And you believe it? Every people, every country scorns the Soviet government. We are not fascists! We will fight for freedom to our last drop of blood. Why are you killing the Hungarian people? In Budapest 60,000 workers, women and children have fallen. All of them victims of Soviet bullets. Soviet soldiers opened fire on a peaceful population. We do not want this kind of Soviet–Hungarian friendship!"[145]

Over 40 years have gone by since the day "help" was given to Hungary. As a result of the democratic transformations in Eastern Europe the Hungarian people, and the Hungarian government, condemn the Soviet political and military leadership of 1956.

Today, by reviewing the international situation, it is possible to understand where we went wrong in 1956. Is it possible that the roots of this mistake go back to 1948, when Stalin forced Hungary to copy the Soviet model and the Soviet pattern with the help of Rákosi and his stooges?

Is it possible that the rapid militarization, misguided industrialization and violent collectivization bankrupted Hungary?

Or did the low standard of living, mass injustice and terror, the humiliation of nations, and the subordination of their interests to the great-power interests of Molotov's foreign policy lead to the tragedy of the autumn of 1956?

Is it possible that, following Stalin's death, the struggle against Stalinism announced by the Nagy government's program in 1953 was not favored by the Soviet leadership?

But other, even deeper, questions also arise. For example, why, from the humane and democratic notion of socialism, was a totalitarian state born which asserted a right to intervene in the internal affairs of other countries?

As we have already mentioned, the Hungarian Parliament has reviewed the earlier analysis of 1956 events. Russian researchers accepted this too. They also saw the events of October–November 1956 as a people's uprising against the Stalinist Rákosi regime, as a broad social movement for national independence and democratic reforms.

It is also true, however, that counter-revolutionary and criminal elements who committed atrocities against Hungarian communists joined the movement and used it for their own ends.

According to the Hungarian Council of Ministers' Information Office, by October 31, 1956, 13,286 prisoners were released from the country's prisons, 9962 criminals and 3324 political prisoners.

The majority of the prisoners joined the armed rebel groups, while the rest perpetrated criminal acts of terror, stealing and looting under the banner of the war for independence.

In a situation such as this, the introduction of armed forces resulted in a great national tragedy for the Hungarian people.

Those who took part in the uprising became victims of the suppression, including Prime Minister Imre Nagy and Defense Minister Pál Maletér, who were executed.

The Old View Is No Longer Valid

In June 1989 the reburial of Nagy and his fellow martyrs hailed the beginning of national reconciliation in Hungary and a radical new look at the events of October–November 1956.

The question also arises of how to evaluate the Soviet Union's role in the events. The old, one-dimensional view is no longer valid which proposes that we extended internationalist aid to the Hungarian nation in a war against counter-revolution, as the role of the Soviet Union, its government, its diplomats in the 1956 events directly contradicts this.

From present-day Hungarian politicians' declarations, it becomes clear that opinions in the Nagy government on the activities of the Soviet troops were not unanimous. Imre Nagy responded to the Soviet intervention by withdrawing from the Warsaw Pact. This declaration was not legitimate as he made it without the approval of Parliament, which had ratified the Warsaw Pact in 1955. From a legal viewpoint the invitation of Soviet military intervention was also illegal. The Hungarian Revolutionary Worker-Peasant Government was appointed by Moscow, and Soviet troops transported it to Budapest. The request for intervention was not ratified by Parliament.

It is true that the measures taken by the Kádár government were later supported and reinforced by the Parliament elected in 1958. The Hungarian Parliament later took a vote of confidence in János Kádár's government.

But the solving of internal problems between the Hungarian government, the people and the army with the help of Soviet troops is impossible to justify from a legal point of view.

Soviet military troop contingents were employed in 1956 as the Hungarian party leadership could not resolve the situation by political means. The Soviet Union's entire party political work was directed at influencing the troops; they tried to convince the army that they were defending the Hungarian people against counter-revolution, that they were fulfilling their internationalist obligations as a friendly country to help defend socialism. During operations Soviet troops worked diligently among the local population and Hungarian army troops. Between November 4 and 9 they distributed more than 15 million leaflets.

The political section of the Special Corps made about 150 radio broadcasts to the people of Budapest between November 4 and 26.

During Operation "Whirlwind" a total of 30 million leaflets were distributed by Soviet troops. By comparison, during the capture of Berlin in 1945, Soviet troops distributed 113 million leaflets.

Soviet troops carried out orders in circumstances where a significant part of the population, rising up to defend its country, was bitterly opposed to them. Yet Soviet troops were convinced that their mission was just, and that they were fulfilling their military and internationalist obligations.[146]

Soviet Troop Losses

During this bloody struggle Soviet troops suffered the following losses: 640 soldiers (85 officers and 555 privates) died, 1251 men (114 officers and 1137 privates and non-commissioned officers) were wounded, and 5 officers, 13 non-commissioned officers and 49 privates disappeared without a trace. Two officers, 2 non-commissioned officers and 11 privates lost their lives for other reasons. According to the author's calculations the total number of dead, wounded and missing was 1982 men. (See Appendix 1 for a detailed breakdown.)

The author's data differs slightly from that appearing in a work entitled *The secret discovered: Soviet Socialist Allied Republic Armed Forces' losses in wars, combat and military conflicts, a statistical analysis,* published in 1993 and edited by G. F. Krivoseyev. In this book losses are put down as 722 men–92 officers and 630 soldiers and non-commissioned officers. These numbers–720 and 722–show that statistical analyses do not differ so much when it comes to the evaluation of Soviet troop losses in Hungary in 1956.[147]

At the same time the higher interests of internationalism and provision for the "endangered" country allowed the agents of repression to violate the rights of soldiers who did not agree with the intervention. Officers and soldiers became hostage to the system. Today we are still not allowed to speak of the black listing made by Lieutenant General Leonov, chief of the KGB Third Main Division, containing the names of 200 such soldiers and their families, from all the military districts and army groups, who dared to diverge from the official line and speak out and who thought the military intervention in the internal affairs of Hungary was a crime.[148]

Despite the "thaw" after the Twentieth Congress of the Soviet Communist Party, the monopoly of the party and state again revealed itself, a monopoly that prohibited organized opposition, limited basic human rights, and employed the ideology of unlimited state violence in the Hungarian war and against any person who thought differently. Officers who did not agree with the intervention suffered from the party committees and the agents of state repression.

The Soviet people received only one-sided information filtered through the state and party organs and were denied access to other perspectives.

Over the postwar years our civilian government sacrificed military leaders, the defenders of our country, more than once, suggesting that they issue criminal orders to their subordinate troops and that, if they did not carry out these orders, then the full force of the law and the contempt of the Soviet people would bear down on them, on generals and privates alike.

Unfortunately very few Soviets thought this through; most of us did not even try to understand or accept it. Soldiers could never question the constitutionality and legitimacy of an order. Thus the party and state nomenklatura could manipulate the armed forces and social awareness to its own interests. Soldiers' heads were filled with formulated ideological themes, instructions given during political training, and they remained reliable cogs in the state machine. Ideology bankrupted morals, but it could not destroy historical memory.

From time to time the question arose: could the troops have renounced this "liberating" mission? If we look at this period in historical context, then the answer is: probably not. Today some are prepared to lay the entire blame on the army. But unfortunately they were neither wise enough, nor brave enough, to point this out at the time.

I would like to believe that an analysis of the Soviet/Russian troops' anti-democratic interventions in Hungary, Czechoslovakia, Afghanistan, Novocherkas, Tbilisi, Baku, Vilnius, twice in Moscow, and in Chechnya, which resulted in many deaths, will help the Russian state and army leadership understand that in future the army cannot oppose the people. The officer and the soldier are an integral part of the country and are always ready to defend their country if an outside force threatens it. But blood need not be spilled and lives lost for the decisions of the leaders and committees, for their unexpected decisions, of which there have been more than enough during our lifetime.

Troops Withdraw, the Graves Stay Behind

Years pass, the world changes, and new relationships form between states, peoples and armies. In Eastern Europe the "doctrine of limited sovereignty" has been replaced by true sovereignty, the independent choice of the road to development, the right of states and nations to govern themselves and non-interference in each other's internal affairs.

In the summer of 1991, Soviet troops withdrew from Hungary, but the graves of the fallen remained. Those party and state leaders who sent people to fight left the fallen on foreign soil in order to conceal from the Soviet people the truth about the undeclared war, as official information contains no trace of them.

Soviet soldiers, in World War II and in Afghanistan, showed the greatest comradeship towards their wounded comrades and felt it their duty to bury their dead.

Not so long ago the paratroopers in Afghanistan–as "Hero of the Soviet Union" Guard Lieutenant Nikolai Kravchenko recalls– scoured the mountains and saved their wounded compatriots from the fire. Weary from war, they descended into the deep craters to lift out their wounded compatriots. Then, lifting their dead comrades onto their shoulders, they went for days through the scorching mountains until a helicopter arrived to pick their sad burden up so that at last the dead soldiers could be decently buried in their own land. There are numerous such episodes. This was the law for paratroopers.[149]

On reflection the events in Hungary in 1956 were not only the beginning of a democratic transformation but also a tragedy for the Hungarian people and Soviet families in the conflict.

After Nearly 40 Years

In the 1990s, after nearly 40 years, Russian historians' work permitted a reevaluation of the role of Soviet diplomacy, government, party and army in the bloody drama of the Hungarian autumn of 1956. First of all, this helps prevent another intervention. Secondly, it is a grave lesson for our state leadership about the political decisions concerning the intervention of armed forces. Thirdly, it allows for the stabilization of Russia's reputation before the world and strengthens trust in Russian–Hungarian relations.

On November 13, 1991, *Izvestia* published TASS's report from the Hungarian 56 Alliance, which said that 2200 Soviet soldiers were shot in the courtyard of the Soviet Embassy because they went over to the Hungarian Revolution and supported the rebels. On November 16, 1991, after a preliminary review at the KGB, Major General A. Boriskin, who supervised rehabilitation issues in the Military Supreme Prosecutor's Office, declared in the newspaper *Krasnaya Zvezda* that the Military Supreme Prosecutor's Office archives had never contained any documents concerning executed Soviet soldiers in the courtyard of the Soviet Embassy or anywhere else. The November 23, 1991, issue of *Pravda* announced that the TASS information was "ill-willed fantasy." Documents and military reports found in the military archives do not point to any mass executions of Soviet soldiers. The author believes that the Hungarian 56 Alliance's report is baseless.

But General Boriskin's reply must be clarified. The Military Supreme Prosecutor's Office should have had data about any mass refusal to carry out orders. Some people did refuse to carry out the criminal orders, but these cases are not reviewed by the Military Supreme Prosecutor's Office, as in such cases those executed are reported as lost. "Disappeared without a trace," as we say.

This was the case when Major S. T. Kochnyev shot Private P. S. Piclitechuk for his cowardice and refusal to obey orders. As is clear from the examination carried out by the division, the death sentence could have been avoided. The officer was merely arrested when he returned to the Soviet Union and sentenced to five days' detention.

But this case not only reveals that the price for a life in our country is five days. It also sheds light on the quality of the legal work carried out by the prosecuting organs for the higher units and units. That is why similar cases were not examined by the prosecutor's office. In this case it would have been better if *Pravda* had kept quiet.

The Price of the Khrushchev-Kádár Agreement

In 1957 the Information Office of the Hungarian People's Republic declared that ' in the period from October 23 until December 1, 1956, 12,971 wounded were treated in the country's surgeries, hospitals and in the Red Cross's temporary institutions." The total number of wounded exceeded this number, as those who were only slightly wounded were treated at home.

Of the 12,971 wounded, 11,513 were treated in Budapest hospitals, surgeries and Red Cross stations, and 1458 were treated in the other towns and settlements. A total of 6731 people ended up in Budapest hospitals, and 559 of them died.

According to the Central Statistical Office the state health service treated nearly 20,000 people wounded in the conflict from October 23 until the end of the year. Of these 67% were hospital patients, 8% of whom died; 25% were under 18 years of age, and more than half were between 19 and 30. According to the book *Hungary 1956: Outlines of the Crisis*[150] the number of wounded between October 23 and December 31 was 19,226.

The Information Office's 1957 report states that between October 23 and November 30, the Budapest district councils registered 1191 deaths due to fighting and murder. This number includes those who died in hospital as well.

But in Budapest, I believe, more people than this died. During the uprising the state funeral services buried 1230 people. Apart from these, about 500 people were interred near apartment blocks and on squares. That is why the number of deaths in Budapest, taking into account the above statistics, but not including Soviet troop losses, was approximately 1800 people. According to the Central Statistical Office report, 2700 people died in the country on October 23 and in the days that followed.

The Registrar's Office registered 2195 deaths, while 307 people were identified on the basis of reports published by the Statistical Office on burials and exhumations. There were likely an additional 100–150 dead who were not exhumed or whose deaths were not registered.

During the entire period 1945 deaths–78% of the total–happened in Budapest. Eighty-five percent of those who were killed in the capital were Budapest residents. Twenty percent of the fallen were less than 20 years old, while 28% were between 20 and 29.

The above data must be subjected to rigorous examination and study. The data found in the Russian military archives allow for such a thorough analysis.

In the data published by the Hungarian Council of Ministers' Information Office in 1957, and then again in 1981 in a separate publication, we find the numbers of Hungarian dead in the various towns. According to the 1981 data 67 people died defending Veszprém. This diverges from the Soviet troop reports, which put the number at 217. Another example is that the archive documents state that in Budapest, in the defense of the Corvin Alley, more than 500 rebels fell.

On the basis of the Chief of Staff Operational Section's documents, the Special Corps and 8th and 38th armies' command and staff reports, we can ascertain that, following the Soviet military intervention, more than 5000 rebels died.*

Added to the human cost was the material cost of the struggle. During the fighting significant damage was done to the buildings, both inside and out. A lot of looting took place, but the country suffered far more from the fall in production and distribution.

Nine billion forints' worth of goods was lost in industry due to fighting, strikes and disorganization; the national income dropped by this

---

* Editors' note: the editors accept the report of the Central Statistical Office, in other words the total of losses was 2700 rather than 5000.

amount in 1956. Looting and destruction caused serious damage in the state stocks, installations, in the transport and trade network, manufacturing machinery and in warehouses.

Five hundred million forints' worth of damage was suffered by trade and public businesses and warehouses; damage to equipment accounted for a further 259 million forints. Total damages amounted to near 800 million forints.

Damage to Hungarian State Railways came to 759 million forints. Looting of military warehouses resulted in damage of approximately 100 million forints. The buildings in Budapest suffered about 1 billion forints' worth of damage. Altogether, the losses suffered because of work stoppages, looting and destruction reduced Hungary's 1956 national income to 11.5 billion forints.

The photographic documents and reports in the military archives on the destruction wrought in Budapest enable today's researchers to correct the data published by the Information Office in 1957.

In 1958 the Hungarian People's Supreme Court condemned Imre Nagy and his followers for conspiring to overthrow the existing system. Nagy died a martyr's death: he was hanged. Kádár's regime condemned approximately 350–500 people to death, and more than 10,000 people to imprisonment for their part in the uprising. About 200,000 Hungarian citizens fled the country.[150] Finally, during the Hungarian tragedy more than 1000 people, including women and children, were deported to the Soviet Union to prisons in Stry and Uzhgorod.[151]

Conclusion

After the Soviet–Hungarian war, unfortunately, the leaders of the Soviet/Russian armed forces and the country showed no improvements. First there was Prague and Brno, then the mountains of Afghanistan, then Baku, Tbilisi, Vilnius, twice Moscow and Chechnya...

The prestige of the Soviet Union, which had defeated fascism, was shattered by the party and state leadership's precipitate and voluntarist decision to militarily intervene and to suppress the national uprising against the Stalinist Rákosi regime for free elections, democracy, and human rights.

The Soviet armed forces were, for the first time in postwar history, subjugated to decisions fed by party ideological ambitions and decided upon as the result of party leadership consensus.

In Hungary, in order to crush the uprising, the Soviet leadership put in 17 divisions–eight mechanized, one tank, two infantry, two air defense artillery, two air force, and two paratroop. More than 60,000 troops took part in "establishing order." This was one of the crimes against humanity in the 20th century.

The Soviet party and military leadership protested against all kinds of aggression. Yet in October and November 1956, the Soviet army, on orders from the Soviet political leadership, carried out aggression in the form of armed intervention against Hungary.

It is obvious by now that these decisions were harmful. The Soviet party and government leadership's actions ran counter to the principles of the peace edict made on November 8, 1917, and turned the country against the 1928 Kellogg–Briand Pact[152] which forbids aggression and makes it unlawful, and contradicts the 1933 London convention and the international rights accords signed in the 1950s.

During the Hungarian war the dishonesty of Soviet diplomatic policy and the absolute contradiction between Moscow's words and deeds became clear. In the name of "historical justice" and "objective necessity," moral doubts were dispelled and moral obstacles destroyed. The Soviet leadership's absence of morals and the immoral totalitarian system denied Hungary an alternative, Hungarian and democratic alternative way forward.

The world, through the UN, condemned the Soviet Union for its military and political intervention in Hungarian affairs. Moscow forced the Soviet-friendly Kádár government on the country and until 1989, it directed the country to further its own interests.

Thus the Soviet Union–ensuring its own geopolitical and strategic interests, preventing the loss of control over the Warsaw Pact states and crushing the people's uprising against the Stalinist–Rákosi tyranny in order to defend the communist totalitarian system–carried out a military invasion in Hungary in 1956 under the banner of internationalism.

Notes

¹ Alexander Mikhailovich Kirov–military historian and candidate in historical sciences–was born in Siberia in a small village in the Krasnoyarsk District in 1956. He completed military political school and military academy. He served as a lieutenant colonel in the Russian Federation Armed Forces' paratroop formations. Researching the history of his formations, he came to the history of the 1956 Hungarian events. He had a scholarship at the post-graduate studies at the Military Arts Political Academy for three years. He defended his dissertation on the 1956 Soviet intervention in Hungary at a closed meeting in 1994 and was awarded candidate status. His research field: military political crises and conflicts in Eastern Europe in the 1950s and 1960s and the Soviet Union's role in their "solution." Following his defense of his candidature, his dissertation and notes were confiscated, and he was relieved of his post in the army. The confiscation of documents occurred, probably, to prevent their usage to persecute Soviet soldiers for having committed war crimes us Hungary in 1956.

² Imre Nagy: *One decade. Selected speeches and writings,* two volumes, Budapest, Szikra 1954.

³ The Russian Federation's Armed Forces Headquarters Central Archive (hereafter: FEVKA) fond (hereafter: f) 32. op. 701 291. d. 15. p. 131.

⁴ Ibid.

⁵ FEVKA f. 32. op. 701 291 d. 15. p. 238.

⁶ FEVKA f. 32. op. 701 291 d. 15. p. 131.

⁷ FEVKA f. 32. op. 701 291 d. supplement (hereafter: supp.) 17. p. 51.

⁸ FEVKA f. 32. op. 701 291 d. supp. 17. pp. 2–63.

⁹ FEVKA f. 32. op. 701 291 d. 15. p. 133.

¹⁰ Ibid.

¹¹ FEVKA f. 32. op. 701 291 d. 15. p. 6.

¹² FEVKA f. 32. op. 701 291 d. 16. p. 31, 45.

¹³ FEVKA f. 32. op. 701 291 d. 16. p. 117.

¹⁴ József Dudás entered the revolutionary events on October 27. He sought out the *Szabad Nép's* headquarters on October 29. [added by J. Györkei and M. Horváth].

[15] The 12th, 17th, and 27th infantry and the 5th mechanized divisions were subordinate to the Hungarian III. Corps. The 8th Békéscsaba infantry division was directly subordinated to the Supreme Command; it was not ordered to Budapest during the revolution [Györkei and Horváth].

[16] FEVKA f. 32. op. 701 291 d 15. p. 133.

[17] The Radio building was recaptured by Soviet and Hungarian troops on the morning of October 25 [Györkei–Horváth].

[18] FEVKA f. 32. op. 701 291 d. 15. p. 226.

[19] FEVKA f. 32. op. 701 291 d. 15. p. 196.

[20] On October 24 not one of the Hungarian People's Army's institutions or sub-units went en masse over to the rebels. Individual soldiers and officers went over to the rebels [Györkei–Horváth].

[21] FEVKA f. 32. op. 701 291 d. 16. p. 220.

[22] They accompanied Mikoyan and Suslov, who had arrived at Veszprém Airport, to Budapest and there supplied the defense of Soviet leaders [Györkei–Horváth].

[23] FEVKA f. 32. op. 701 291 d. 16. p. 121.

[24] FEVKA f. 32. op. 701 291 d. 16. p. 48.

[25] *Izvestia,* October 25, 1956.

[26] FEVKA f. 32. op. 701 291 d. 16. p. 150.

[27] *Krasnaya Zvezda,* October 25, 1956.

[28] *Izvestia,* October 26, 1956.

[29] FEVKA f. 32. op. 701 291 d. 15. p. 298.

[30] FEVKA f. 32. op. 701 291 d. 15. p. 280.

[31] FEVKA f. 32. op. 701 291 d. 15. p. 197.

[32] FEVKA f. 32. op. 701 291 d. 15. p. 226.

[33] *Izvestia,* October 28, 1956.

[34] The construction battalions mentioned did not join the rebels in any organized way, but they did not fight against rebels either. At various times 40–50 officers and men took part in the fight against Soviet troops on the side of the rebels in the Kilián Barracks [Györkei–Horváth].

[35] FEVKA f. 32. op. 701 291 d. 15. p. 134.

[36] FEVKA f. 32. op. 701 291 d. 15. p. 141.

[37] FEVKA f. 32. op. 701 291 d. 15. p. 390.

[38] FEVKA f. 32. op. 701 291 d. 16. p. 235.

[39] FEVKA f. 32. op. 701 291 d. 16 p. 16.

[40] FEVKA f. 32. op. 701 291 d. 15. p. 138. The 37th Kiskunhalasi regiment, according to Hungarian sources, arrived in Budapest on October 26, at the designated time, and later did not go over to the rebels either. For their active part in suppressing the uprising, the regiment led by Major Imre Hodosán received the title "revolutionary regiment" from the Kádár government. Until

October 26 the 46th air defense artillery division did not go over to the rebels either. An attempt was made by the 8th regiment's Törörkbálint-felső battery, subordinate to the division, where 30 privates and eight cannons wanted to go out onto the Balaton road in order to fire at Soviet tanks processing along it. The leadership of the regiment managed to prevent this except for one cannon. The eight soldiers who took the cannon out brought it back voluntarily the following day [Györkei–Horváth].

FEVKA f. 32. op. 701 291 d. 15. p. 171.
FEVKA f. 32. op. 701 291 d. 17. p. 35.
Izvestia, October 30, 1956.
FEVKA f. 32. op. 701 291 d. 15. p. 139.
FEVKA f. 32. op. 701 291 d. 15. p. 226.
FEVKA f. 32. op. 701 291 d. 15. p. 392.
FEVKA f. 32. op. 701 291 d. 17. p. 44.
Izvestia, October 31, 1956.
FEVKA f. 32. op. 701 291 d. 15. p. 139.
FEVKA f. 32. op. 701 291 d. 17. supp. p. 31.
FEVKA f. 32. op. 701 291 d. 15. p. 143.

During the attack on the Budapest Politburo on Köztársaság Square, the greatest losses were suffered by the state security forces ordered to defend it. Some of the state security soldiers fell in the battle, while others fell victim to mob violence as the building was stormed. The majority of the party workers in the building escaped.

The divided state security authorities stopped guarding József Mindszenty, and thus he did not even have to be released. Mindszenty, on orders from the government, was escorted by the Rétság tank regiment officers [Györkei–Horváth].

FEVKA f. 37. op. 697 193. d. 13. p. 141.
FEVKA f. 32. op. 701 291 d. 15. p. 140.
Krasnaya Zvezda, November 1, 1956.
FEVKA f. 32. op. 701 291 d. 16. p. 60.
FEVKA f. 32. op. 701 291 d. 16. p. 153.
FEVKA f. 32. op. 701 291 d. 17. p. 35.
FEKVA f. 32. op. 701 291 d. 17. supp. p. 3.
FEVKA f. 32. op. 701 291 d. 17. supp. p. 11.
Izvestia, November 1, 1956.
FEVKA f. 32. op. 701 291 d. 16 p. 16.
FEVKA f. 32. op. 701 291 d. 16. p. 153.
FEVKA f. 32. op. 701 291 d. 16. p. 48.
FEVKA f. 1317. op. 891819 d. 1. p. 4.
FEVKA f. 37. op. 647 193 d. 13. p. 142.

[67] FEVKA f. 1317. op. 891819 d. 1. p. 6.
[68] FEVKA f. 37. op. 647 193 d. 13. p. 142. The organization of the Transdanubian Army had faltered from the very beginning. No military organization with this name was active during the revolution [Györkei–Horváth].
[69] FEVKA f. 32. op. 701 291 d. supp. 17. p. 3.
[70] *Izvestia*, November 3, 1956.
[71] Ibid.
[72] FEVKA f. 32. op. 701 291 d. 15. p. 293.
[73] FEVKA f. 32. op. 701 291 d. supp. 17. p. 25.
[74] *Izvestia*, November 3, 1956.
[75] Ibid.
[76] *Izvestia,* November 4, 1956.
[77] FEVKA f. 32. op. 701 291 supp d. 16. p. 61.
[78] FEVKA f. 32. op. 701 291 supp d. 16. p. 19.
[79] FEVKA f. 32. op. 701 291 supp d. 16. p. 124.
[80] FEVKA f. 1317. op. 891 819 d. 1 p. 7.
[81] FEVKA f. 37. op. 647 193 d. 13. p. 145.
[82] FEVKA f. 108. gv. PDP. op. 733 990 d. 35. p. 5.
[83] FEVKA f. 1317. op. 891 819 d. 1 pp. 113–115.
[84] FEVKA f. 37. op. 647 193. d. 13. p. 145.
[85] FEVKA f. 32. op. 7001 291. d. 15 .p. 20.
[86] Before the revolution the Gyöngyös 4th mechanized division, in accordance with its orders, went out of existence on October 25. Therefore after November 4 it could not have gone over to the Soviet side as a fully combat-ready division [Györkei–Horváth].
[87] FEVKA f. 32. op. 701 291 d. 16 p. 62.
[88] Ibid.
[89] FEVKA f 32. op. 701 291 d. 16 p. 304.
[90] FEVKA f 32. op. 701 291 d. 16 p. 310.
[91] FEVKA f 32. op. 701 291 d. 16 pp. 55–56.
[92] *Izvestia*, November 6, 1956.
[93] FEVKA f 32. op. 701 291 d. supp. 17. p. 45.
[94] FEVKA f 32. op. 701 291 d. 15. pp. 120–122.
[95] FEVKA f 32. op. 701 291 d. 15. p. 13.
[96] This appeal was put out by the Dunapentele Revolutionary Committee on behalf of the Transdanubian Military Command. In reality no such command existed [Györkei–Horváth].
[97] *Izvestia*, November 6, 1956.
[98] Ibid.
[99] FEVKA f 32. op. 701 291 d. 15. p. 202.

[100] FEVKA f 32. op. 701 291 d. 15 p. 20.
[101] FEVKA f 32. op. 701 291 d. 15 p. 21.
[102] FEVKA f 32. op. 701 291 d. 15 p. 202.
[103] *Krasnaja Zvezda*, November 8, 1956.
[104] FEVKA f, 2252, op. 663 367 d. supp. 2. p. 2.
[105] FEVKA f 32. op. 701 291 d. 15. p. 4–table.
[106] FEVKA f 32. op. 701 291 d. supp. 17 p. 67.
[107] FEVKA f 32. op. 701 291 d. supp. 17 p. 5.
[108] *Izvestia*, November 9, 1956.
[109] FEVKA f 32. op. 701 291 d. 15. p. 186.
[110] FEVKA f 32. op. 701 291 d. 15 pp. 153–154.
[111] FEVKA f 32. op. 701 291 d. supp. 14. p. 41.
[112] FEVKA f 32. op. 701 291 d. 16. p. 50.
[113] Ibid.
[114] FEVKA f 32. op. 701 291 d. 17. pp. 19–23.
[115] FEVKA f 32. op. 701 291 d. 17. pp. 258–271.
[116] *Izvestia*, November 11, 1956.
[117] FEVKA f 32. op. 701 291 d. 16. pp. 26, 27.
[118] FEVKA f 32. op. 701 291 d. supp. 17. p. 78.
[119] FEVKA f 32. op. 701 291 d. supp. 17. p. 23.
[120] FEVKA f 32. op. 701 291 d. supp. 17. p. 49.
[121] FEVKA f 32. op. 701 291 d. supp. 17. p. 26.
[122] FEVKA f 32. op. 701 291 d. 15. p. 45.
[123] FEVKA f 32. op. 701 291 d. 15. pp. 75, 77.
[124] FEVKA f 32. op. 701 291 d. supp 17. p. 23.
[125] FEVKA f 32. op. 701 291 d. 15. p. 202.
[126] FEVKA f 32. op. 701 291 d. 16. p. 331.
[127] FEVKA f 32. op. 701 291 d. 15. p. 93.
[128] FEVKA f 32. op. 701 291 d. 15. p. 94.
[129] FEVKA f 37. op. 647 193 d. 13. pp. 147–148.
[130] FEVKA f 32. op. 701 291 d. supp. 17. p. 2.
[131] FEVKA f 32. op. 701 291 d. 16. p. 34.
[132] FEVKA f 32. op. 701 291 d. supp. 17. p. 61.
[133] FEVKA f 32. op. 701 291 d. supp. 17. p. 7.
[134] FEVKA f 32. op. 701 291 d. supp. 17. p. 17.
[135] FEVKA f 32. op. 701 291 d. supp. 17. p. 9.
[136] FEVKA f 32. op. 701 291 d. supp. 17. p. 15.
[137] FEVKA f 32. op. 701 291 d. supp. 17. p. 60.
[138] FEVKA f 32. op. 701 291 d. 15. p. 159.
[139] FEVKA f 32. op. 701 291 d. supp. 17. p. 1.
[140] FEVKA f 32. op. 701 291 d. supp. 17. p. 8.

141 FEVKA f 32. op. 701 291 d. supp. 17 p. 1.
142 FEVKA f 32. op. 701 291 d. 1. p. 2.
143 FEVKA f 32. op. 701 291 d. 3. pp. 45–59.
144 A 15-member committee led by Imre Pozsgay and set up by the HSWP Central Committee was commissioned to work out a new program and analyze the history of recent decades and the situation that arose in 1989. The working committee's report, entitled "Our Historical Path–On the Historical Reasons for the Present Situation by the Working Committee," deals with the development of the Hungarian crisis and the October 1956 uprising in its second part. *Társadalmi Szemle* (Social Review), the Hungarian Socialist Workers Party's analytical and political periodical, No. XLIV (1989), special issue.
145 FEVKA f 32. op. 701 291 d. 17. p. 311.
146 FEVKA f 32. op. 701 291 d. 17. p. 49.
147 *Grif sekretnosti sniat: Poteri Vooruzhonnykh Sil SSSR v voinakh, boievykh deistviyakh i boievykh konfliktakh: Statisticheskoye issledovaniye:* Edited by G. F. Krivosheyev. Voenizdat, Moscow, 1993, p. 397.
148 FEVKA f 32. op. 701 291 d. 37. pp. 192–340.
149 *Solidatskaya Pravda* No. 2, August 1990, p. 8.
150 *Hungary–1956. Outlines of the Crisis.* Nauka, 1993, p. 163.
151 E. I. Malashenko: *Osobij Korpus v ognye Budapest. Voyenno-istoricheskiy zhurnal* No. 1, 1994, p. 35.
152 Briand, Aristide (1862–1932), French statesman and diplomat. His name is linked to the Kellogg–Briand Pact made in 1928. In 1925 he signed the Locarno Agreement on behalf of France. Kellogg, Frank (1856–1937) U.S. secretary of state. On the proposal of Kellogg and the French foreign minister, the agreement was established in which signatory states rejected war as a means of settling international questions. They announced that the problems arising between states would only be solved by peaceful means. On August 27, 1928, the United States, France, Great Britain, Germany, Italy and others signed–15 states in all. The Soviet government also signed the pact.

Tables

Table 1. Total account of Soviet troops taking part in military operations in Hungary

Military formation	Permanent base	Time of combat readiness*	Time of border crossing*
Special Corps sub-ordinates and back up	Hungary	October 23rd 1956 20:00	–
2nd mechanized guard division	Hungary	October 23rd 1956 20:00	–
17th mechanized guard division	Hungary	October 23rd 1956 20:10	–
177th bomber air division	Hungary	Night of October 23rd-24th 1956	–
195th fighter air division	Hungary	October 23rd–24th 1956	–
128th infantry guard division	Soviet Union, Carpathian Military Zone	October 23rd 1956 19:45	October 24th between 00:15 and 07:00
33rd mechanized guard division	Romania	October 23rd 1956 22:35	October 24th 1956 between 11:00 and 12:00
8th mechanized army forces ordered to Hungary	Soviet Union, Carpathain Military Zone	Night ending October 28th 1956	October 28th until November 4th
70th infantry guard division	Soviet Union, Carpathian Military Zone	October 26th	October 28 06:00
32nd mechanized guard division	Soviet Union, Carpathian Military Zone	October 27th	October 28th–29th
60th air defence artillery division	Soviet Union, Carpathian Military Zone	October 27th	October 30th–November 1st
11th mechanized guard division	Soviet Union, Carpathian Military Zone	Night ending October 28th	November 1st
31st tank division	Soviet Union, Carpathian Military Zone	Night of November 1st	November 3rd 08:00
35th mechanized guard division	Soviet Union, Odessa Military Zone	October 31st 18:45	November 4th at dawn through Romania

Military formation	Permanent base	Time of combat readiness*	Time of border crossing*
38th total army services ordered to Hungary**	Soviet Union, Carpathian Miliary Zone	October 23rd 19:45	October 24th until 27th 08:00
39th mechanized guard division	Soviet Union, Carpathian Military Zone	October 23rd 19:45	October 24th
61st air defence artillery division	Soviet Union, Carpathian Military Zone	October 23rd 19:45	October 24th
2nd mechanized division	Soviet Union, Carpathian Military Zone	October 27th	October 27th 08:00
7th paratroop guard division	Soviet Union, Baltic Military Zone	October 19th	October 30th 17:30 Tököl airport
3rd paratroop guard division	Soviet Union, Carpathian Military Zone	October 28th 10:00	October 30th Veszprém airport
1st railway guard brigade	Soviet Union, Carpathian Military Zone	October 27th	October 29th

* Times are given according to Hungarian time
** The main forces of 17th mechanized guard division, subordinate to the Special Corps, came under the 38th total services
Source: FEVKA, 32. f. 701 291. op. 15-17.d.

Table 2 Summary of Soviet

Military formation	Died				Wounded	
Rank*	officer	warrant officer	private	total	officer	warrant officer
2nd mechanized guard division	11	10	59	80	26	30
17th mechanized guard division**	5	4	19	28	5	7
33rd mechanized guard division	31	62	171	264	42	151
128th infantry guard division	6	8	26	40	10	16
177th bomber air division	3	-	-	3	-	-
195th fighter air division	-	-	-	-	-	-
Special Corps subordinates and back-up in total	56	84	275	415	83	204
31st tank division	4	13	44	61	2	9
11th mechanized guard division	3	5	10	18	1	3
32nd mechanized guard division	6	3	18	27	-	-
35th mechanized guard division	-	1	1	2	-	-
70th infantry guard division	3	3	4	10	1	3
301st artillery regiment	2	1	6	9	-	-
93rd independent signal regiment	1	-	1	2	2	-
Army political staff	1	-	-	1	-	-
8th mechanized army forces ordered to Hungary and back-up total	20	26	83	129	6	15
27th mechanized division	-	2	3	5	2	3
39th mechanized guard division	-	-	5	5	2	3
38th total services army forces ordered to Hungary and back-up**	-	2	8	10	4	6
7th paratroop guard division	4	36		40	15	131
31st paratroop guard division	5	5	35	45	6	21
1st railway guard brigade	-	-	1	1	-	-
Soviet troops total	85	555		640	114	1137/9 ***

*Ranks: officer, warrant officer, private   ** After October 28th the 17th mechanized guard division, belonging to the Special Corps, came under the 38th total services army. As the majority of its losses were suffered before October 28th it appears as part of the Special Corps on this table.
***The dead and wounded indicated in the denumerator did not result from war activities.
Source: FEVKA, f. 32. op. 701 291. d.15-16. , f. 37. op. 647 193. d.13., f. 1317. op. 732 798. d.41., 44. , f. 2252. op. 663 346. d.1.

troop losses in Hungary 1956

(Wounded)		Disappeared				Died but not in fighting				Total
private	total	officer	warrant officer	private	total	officer	warrant officer	private	total	TOTAL
1=8	194	3	5	18	26	-	-	-	-	300
2	39	-	-	-	-	-	-	-	-	67
3-5	568	2	7	19	28	-	-	-	-	860
66/2	92/2 ***	-	-	-	-	-	-	0/2 ***	0/2 ***	132/4 ***
5-1	5/1 ***	-	-	-	-	-	-	-	-	8/1 ***
	-	-	-	-	-	0/2 ***	-	-	0/2 ***	0/2 ***
6T/3	898/3 ***	5	12	37	54	0/2 ***	-	0/2 ***	0/4 ***	1367/7 ***
8	30	-	-	1	1	-	0/2 ***	0/6 ***	0/8 ***	92/8 ***
-	11	-	-	-	-	-	-	-	-	29
	8	-	-	-	-	-	-	-	-	35
	-	-	-	-	-	-	-	-	-	2
12	16	-	-	-	-	-	-	-	-	26
	-	-	-	-	-	-	-	-	-	9
	2	-	-	-	-	-	-	-	-	4
	-	-	-	-	-	-	-	-	-	1
6	67	-	-	1	1	-	0/2 ***	0/6 ***	0/8 ***	197/8 ***
3	8	-	-	-	-	-	-	-	-	13
3	13/4	-	-	-	-	-	-	0/3 ***	0/3 ***	18/7 ***
1/4	21/4 ***	-	-	-	-	-	-	0/3 ***	0/3 ***	31/7 ***
	146	-	1	11	12	-	-	-	-	198
2	119	-	-	-	-	-	-	-	-	164
C2	0/2 ***	-	-	-	-	-	-	-	-	1/2 ***
	1251/9 ***	5	13	49	67	0/2 ***	0/2 ***	0/11 ***	0/15 ***	1958/24 ***

THE SPECIAL CORPS UNDER FIRE IN BUDAPEST

MEMOIRS OF AN EYEWITNESS

Y. I. Malashenko

Lieutenant General Yevgeny Ivanovich Malashenko *was born in Ukraine in 1924. He served in the Soviet armed forces since 1941.*

During World War II he was the platoon commander of a reconnaissance company at the front, the leader of the reconnaissance services for the navy infantry brigade and the air mobile division.

After the war he graduated from the Frunze Military Academy and then the General Staff Academy.

He served as a deputy chief of staff on corps, army and district staffs.

In 1956 he led the operational section of the Special Corps Headquarters stationed in Hungary, then in 1967, after the Arab–Israeli War, he was a chief military adviser to the chiefs of staff of the Egyptian armed forces. Following this he was the chief of staff of the Carpathian Military District, the chief of deputy staff for the United Armed Forces Headquarters of the Warsaw Pact states. Later he worked as an adviser to the Operative Strategic Research Center of the Soviet Union's Armed Forces Headquarters. He is now retired.

To the Reader

The events that took place in Hungary in 1956 shocked the whole world.

This was the first time after World War II that an armed uprising broke out against the socialist system.

Hungary became the scene of tragic events. In Budapest and around the country an armed struggle was waged for three weeks. The existing social order was restored with help from the Soviet Union.

On the eve of the uprising, and during it, I was serving in Hungary, fulfilling my duties as chief of staff of the Special Corps, and as such I met political leaders, military commanders and active participants in the events.

As a witness to events in Budapest, I will try to give an account of what took place and about the Soviet troops' Hungarian operations.

I know the Special Corps' Budapest actions in detail, because the most important events took place there and the Corps' operations were of decisive import.

Today people who were not present and did not take part in the events write about Soviet operations in Hungary from hearsay. This makes an objective look at the subject difficult. On the other hand, many of those who were actually there do not know all the circumstances and factors involved.

Most memoirs were written immediately after the events on the basis of a few documents about the period in question. I will account for what I saw and what I knew at the time. I do not write about events as a historian but as a direct participant in events. This presentation of events that happened 40 years ago may be of interest to historians too, as it is not always possible to piece together the truth based on documents alone. Official sources, for various reasons, do not reveal the whole picture of what happened.

The accusation is often made that the Soviet army acted unlawfully. This is very far from the truth.

Soldiers and officers obeyed orders.

It is not the army that must be blamed. Responsibility lies with the Soviet Union's politicians, who decided to send in forces, and with those Hungarian leaders who requested their help. But we must not overlook the circumstances affecting our countries at that time.

Understandably, the opinions of those on the other side of the barricades will always remain somehow subjective, and there will be certain inadequacies.

The fact that the important orders coming from Moscow arrived by word of mouth, through the government liaison lines of communication, as was customary in our country, and given that numerous documents were destroyed, or are kept in closed archives even today, hinders a more complete, broader look at the 1956 events.

I would like to thank the publisher for undertaking to publish my memoirs and express my gratitude to military historian Jenő Györkei, without whose cooperation my memoirs would have never seen the light of day.

Moscow, June 1995

Y. I. Malashenko

Chapter I

On the Eve of the Events

In Hungary—In the Special Corps Staff

The stationing of Soviet troops in Hungary was based on an Allied Powers agreement, which was laid down in a document on the capitulation of the armed forces of fascist Germany. Later, as was laid down in the 1947 Paris Peace Treaty, the reason for the presence of Soviet troops in Hungary was to back up Soviet troops stationed in Austria.

After the peace treaty with Austria in 1955, Soviet troops did not withdraw from Hungarian territory, but remained stationed there by way of the Warsaw Pact, which was signed a day earlier.

In 1955 our troops in Austria were transported to the Soviet Union. After the abolition of the Central Austrian Army Group which had commanded them, a smaller command center had to be established for troops stationed in Hungary.

The title "Military Group and Separate Army" did not suit the leaders of the Soviet Ministry of Defense, as they thought that, while military groupings were withdrawing from Austria, they would relocate the armed formations in Hungary. In any case, they had already established a Separate Army command center in Romania.

Marshal G. K. Zhukov proposed calling the center the Special Corps, as an analogy to the Special Corps of Soviet troops in Mongolia which he himself had commanded in 1939.

In September 1955 the Special Corps center was formed.

No special duties were given to it; only its composition was unusual. Every Soviet troop who had been in Hungary previously was subordinated to it: the 2nd and 17th mechanized guard division, the 195th fighter air division, the 177th bomber air division, the 20th pontoon bridge regiment, the air defense artillery unit and various, additional units and the formations and institutions of the logistical service corps.

These units were stationed in Győr, Körmend, Szombathely, Pápa, Székesfehérvár, Kecskemét, Szolnok, Cegléd, Debrecen and other towns. We had no troops in Budapest, but our military command, the political section of the special units, and the hospital and military commercial leadership had their headquarters there.

The Special Corps were called upon to cover the Austrian border with Hungarian troops and collect information.

The Special Corps command was approximately the same size as the leadership of a field army.

But there were also units under its command, such as the air force division, the air service and other special services, logistical service units, which supplied most of the institutions and units of the Soviet troops stationed in Hungary.

The Special Corps was under the direction of the Soviet Ministry of Defense. The command of the Special Corps was to be located in Székesfehérvár.

In 1955 I served the General Staff of the Central Army Group in Baden as a section leader. At the beginning of September they appointed me head of reconnaissance, deputy to the chief of staff of the Special Corps. I was given the duty of locating the Special Corps staff to Székesfehérvár, as the leader of a group of officers. There were no available apartments for the Special Corps officers and their families.

To relocate the corps' command we took over a few buildings and military objectives of one of the regiments of the 2nd mechanized division.

The Special Corps Command was filled with officers and servicemen who had belonged to the Central Army Group and the group's air force troops in Austria.

Lieutenant General Piotr Nikolayevich Lashchenko was appointed the head of the corps. During the war he had led an infantry division and had been decorated with the "Hero of the Soviet Union" merit order. He came to us from the Baltics, where he had served as command officer of an infantry division. When he arrived he took control of all troops under him and organized the complicated work of the Special Corps with great precision, as well as the battle training of units and staff.

General Lashchenko took the combat readiness of troops, military training, and the development of instructional material very seriously.

The chief of staff was Brigadier General G. A. Shchelbanyin.

As the corps did not have a deputy chief of staff commander of independent status, and given Shchelbanyin's advanced age, I had to deal with the various operative and organizational problems.

I was completely taken up with supplying the headquarters, becoming acquainted with the troops' positions and their preparedness, directing military training for the motorcyclists' reconnaissance battalions and companies, taking part in command meetings, drafting and supervising combat plans and studying and receiving situation reports.

In the summer of 1956, due to Shchelbanyin's holiday and then illness, the duties of chief of staff fell temporarily on me. This was the first time I had to act as chief of staff when, during a military exercise, the 2nd mechanized division forced a crossing of the Danube.

General Lashchenko had taught the troops what was necessary in times of war. During all exercises he demanded that things be done as if a real battle was going on. When preparing for an attack we had to organize the destruction of the enemy "defense." If we were ordered to defend, we had to dig trenches and build dug-outs and barricades; all the artillery systems had to form and organize the cooperation of the units and sub-units. This was all completely unexpected and strange for the commanders of heavy artillery.

The difficult part of the division's military exercise was the forced crossing of the Danube. During the exercise, after capturing the bridgehead, we put two ferries on the water, and the main forces of the division crossed the Danube in eight hours, which required a high degree of preparation from the division's engineering forces and the 20th pontoon bridge regiment. The exercise went off without any undue disturbance.

For leading the exercises I was awarded a gold watch, which is a prized family possession to this day.

As commanders of the Special Corps we all tried to prepare the fighters for what was necessary in military operations. This included one winter military exercise held for some of the reconnaissance forces, when tanks could hardly cross the river as they couldn't get a grip on the layers of ice that covered the banks. I persisted to the end of the action, even when one of the tanks was caught in the current and was not able to make it to dry ground for a long time. Obviously there were some unpleasant moments, but in the end everything worked out well. I also learned that we must select better reconnaissance officers and train them more thoroughly so that they would be capable of fulfilling any duty that might arise in a war.

In the summer of 1956, our units and higher units took part in military and political training night and day. They trained hard; took part in numerous military exercises, including shooting practice; received artillery, tank, armored and motor vehicle driving training; and carried out exercises.

We concentrated on high-standard summer training for the air forces staff, on preparing experts for the services, and on supervising weapons and military techniques. Our troops started preparing for the autumn exercises review.

In the same year our soldiers helped the Hungarian population during the great flood along the middle section of the Danube. They saved people, livestock, and state and private property. The Hungarian government decorated several soldiers for their efforts.

During their years in Hungary, our military formations forged relations with the factory and cooperative collectives and with formations from the Hungarian People's Army. We organized meetings between our personnel and the Hungarian population and Hungarian army soldiers, and our amateur artist groups held performance evenings for each other.

Our officers and soldiers helped Hungarian officers in their military technique studies and in equipping exercise sites. We passed on our experience in the training of soldiers, and we asked Hungarian commanders to our meetings, military exercises and drills. We often held joint sports competitions and other events.

The Soviet soldiers and civilians living in Hungary respected the Hungarian population; they did not provoke conflicts. They worked hard to avoid any damage to agriculture, roads, bridges or woods during their exercises, and if damage occured, they compensated for it.

All in all it seemed as if relations were not so bad between the Hungarian population and our military formations and soldiers.

Yet our officers, soldiers and their families in Hungary, as elsewhere abroad, lived somewhat isolated lives.

Our relations were exclusively with the leaders of the local party and state organizations and with the commanders of the Hungarian formations and units. We were regularly invited to official occasions, such as on April 4 to Budapest, on September 29 to Árpád Hill, near Lake Velence, for People's Army Day.

With my family I tried to visit as many museums and theaters as possible in Budapest and Székesfehérvár. On such occasions we traveled to the capital, to the Embassy, and lunched in the Embassy restaurant. We took the children to the zoo, went walking on Margit Island and traveled to Lake Balaton.

Sometimes we went to the Népstadion (People's Stadium). At that time the famed Puskás, Kovács, Czibor, Hidegkuti, Farkas and others played for the Honvéd team.

Our officers living in private apartments forged good relations with their landlords.

Even so all our meetings were somewhat limited; we did not know the lives and feelings of the Hungarian citizens from all perspectives. The absence of a common language prevented relations from deepening—we did not speak Hungarian, and the Hungarians did not speak Russian.

Right up until the summer of 1956 we had good relations with the Hungarian population. The complicated internal political situation, caused by propaganda circulating among the Hungarian population and army, only began to be felt later. But there were seemingly insignificant signs: previously not everybody had managed to get into our concerts, as we always enjoyed a full house, but now we hardly saw anyone. There had been full houses too at joint football matches, even in Budapest. Now the bleachers were half-empty, and those who came to cheer behaved towards us in a way that they never had before.

Among the population anti-Soviet remarks became common and false stories were spread. Colonel M. Y. Kuziminov, the Budapest city commander, reported displays of hostility.

We collected data and received information about the Hungarian situation, and we knew that the political atmosphere in the country was becoming increasingly acrimonious.

Mistakes and Consequences

The Rákosi–Gerő leadership did not take Hungarian circumstances into account when they determined the duties and methods for building socialism. Thus there was serious dissatisfaction among workers. The leaders copied and introduced to Hungary the Soviet Union's slogans for rapid industrialization. They utilized a great deal of material wealth to establish great factories in order to create all branches of industry, including those that had no source of raw materials. They did not bother much with agricultural development or raising the living standards of the workers.

The violations of the law committed during the Rajk trial and other similar trials caused many innocent party and state officials to suffer.

Furthermore, some decisions permitted by the leadership offended the national feelings of the Hungarian people. Many streets in Budapest had their names changed to the names of Russian and Soviet writers, Soviet-style military uniforms were introduced, and the school system was based on the Soviet model.

The serious mistakes made by the Hungarian Workers Party caused enormous dissatisfaction among the masses.

During the HWP's July plenum Rákosi was relieved of his duties as first secretary, and new party political principles were adopted in order to correct the mistakes. However, it soon became clear that this line was mistaken. The opposition profited from the fact that the Rákosi–Gerő leadership's mistakes could not be rectified and the increasing dissatisfaction of the masses could not be redressed. They condemned the mistakes ever more loudly, and anti-party, -government and -regime propaganda became increasingly shrill. Alongside the legitimate complaints, nationalist motives became increasingly apparent.

The weakness of the party and people's power and the increasing number of those dissatisfied with the regime created favorable conditions for the uprising. During this time HWP membership accounted for 900,000 people, which was 10% of the total population. But many of its members did not sympathize with party policy; indeed, there were many careerists who influenced the various ideological currents and feelings.

The opposition led by Imre Nagy and Géza Losonczy played a big part in the leadup to the October events, as they determined the tasks and means of action to be taken. Géza Losonczy, writing in *Művelt Nép* (Cultured People), said Hungary's further development depended on a review of the entire policy of the HWP.

The center of dissatisfaction was the Hungarian Writers Alliance.

Within the Petőfi Circle they drafted a 16-point statement[1] of their demands to the party and government.

Certain circles in the West also aided the preparations for an antigovernment stand. Emigré centers and leaders in numerous countries renewed their activities. Western radio stations–the Voice of America and Radio Free Europe–spurred on the overthrow of the existing order. Radio Free Europe contributed to the increasing dissatisfaction both with its programs and by sending out balloons filled with leaflets.

The Soviet ambassador, Yuri Vladimirovich Andropov, informed us of the domestic situation in Hungary. In a speech to the commanders of the Special Corps in Székesfehérvár, on the eve of the HWP July plenum, he told us how complicated the situation was in the party and in the country. He spoke of the presence of the opposition and the hostile atmosphere. He prepared us for the possible turn events might take and said that the Hungarian government might turn to us for help. Looking back now, after so many years, I do not think it impossible that Andropov initiated certain steps to aid the Hungarian government and to prevent Hungary from breaking away from the socialist camp. It is also possible that Andropov, knowing the opinion of the higher party leadership, made proposals accordingly, which Moscow then supported. On two occasions, in July and October, his announcements followed orders from Moscow.

The Drafting of the Plan for Restoring Social Order

In July we received the order from Moscow to work out the Special Corps plan for maintaining and restoring order in Budapest and on Hungarian territory. At the same time we were given the duty of gathering intelligence about the most important state and military leadership's objectives. The agreement with Hungarian troops on the possible military operations was entrusted to Lieutenant General M. F. Tikhonov, the chief adviser to the Hungarian Ministry of Defense.

I was asked to work out the plan, and when I sought out Tikhonov to clear up a series of questions, he did not receive me with much pleasure. He was not prepared for my questions, could not answer one of them and asked me to come back in a few days. I used this time to become acquainted with the town, with the location of the most important objectives and possible approaches to them. When I again went to see Tikhonov two days later, he took three thick bundles of paper out of his safe and told me to look at what I was interested in.

These were the plans for restoring social order worked out by the Hungarian People's Army Headquarters, state security services and the police.

The documents proffered information on the main objectives and their defense on the occasion of marches and big protests. They also listed all the Hungarian military and police forces and means to be used against armed groups in the event of an anti-government action.

After I had studied the documents and taken notes from them, I told General Tikhonov that due to lack of troops, our men could only assume the defense of main targets and could not take part in maintaining order if there were protests or gatherings.

Tikhonov replied that the Hungarians had a strong state security service and army at their disposal, so that they could maintain order themselves quite easily. Our help would not be necessary. But I maintained that it would be good if everything would go off smoothly, and then there would be no need for us to intervene at all, and the plan would remain a plan on paper only.

With this we parted.

The Hungarian army therefore already had a complete plan for restoring order by July. I saw this plan myself in Russian translation; I worked with it and took the necessary notes from it.

As became clear later, neither Hungarian Minister of Defense István Bata nor Chief-of-Staff Lieutenant General Lajos Tóth knew what the plan contained. Most likely, they signed it without reading it, and only the commander of the operational leadership, Brigadier General István Kovács, knew what military operations it contained.

After I had studied the objectives once more and the notes I had made from the Hungarian plan, I finished the draft for the plan for the "operations to be carried out by the Special Corps to maintain order on Hungarian territory" a few days later.

I worked it out on a Budapest map, with a list of the capital's main objectives, the defense of which was officially entrusted to our units and higher units, and added a separate order.

On the map the routes and departure points of our units' march into Budapest were marked, as were the pace of the march and the time of arrival in the capital.

I had marked the objectives to be defended by our troops on the plan. There were about 40 of them, including the HWP Central Committee building, Parliament, the Foreign Ministry, the Radio, the central telephone exchange, the National Bank, the railway stations, the Danube bridges, the munitions factory, large warehouses, defense enterprises, the Soviet Embassy, our city command and other public buildings. All the objectives were marked out in red on the sketch.

Formations of platoon and company size were ordered to defend every single objective. Apart from these there were about 30 other items, patrol routes, reserve staff and bases, and the control bases of the units marked on the plan. We aimed to place the control bases close to the objectives in order to maintain contact with the units, and in every objective we would place a liaison officer.

We gave special attention to the restoration of order in Budapest. We divided the capital into three sectors—central, northern and southern—which were more or less the same size. Each sector contained about the same number of important establishments.

The task of restoring order in Budapest fell to Brigadier General S. V. Lebedev's 2nd mechanized guard division. According to the plan the division would set off from the Kecskemét zone to Budapest and defend the capital's main objectives. It had already been determined which of the capital's buildings had to be defended primarily by the above division's units and what forces and means could be used to do so.

Brigadier General A. V. Krivosheyev's 17th mechanized guard division had to cover the Austrian border and secure order in western Hungary, particularly Győr, Szombathely, Kőszeg, Körmend and Nagykanizsa.

The units stationed at Hajmáskér were to make up the reserves; we intended them primarily for Budapest.

The air force formations, air defense and other special units had to secure order in their areas and garrisons, to defend their objectives, airports, warehouses and other establishments.

If military operations were set in action to maintain and restore order in Hungary, then we had a special command at our disposal. This determined the order of combat activities of the units and sub-units within the town, the method of defending and guarding objectives, when weapons could be used, how to cooperate with Hungarian formations, how to maintain contact with the Hungarian military units' and sub-units' commanders and with government organs locally, etc.

The plan was approved by Lieutenant General Lashchenko, commander of the Special Corps, on July 20. The plan was given the code name "Volna" ("Wave") and was initiated with the code word "Compass."

After the plan was drafted, the division commanders decided what tasks and orders had to be given in order to introduce units to restore and maintain order in Budapest and other towns. There were also a series of measures to be taken connected with carrying out the plan. We told the commanders that they must study the objectives and the possible approaches to them very thoroughly and must keep in contact with the Hungarian party and state local services, and with the Hungarian commanders of the garrisons.

I must note that we counted on cooperating with the Hungarian formations, state security forces and the police when the plan was drafted. But one version of the plan also made provisions for the eventuality of our troops having to work alone. As events show, it was a good thing we did.

Although a plan was drafted and resulting measures taken, many Hungarian leaders, and Hungarian and Soviet generals, did not believe that an armed uprising could take place in Hungary.

The Soviet ambassador, the Budapest city commander, leaders of the Hungarian People's Army formations and units and others informed us of events outside the party, in the country and in the People's Army and of the atmosphere among intellectuals and students.

We essentially understood the situation in the country, the atmosphere among the population, but particularly among intellectuals; we knew about the student actions and the preparations for protest. Captain V. I. Fomin, the instructor who dealt with special propaganda in the corps' political section, and the corps staff's interpreter V. Y. Sokolov, monitored the press and radio and played an important role in relaying information.

A few days before the events began, we sent a report to Moscow headquarters in which we included several previously mentioned facts and several pieces of data at our disposal and pointed out the possibility of an "isolated" armed action in the near future. It was then that Lashchenko crossed out the word "isolated," making our report an objective mirror of subsequent events.

Meanwhile events in the country accelerated. László Rajk's burial on October 6, 1956, had led to a whipping up of passions, the deepening of the party's ideological crisis, and an increase in the uncertainty of the masses.

The party leadership and the Hungarian government did not take the necessary measures in this situation. Indeed, they were incapable of realistically evaluating the situation. One of the party leadership's representatives announced at a meeting of party activists at the Csepel Works on October 22 that they could suppress any kind of action in 30 minutes.

The party leadership's confidence also meant that, although the Hungarian People's Army and other armed bodies were put on alert on October 20, this order was rescinded the next evening. The incompetence of the party and state leadership became completely obvious to the opposition and the people.

On October 22 General Lashchenko, appraising the Hungarian situation, closed his command briefing by saying that everybody must be at their post in order to carry out the necessary measures as urgently as possible.

On the evening of October 22, I traveled to Budapest to clarify the situation. I went to the Embassy and to the Soviet City Command, and I found out that a protest was planned for the next day, October 23. On October 22 large meetings had been held in several colleges and universities, in which, apart from the protest, they had also taken a stand. Representatives of the colleges and universities were also present during the meeting of the Petőfi Circle's leadership, and they decided to protest.

Over those days we had a good idea of the events taking shape. But what actually took place went far beyond our imaginings and expectations.

The Protests and the Armed Uprising in Budapest

On the morning of October 23, it was announced that the government of the Hungarian People's Republic forbade the protest in Budapest. Despite this numerous students from the colleges and universities persistently demanded permission and urged a protest against the ban. At noon it was announced that the government had allowed the demonstration to go ahead anyway and that the Hungarian Workers Party had ordered its members to take part in it.

On October 23, 1956, at 1 o'clock, the protest began in Budapest. More than 10,000 people took part in the march. The majority of the protesters were students and intellectuals, but workers, clerks, soldiers and some party members also took part.

The protesters marched to the Bem and Petőfi statues. Several columns marched with red flags and with placards expressing Soviet–Hungarian friendship, demanding the appointment of Imre Nagy to the government, etc. But the protest slowly took an anti-government tone. The marchers shouted out slogans in the spirit of the 16 Points drawn up by the Petőfi Circle. They demanded the return of the national coat of arms, the end of Russian language teaching, and the return of old national holidays in place of the April holiday [marking the Soviet liberation of Hungary in 1945].

Apart from this they demanded free elections, the formation of a new government headed by Imre Nagy and the withdrawal of Soviet troops from Hungary.

From time to time whistles and shouts came from their ranks: "We don't need the Soviet school system!" "Down with the red star!" "Down with communists!" The marchers tore the coat of arms of the Hungarian People's Republic out of the national flag, and they started to burn red flags and similar items.

On October 23, at around 17 hours, the Soviet ambassador, Andropov, called Lieutenant General Lashchenko on the military telephone and informed him of the situation in Budapest. He asked him if he could send his troops to help liquidate the disorder in the capital. I myself heard Lashchenko reply that that was a task for the Hungarian police, state security services and Hungarian soldiery, because, for one thing, intervention went beyond his authority, and for another it was not desirable to bring Soviet troops into something like this. He told the ambassador that our troops could only be ordered into action by the Soviet minister of defense and the chief of staff, by a decree of the Soviet government. General Lashchenko had said something similar to the ambassador just before the HWP Central Leadership's July plenum.

Within one hour an order arrived from the Soviet Armed Forces Headquarters for the units and higher units of the Special Corps to be ready for combat.

Meanwhile armed groups had started to attack the Hungarian Defense Alliance's district headquarters in Budapest, the district police stations, the barracks, military depots and munitions depots to get hold of weapons and ammunition. They also took ammunition and weapons from Hungarian soldiers.

Budapest's city commander, Colonel Kuzminov, announced that the armed groups had seized important objectives. Weapons and ammunition were being handed out from trucks on the streets and squares. The motor vehicles carrying Hungarian soldiers could not break through the lines of protesters to get to their posts. In many places they had been disarmed or had themselves joined the rebels. At 8 p.m. Ernő Gerő, the HWP Central Leadership's first secretary, gave a speech on the radio. Gerő pointed out the counter-revolutionary nature of the Budapest uprising, although he lumped all resistance elements together, including those who were merely dissatisfied and demanded the righting of wrongs.

He did not indicate any way out of this situation and did not make an appeal to the workers or the communists either. Gerő's radio speech had a negative effect on the further development of events.

News spread through the city in the evening that the state security organs were shooting protesters by the Radio building. Not long afterwards the attackers seized all the Radio buildings.

When news started to come to the main police station that protesters had appeared at the district police stations and demanded weapons, the police chief, Sándor Kopácsi, ordered them not to shoot at rebels or to get mixed up in events.

The crowd also appeared outside the main police station. They demanded that prisoners be released and that the red star be taken down from the building's facade. Their demands were fulfilled. Police Chief Kopácsi's actions were greeted by the crowd with joy.

The armed uprising in Budapest had begun.

Chapter II

Soviet Troops in Budapest

The Hungarian Government Requests Help

On the night of October 24, Imre Nagy became head of the government and became a coopted member of the HWP Central Committee's Politburo. His followers took up important positions in the state and party apparatus.

On the same night, at the HWP Central Leadership's extraordinary session, a proposal was drafted for the government on the necessary and decisive measures to restore order and defend the People's Republic. The government was advised to arm the workers immediately and to act against the counter-revolution, suppress the uprising with the help of Soviet troops stationed in Hungary, and introduce a state of emergency.

In accordance with these decisions, the Hungarian government, with Imre Nagy's agreement, asked the Soviet government to allow Soviet troops to help restore order in Budapest.

Sometime later, Soviet ambassador Andropov announced that the Hungarian Council of Ministers had sent the following telegram to the Soviet government: "The Hungarian People's Republic Council of Ministers requests the government of the Soviet Union to kindly send Soviet troops to Budapest in order that they might help liquidate the disturbances there, restore order quickly and create conditions for peaceful work."[2]

On October 23 at 21 hours the chief of staff of the Soviet Armed Forces Headquarters, Marshal Sokolovsky, gave a direct order to the commander of the Special Corps over a military telephone for Soviet troops to march into Budapest and help Hungarian troops restore order.

In accordance with the order, at between 22:30 and 23:00 Budapest time, our formations, units and higher units immediately started for Budapest from Kecskemét, Cegléd, Szolnok, Székesfehérvár, Sárbogárd and other towns. A 75–120-kilometer march lay ahead of them.

The commander of the Special Corps, General Lashchenko, traveled with his staff operational group from Székesfehérvár to Budapest. Our military column consisted of a few cars, a radio transmitter, an armored transport vehicle and two tanks. When we arrived in Budapest we saw considerable movement in the town despite the late hour. Vans transported armed civilians from one street to another. Gatherings were still going on near the center of the city, in which many people took part with torches, flags and placards. From every direction the sharp whistle of shots and sub-machine-gun fire could be heard.

We could not approach the Ministry of Defense building through the streets of the inner city. Great crowds had gathered at Parliament, the City Park, the National Museum and in other places. Proceeding down the narrow streets and alleys, violating the traffic laws, we reached the Ministry of Defense only with great difficulty.

As there were many Soviet-made cars in the town, our cars traveled virtually unnoticed. But one of our radio transmitters was separated from the convoy in Buda, as it was attacked straight away. The transmitter commander suffered a head wound, one of the radio operators was killed and the station itself was turned over and set on fire. The two tanks and our armored vehicle rescued the remaining men.

At midnight on October 24, when we arrived at the Ministry of Defense, we were told that the Radio building, the telephone exchange, the editorial offices of the *Szabad Nép* newspaper, munitions depots and munitions factories, railway stations, police stations, several army barracks, and the air defense cannons in Buda had been attacked on the evening of the 23rd. Protests continued in the center of town, while the western part of the city, Buda, remained relatively calm. The rebels' main forces were in the center, in Districts VIII and IX.

The Special Corps headquarters organized its military operations center in the Ministry of Defense, since a military cable there connected us with Moscow, and we could more easily organize cooperation with the Hungarian command from there.

General Lashchenko entrusted me with the leadership of the military operations group and the duties of the corps staff chief.

There was great tension and confusion within the Ministry of Defense. Conflicting data was coming in about the events and the activities of the rebels, the Hungarian formations and the police.

Minister of Defense István Bata, and especially Lieutenant General Lajos Tóth, panicked and issued orders completely contradicting each other. So for example, when the munitions depots were attacked, headquarters gave the order not to shoot. After the attackers had already opened fire, there were still Hungarian military formations who had been sent to defend their objectives without ammunition and whose weapons were taken away by the rebels.

We received news that they were holding out at the Radio building. To strengthen their defense they sent tanks and a battalion of infantry. As became clear later, a small group of state security forces and soldiers were inside, and the buildings had all been seized. Nobody knew why the police and the Hungarian army did not act to restore order.

As we arrived at the Ministry, a mass of requests were fired at us from the Central Committee, the Hungarian government and from our own military adviser, Lieutenant General Tikhonov. They demanded that we reinforce the defense of the main objectives, and they asked us to defend the district party committee buildings, the police stations, the barracks and various warehouses and even asked us to defend certain peoples' private apartments. Naturally, all this would have required a greater military force than we actually had. More importantly, it would not have solved the basic question–the crushing of armed groups and the restoration of order.

They could not answer us as to why the police and army could not defend their own buildings and barracks.

The Ministry of Defense did not know the circumstances well enough. In Budapest there were about 700 soldiers and 50 tanks which were divided between 40 to 50 objectives, and in the Hungarian headquarters nobody knew where, or how big, the forces were that they had at their disposal. Thus they did not put them into active combat against the armed groups. The main reason for this inactivity was that no decisive orders were issued by the leadership, so they did not know what to do or how.

The situation reports we received from the Hungarian comrades continued to be contradictory.

The situation in Budapest meant that an operational plan had to be defined earlier than originally thought, as we could not rely on the cooperation of the Hungarian police and soldiery. First of all we had to get the armed groups out of the captured objectives, we had to defend all the important institutions in the town and liquidate the armed groups in the town center and Districts VIII and IX.

In regard to the situation in the city center, where protests were going on and where the main rebel forces had gathered, and, at the request of the formations from Cegléd and Szolnok who, according to the plan, should have defended the institutions of the inner city, the duties of General Lebedev's division's units were to be defined more exactly.

We redirected an armored and a mechanized regiment, which should have been occupying the districts of Buda, to combat in the city center.

We sent Colonel S. Y. Kuzmin, the corps artillery commander, and Colonel A. A. Fukavcev, the operations section's deputy, to receive the approaching formations in order to define their duties and so speed up their arrival.

(The route of the units into Budapest can be seen in Map 1.)

The Beginning of Combat Operations

Formations arriving in the city were greeted with a hail of bullets and stones. There was a great crowd on the streets, and barricades had gone up in several places in the suburbs.

Despite these attacks on us, our troops did not open fire. Captain Petrochenko, commander of the motorcyclist battalion, on seeing the barricades, sent a man with a message to kindly let them pass. This soldier was shot by rebels. Heavy fire greeted the approaching units on Üllői and Markusovszky Roads, on Hungaria Boulevard and near several objectives.

On October 24 at 4 o'clock in the morning Colonel Bichan, the deputy commander of the 2nd mechanized guard division, arrived in Budapest at the head of a tank regiment, and Lieutenant Colonel G. T. Dobrunov arrived leading an independent reconnaissance battalion.

Dobrunov received the order to do reconnaissance work around the main roads in the town center, to determine the active centers of the armed groups and what forces they had at their disposal, and what the population, the police and the Hungarian army were doing. The order decreed that they should fire only if attacked.

The 37th tank regiment was entrusted with defending the HWP Central Leadership building, Parliament, the Soviet Embassy and the Danube bridges, and they were ordered to liberate the Radio building.

Hungarian officers were designated to lead our sub-units to the objectives. One of them, who was to have led our soldiers to the Radio building, disappeared en route.

At 4 o'clock the 2nd mechanized division's main forces approached Budapest. They were slightly held up by dense fog and the uncertainty of the division's leadership. The division's command and staff arrived in the city very late, as during a short rest everybody in the command car had fallen asleep and the staff chief had not been vigilant enough. Therefore arriving formations received their orders directly from the commanders of the units and sub-units.

The 7th mechanized regiment had come in from Szolnok, followed by a heavy-tank–self-propelling assault gun regiment from Cegléd.

The division's units were ordered to reinforce the defense of the Central Leadership, the Parliament building and the Foreign Ministry; to guard the National Bank, the airport, the munitions depots; to win back the telephone exchange and the *Szabad Nép* newspaper editorial offices; to disarm armed groups; and to hand captured rebels over to the police.

The arriving formations clashed with rebels while still marching. They cleared many institutions of armed groups, and they seized the railway stations, and the bridges and a few warehouses. During the day they managed to defend several important government establishments: The Hungarian Workers Party Central Leadership building, Parliament, the City Council and the City Party Committee, the National Bank, the State Post Office, the stations and the Danube bridges as well as the Soviet Embassy and the City Command.

The tank regiment sub-units managed to clear one of the Radio buildings of rebels. But there was not enough infantry to recapture all the radio buildings. During this conflict the regiment had four tanks shot down. It continued to fight in the town center and in the southeastern parts, by the Radio, around the Corvin Cinema and on Üllői Road.

On October 24, at around noon, the following picture had formed of the situation in the city:

A series of objectives were in the hands of the armed groups. The police did not do anything anywhere; Hungarian military formations had not received orders for active operations. A few sub-units and many privates had gone across to the rebels, but the rest continued to fight fiercely. Armed groups were active in Óbuda, on Széna Square, in Maros Street, in the inner city, in Petőfi Sándor Street, in Districts VIII and IX, in Práter Street, in Corvin Alley, in the Kilián Barracks, on Rákóczi Road, on Museum Boulevard, on Köztársaság Square and in other districts.

Active combat was being waged by armed groups in Districts II, VIII and IX. Later events showed that reconnaissance work had already discovered the main armed groups' centers and determined their areas of operation on the very first day. The total number of these identified groups approached 2000 people.

It must be admitted that there were certain difficulties in collecting information. We did not have enough reconnaissance sub-units at our disposal. The city command did not understand its new duties and did not deal with information-gathering. Not one of the Hungarian officers was willing, and they did not give us accurate information about the situation.

I had to put all my efforts and persistence into gathering the necessary information, analyzing it and summarizing it, and activating the activities of the reconnaissance sub-units who were gathering intelligence. Despite the complicated situation in the city, in the absence of the usual front line, and given the time limitations, the reconnaissance battalion under Lieutenant Colonel Dobrunov's command worked well. He sent out tanks, armored transport vehicles and motorcyclists on reconnaissance patrols, while he himself headed the reconnaissance group working in the city center.

In order to observe the traffic crossing the Danube bridges, he posted a reconnaissance group equipped with a radio transmitter.

In order to find out where the armed rebels were operating, the reconnaissance battalion often used the "cavalry method": the enemy opened fire on a rapidly moving patrol, and then the command was able to observe where the rebel strongholds and hiding places were.

Interrogations of captured rebels allowed us to determine the armed groups' situation and the size of forces.

Until the afternoon Dobrunov essentially fulfilled his duty, which contributed greatly to clarifying the situation in the city.

On the first day in Budapest, our troops suffered 20 dead and 40 wounded; four tanks and four armored transports were shot to pieces, and a few of our motor vehicles were set alight.

On October 24 we captured about 300 armed rebels, disarmed them and handed them over to the Hungarian police services. But numerous armed groups–a total of more than 3000 people–continued fighting in the city. There was no way of crushing them without the Hungarian police and military formations.

On October 24 the total number of Soviet armed forces arriving in Budapest was not more than a division, which meant about 6000 men.

In a big city with more than one million inhabitants, this military force was not even enough to maintain order.

Panic and confusion continued to overwhelm the Hungarian Ministry of Defense. When the Hungarian government accepted a decree to arm the factory workers, the Ministry's leadership announced that there was no way of arming workers, that this could only happen later, once they were able to locate weapons. They were incapable of getting weapons to their destination, and so many weapons fell into rebel hands.

The Hungarian military formations were given no duties in the suburbs; they were not even ordered to defend the main targets.

Later in the day, the 17th mechanized division's tank and mechanized regiments were ordered to maintain order in Buda and to defend the Danube bridges.

At noon Hungarian Radio announced that the government had declared a state of emergency in Budapest. A curfew was introduced, the city inhabitants were forbidden to be on the streets before 7 o'clock in the morning, meetings and gatherings were forbidden and summary military courts were set up. On October 24 appeals were made for an end to the fighting and for a laying down of arms.

We hoped that these measures would facilitate the liquidation of the armed groups and a rapid return to order.

Our units and sub-units defended the most important social institutions and objectives and patrolled the city streets, where they were often attacked and came under unexpected fire.

Towards the end of the day, the situation was such that the press in several countries reported that the uprising in Budapest had suffered a defeat. We thought that the emergency measures and the aid of our troops would prevent the armed groups from increasing their operations.

But on the night of October 25, more disturbing news came in: Prisoners had been released from several prisons, and émigrés and armed groups were flooding across the border from Austria without coming into conflict with border guards.[3]

Imre Nagy, without the knowledge of the party leadership and without permission from the Soviet command, rescinded the curfew. This set back the liquidation of the armed strongholds and allowed once more for the organization of marches.

Within a short time several groups of protesters marched out of the side streets onto the main roads. The several-thousand-strong crowd set off for Parliament with the national colors.

The Hungarian officers guarding Parliament appealed to the crowd to disperse, but to no avail. The lively flood of people surged forward like an avalanche and mixed in with our officers and sentries. Many went over to the tanks, climbed up on them and stuck flags in their gun barrels. Then fire was opened from the rooftops of the buildings opposite Parliament onto the crowd and Soviet soldiers. The two Hungarian tanks accompanying the crowd fired a few shots and then disappeared. They shot one of the commanders of our sub-units. Soviet soldiers and the state security forces guarding Parliament fired back at the rooftops. Indescribable panic broke out on Kossuth Square. The crowd, hearing the first shots, started to flee; seeking cover, many of them flattened themselves against the Parliament walls. Ten to twelve minutes later, the shooting stopped. Seizing this opportunity, many of the marchers ran from the square. Twenty-two protesters were shot, many were wounded, and we also lost a few soldiers and several Hungarian police.

The news went round the town that ÁVH men and Soviets had fired on the unarmed crowd in front of Parliament!

During this period we were informed that there were disturbances outside of Budapest as well. To maintain order we were forced to leave artillery and air defense sub-units in Székesfehérvár, Kecskemét and Szekszárd and in other towns too.

The Arrival of Soviet Political and Military Leaders in Budapest

The president of the KGB, I. A. Serov, and the first deputy to the Armed Forces chief of General Staff, General of the Army, M. S. Malinyin, unexpectedly arrived in the company of Soviet generals and officers at our staff headquarters in the Ministry of Defense. Without waiting to hear our reports, they expressed their dissatisfaction with the indecisiveness of the Soviet operations, as they had proved incapable of dealing with armed student groups. Serov reported all this to the highest political and military leaders over a direct military phone. It came as a surprise that he used the familiar form of address with them and that he made his report without knowing any of the real facts.

When he had finished his call, without taking into account the consequences, I plunged in like a young hothead:

"Ivan Alexandrovich, you are not familiar with the situation. There is fighting going on all over town; we need more forces to take decisive steps. We have essentially only one division. Let us go now and circle the city in tanks and armored transports."

Serov agreed. I also took Brigadier General Pavoli, who had arrived not long before. We were twice fired on with machine guns, and several times our paths were blocked; then we returned to the Ministry of Defense. After this they understood what was really going on.

Lashchenko was pleased that I was not afraid of Serov and told me not to be afraid a second time either: he would defend me although he had nobody to defend him.

After this they made a much more objective report to A. A. Mikoyan and M. S. Suslov. Our reports concerned the military operations in Budapest; at the same time we noted that the inactivity of the police and the Hungarian soldiery allowed for the increased activity of the armed rebel groups.

After we had returned to the Ministry, Generals Malinyin and Lashchenko went to Parliament to introduce themselves to the Hungarian head of government, Imre Nagy, and to inform him of our division's arrival in Budapest and to speak about the cancellation of the curfew.

In the meantime a phone call from the Embassy told us that Andropov had set off to meet Mikoyan and Suslov, but that fire had been opened on his car near one of the Danube bridges. He requested an armored car so that he could go to the airport. On the same day Mikoyan and Suslov arrived in Budapest. Following their meeting with Imre Nagy and János Kádár en route to us, they stopped in front of the Ministry building and spoke to our officers and soldiers. General Lashchenko and I received them, so we were eyewitnesses to the exchange.

Mikoyan behaved simply and directly. He asked about the difficulties of military service, what provisions were like, and where the soldiers slept. They told him that they slept either in the vehicles or under them. They were forbidden to enter the houses, which was not a problem in itself—it was just that they never got enough sleep.

Suslov's conversation with the staff reminded me of a sermon. He spoke of our duties, of the Soviet Union's internationalist aid to the Hungarian people. One of the officers asked why they were shooting at us if they had asked for our help. Later the staff of the Special Section sought this same officer out, whether as preventative action or on the command of a higher authority, I don't know.

During his talks with soldiers, Suslov also said that we could not abandon Hungary; otherwise the Americans and NATO allies would enter immediately.

During talks with us they asked about the Soviet and Hungarian troops' Budapest operations.

The next day Imre Nagy asked Lashchenko to Parliament. Lashchenko telephoned from the Embassy where he was meeting Mikoyan and Suslov. He asked me to urgently deliver a series of documents to him in Parliament, including the map of the Budapest conflicts, information on our troops, a description of the bloody events on Kossuth Square and other things.

Inside the Parliament building a working meeting led by Imre Nagy was underway. Antal Apró, István Kovács (HWP), Károly Janza and others were present. After Interior Minister László Piros's address the following question was put to Lashchenko:

"Have Soviet tanks fired on protesters?"

"Those who maintain that they have not fired are correct," replied Lashchenko, commander of the Special Corps.

After this Imre Nagy requested that Soviet troops not open fire in the city. Lashchenko replied that this request would make his task more difficult.

We were given permission only to return fire.

I still remember Nagy's imposing figure today; he gave the impression of being a clever, crafty Hungarian.

The Hungarian government later gave us many contradictory requests, essentially asking that our troops not shoot, not pursue active operations, yet carry out the task at hand.

As our orders were originally issued because the Hungarian government had called us in to help, we fulfilled our duties in accordance with their wishes. This, of course, did not make our task easier, and it contributed to the increase in rebel forces.

In the initial days it was difficult to properly evaluate events. The workers' legitimate protest against the mistakes committed by the Rákosi–Gerő leadership and the Nagy government's ambition to right these wrongs were both factors. But later open experiments were made to change the existing order, or, even more, to restore the previous order.

The military committee, headed by Antal Apró, did not fulfill its duties and could not influence the shaping of power relations. It urged the Hungarian People's Army to exercise caution and the police to remain passive.

The Arrival of New Formations and the Soviet Troop Operations in Budapest

On the morning of October 25, the 33rd mechanized guard division arrived in Budapest from Romania under the command of Brigadier General G. I. Obaturov. By that night the 128th infantry guard division arrived under Colonel N. A. Gorbunov. They had come from the Carpathians.

At that time the rebels in the city center were putting up even stronger resistance. That is why the 33rd mechanized guard division was given the task of clearing rebels out from the central part of the city, from the areas of Üllői Road, Kőbánya and the roads leading to the Danube, the Radio buildings, the Kilián Barracks and the Corvin Cinema. The division's advance detail, consisting of the 104th mechanized regiment, reached Parliament first by fighting its way down the embankment.

At sunset on October 25, the 315th infantry regiment of the 128th infantry guard division arrived in Budapest under Lieutenant Colonel

N. S. Nikiforov and received the order to destroy the armed groups in Buda and restore order there.

The armed groups had built up a resistance center in the inner city and fought fiercely. They used armor-piercing and air defense weapons, armor-piercing shells and bottles filled with flammable liquid, so-called Molotov cocktails, against the armored transports and tanks.

At the beginning the units of Obaturov's division, who were advancing without either cover or reconnaissance work, suffered great losses. Two regiment commanders' vehicles were hit, and the staff's radio transmitter was destroyed. The artillery regiment on Ferenc Boulevard came into bitter conflict with the rebels, and the 2nd artillery battalion suffered serious losses. The commander of the regiment, Colonel E. N. Lokanovich, was mortally wounded.

The division commander, General Obaturov, and his staff, under the leadership of Chief of Staff Davidov, organized the reconnaissance of the resistance strongholds and their military activities on the following day.

In the days that followed, the division's formations cleared numerous residential areas in the center of town. But they did not manage to clear the resistance center in Corvin Alley and the Kilián Barracks where there were several thousand people, a few tanks and other military equipment. The resistance's strongest group was here, the most important stronghold of the uprising, the liquidation of which would have been of decisive significance in the crushing of the armed groups in Budapest.

The military action to destroy resistance strongholds in the Corvin was set by the Soviet and Hungarian formations for the morning of October 28. On the Hungarian side the 5th and 6th tank and mechanized regiments under Colonel András Márton, commander of the Hungarian Military Academy, would have taken part in the joint operation.[4]

At dawn, directly before the attack, the Hungarian units were told that the Hungarian government had withdrawn all military operations, as the rebel groups–so they said–were ready to lay down their arms, and so they were negotiating with them. But the rebels did not capitulate. Nevertheless, the operation to crush the rebels around the Corvin Cinema did not take place.

Following negotiations with the leaders of the armed groups–Iván Kovács, Gergely Pongrácz and others–Imre Nagy accepted their demands, and half an hour before the operation was due to start, he phoned the Ministry of Defense and said that if they did not put a stop to the attack, he would resign. This saved the Corvin armed groups.[5]

On October 26 heavy fighting took place in Buda. In the meantime the 128th infantry guard division had arrived, headed by Colonel Gorbunov. He was given the task of relieving Brigadier General Krivosheyev's units, who were then directed to the western border to Szombathely, and to destroy the rebels in Buda and maintain order there.

At that time three of our divisions were operating in Budapest: two mechanized and one infantry division. Our total number exceeded 20,000 men, although in the divisions' regiments there were 600–800 infantry in all. The headquarters staff that had come in from Moscow, headed by General of the Army M. S. Malinyin, helped the operational staff in Budapest.

One of the headquarters' officers, Major General M. I. Pavoli, was with us and continually and regularly informed us of the situation in Hungary. He was given information and informed of decisions by our headquarters in Moscow on the Ministry of Defense's decrees, measures, the troops that had been ordered to the Special Corps, their time of arrival, and it was he who unified the direction of our operations and the tasks involved. We got to know each other's reports, which we sent to Moscow for the General Staff, and more than once we wrote them together. Pavoli reported on his experiences of the formations' supervision, on any deficiencies and gave us advice.

General of the Army M. S. Malinyin spent most of his time with General Lashchenko, with Andropov and Serov and members of the Hungarian government. He would usually appear unexpectedly to define the duties of the troops and give advice on how to carry them out. Malinyin often reported to the chief of General Staff, Marshal V. D. Sokolovsky, saving us from direct talks with the General Staff.

G. K. Zhukov, defense minister and marshal of the Soviet Union, did not interfere in the Special Corps' operations; he did not use the military phone lines, did not send messages and orders containing veiled threats, and did not abuse us. Obviously he knew about the complicated political situation and of our difficulties. Perhaps he reacted in the same way to Khrushchev's decision to invade Budapest.

Our press reported every day on how Western powers were behind the uprising in Hungary and how the majority of the rebels were Horthyist officers and police, and that anarchist elements introduced by the West were taking part. Of course, these forces really played a role in the armed struggle.

But I have to say that the uprising was mass in character. Tens of thousands of workers took part who were dissatisfied with the Rákosi–Gerő leadership and system.

The Voice of America and Radio Free Europe did not remain idle during the struggle. They urged more active participation. And although they reported objectively on a lot of events, they also distorted a lot of facts for propaganda reasons. For example, in the October 25 Parliament protest, they said Soviet units had fired on the protesters. Radio Free Europe concealed the facts of the cruel terror. They even spoke of the destruction of the Budapest party committee and its defenders as if it had been a necessary step, as an expression of the "legitimate passion of the masses."

The 17th mechanized guard division, which belonged to the Special Corps, covered the Austrian–Hungarian border, with its main forces, around Lenti and Szengotthárd, a 125-kilometer stretch of land.

On the decision of Brigadier General A. V. Krivosheyev, the division commander, mobile troops and border guard were established to secure the border. The division's units also provided garrison services in the Győr, Vác, and Veszprém zones and maintained local order.

Our operational group in Budapest received regular situation reports from Colonel G. I. Zerebsov, a staff officer in the 17th division's headquarters.

The 57th mechanized, the 83rd tank, and 1043rd artillery regiments under Colonel Kuznesov, the division's deputy commander, were active in Buda. Then, during the last days of October, they returned to Hajmáskér. The trainee tank battalion defended the Special Corps staff until the 38th army's forces arrived. Then it carried out its duties in Székesfehérvár under the 38th army staff.

The 17th mechanized guard division joined this army on November 1.

Lieutenant General Piotr Nikolayevich Lashchenko undoubtedly played the most important role in leading the operations in Budapest. He directed the units and higher units soberly, calmly and determinedly, and did not change any of the decisions.

His combat experiences, gained during his command and General Staff work in the war, his preparedness, his grasp of reality and sobriety, all meant proper direction for the troops and allowed our formations to carry out duties in the shortest possible time and with minimal losses. The leaders who came to visit us were calm, but sometimes the political leaders and the responsible staff of the KGB made things more difficult by interfering in our operations. He found these interruptions unnecessary and unacceptable.

He trusted me and allowed me to sign countless documents. He also listened to my proposals, thus easing my work considerably.

The Budapest Operational Group was small, about 30 strong. In the beginning, the fact that the circumstances were unusual and that there were many different kinds of duties, new divisions and unknown commands and staff, all affected our work.

Most of the personnel on the Special Corps staff remained in Székesfehérvár. Maintaining communication was difficult because of problems with the inter-city telephone exchanges. As a result they could not always act accordingly and could not help in directing troops. In the absence of typists and draughtsmen, all technical work was done by the officers. Many of us were forced to work for days on end–with three to four hours of sleep. There were also those who could never be found when they were most needed.

Our work directing troops was significantly aided by the telephone lines in Budapest, which we used to gather information about the situation, and for the commanders and staff of the higher units and units to send orders.

Later the operations staff work became more organized and by the time most of the staff had arrived in Tököl, all our work had become easier and circumstances had improved.

The Hungarian government had turned to the Soviet troops for help and yet took no decisive steps to restore order.

In political and state leading circles there was no decisive evaluation of events; I have already mentioned Gerő's October 23 radio speech.

At the beginning Imre Nagy and János Kádár had condemned counter-revolutionary elements. After Soviet troops had been brought in and the people had expressed their dissatisfaction at this, the Hungarian government did not order their own troops to restore order. They withdrew the curfew, thus aiding the operation of the anti-government elements.

After withdrawing the curfew they only permitted fire to be returned. Later they did not allow fire of any kind. Finally they also stopped the attack against the main center of resistance around the Corvin Alley.

Obviously, under such circumstances Soviet troops could not fulfill their duty to restore order in Budapest. This duty was, in any case, beyond the power of our forces.

The armed groups tried to disarm our soldiers and smaller sub-units. General Lashchenko ordered the most determined resistance. The unit commanders were warned that they would be severely punished if they did not prevent arms and military equipment from being handed over.

The armed groups were often led by people who knew the art of street fighting. Their commanders were former Horthy officers and policemen.

Events changed with alarming speed in Hungary during those days and determined the complicated military-political situation facing our troops in Budapest.

We did not know all the details of the events, but we felt that the Hungarian government was not united in the struggle against the rebels and in the question of restoring order.

Such entangled circumstances caused difficulties for our commands and troops.

The Hungarian People's Army formations did not resist the rebels. They did not receive orders for active and decisive action, so they became, at best, passive observers. Some Hungarian formations and several officers went over to the rebels.

Our soldiers and officers, despite the losses we suffered, were not hostile to the Hungarian population. During those grim days I met not only Soviet and Hungarian leaders and military commanders, but also a few participants in the armed uprising.

I remember on October 26 or 27 it was announced that the leader of the Hungarian National Revolutionary Committee, József Dudás, requested that the commander of the Soviet troops stationed in Hungary receive him. I had to speak to him instead of General Lashchenko.

Dudás was disappointed that the commander did not receive him. I told him that I was there in his stead and that I would mediate all his requests. Dudás announced that he was the president of the National Revolutionary Committee and the commander of all the armed groups. He was acting against the Imre Nagy government, and he requested that we recognize the Committee as Hungary's highest authority. He also said that during the war he had taken part in the anti-fascist movement, and that he was a member of the delegation which in 1944 negotiated the Hungarian surrender in Moscow, then later suffered retribution. Now he headed all the armed groups, he published a newspaper, and his headquarters could be found in the *Szabad Nép* newspaper editorial offices. The commander of every significant armed group was directed by him, including János Szabó and Iván Kovács. At that time he really did hold political and military power. At that moment he was not fighting against Soviet troops.

I replied that he had to clear it up with the government who was actually in power. The Hungarian government had called Soviet troops to Hungary, and understandably we recognized their authority. We did not know about any kind of National Revolutionary Committee, and it was not our job to deal with political questions.

When he announced that he was the commander of all the armed groups, I warned him that we knew of instances when his groups had attacked our troops and formations, and that they were breaking the law by so doing, and that they arrested Hungarian state security staff and party workers. If he did not end the armed struggle and his infringements of the law, he would have to answer for his actions in court. Dudás denied that his groups had attacked and killed; he gave the impression of being a political adventurer. Despite this I felt it would be improper to arrest him, as he had come voluntarily to negotiate with us.

Once a woman came weeping to me, asking me to release her son who had been captured by our soldiers. I immediately telephoned the city command. It turned out that her son had really been arrested for armed resistance; he had had a pistol and fired at our soldiers with it, but on the previous day we had handed him over to the Hungarian authorities.

I had many similar experiences.

On the evening of October 28, Imre Nagy made the following announcement on the radio:

"The government condemns those views that say that the present people's movement is a counter-revolution...

"In order to maintain order and public safety, we will establish a new public safety service from the army, the police and workers and young people from the armed groups..."

Szabad Nép, the party's press organ, called the events "a people's democratic movement" and the armed rebels "freedom fighters."

The newspaper reported on the new local authorities throughout the county, in the capital and the provinces, and on the workers' councils being formed in the factories.

In October the Hungarian leadership tried to give Soviet troops the difficult and thankless task of fighting the armed rebels. Now it became clear that all those who had stood by the previous authorities, and the Soviet troops who had taken part in operations at the request of the Hungarian government, were now really fighting against a mass democratic movement.

Immediately after this Imre Nagy declared that the "Soviet troops have already began to withdraw to their bases." A hysterical, hostile campaign was started against the Soviet forces; Soviet troops were told to leave Budapest and the whole country immediately.

During these days Ambassador Andropov visited us in the Ministry of Defense. Lashchenko invited him to breakfast with us. The ambassador accepted the invitation and asked for tea; during breakfast we spoke to him.

On the same day we told Andropov that Imre Nagy and his followers called the rebels "freedom fighters." "Does that mean we were fighting against freedom?"–we asked the ambassador.

Andropov told us that he had informed Mikoyan and Suslov that a counter-revolution had broken out in Hungary and that the uprising was headed by Imre Nagy.

The others agreed with Andropov but reminded him that Imre Nagy was an old communist, that he had been at the siege on the Winter Palace[5] and worked for the Communist Internationale. The ambassador replied:

"It is possible that Imre Nagy was an internationalist, but now he is shaking the foundations of people's democracy. It is Soviet troops who are carrying out the orders of internationalism."

Andropov said that the Hungarian armed uprising tended to be against socialism. Only a handful of workers had been found among the protesters; the majority were Horthy officers. They were recruited from counter-revolutionaries, déclassé elements and agitators from the West who had come over the border.

It was my impression that Andropov had a one-sided view of the Hungarian events. Of all the factors involved he only noticed the anti-socialist phenomena, and he did not recognize as legitimate any of the Hungarian people's demands. He gave his opinions very forcefully. His standpoint was certainly accepted, not only in Moscow, but also among the political delegates who were arriving in Budapest.

Then we came to the most important question: what to do concerning the demand for our troops to withdraw from Budapest.

Lashchenko said that our troops must withdraw–under the circumstances–as they were in any case confined to a passive role.

To Andropov's question of whether we should let the people's power of the communists and the patriots be overthrown, Lashchenko replied that they should defend themselves, they should fight for their own truth. "We do not need to fight for them. Anyone who wants to can come with us."

"If Soviet troops withdraw from here," said Andropov, "by the next day the United States and its allies will be here. We must crush the armed rebel groups–only then will order be restored." With that we said goodbye.

During the last days of October, reactionary forces and those who wanted to restore the old order, who had previously been hidden, took a more open part in the struggle for power. At their request Imre Nagy increasingly modified and expanded the government; he closed the State Security Authority and its organs.

Suslov and Mikoyan, who were in Budapest, advised the government to reject every demand the opposition made. They thought that Soviet military aid–even if its prestige was reduced among the people–was still a better method for restoring order than the uncertain revisionist measures Imre Nagy had taken, which tended towards expanding the composition of the government, establishing coalition parties and fulfilling the rebels' demands.

Both Suslov and Mikoyan were outraged by the Hungarian leadership's intention to even raise the question of a Soviet troop withdrawal from Hungary. Like the Soviet ambassador they believed that was tantamount to an American invasion of the country.

Andropov could not allow this to happen, as he would have ruined not only his ambassadorial work, but his whole career. Moreover, as

Lashchenko later pointed out, Yuri Vladimirovich Andropov wanted to write his name in the history books.

The ambassador's views most likely accorded with the viewpoint of the Moscow leadership and with the reports of previous Hungarian politicians as well.

According to Suslov and Mikoyan, the situation in the country was increasingly disastrous, and that is why further military aid had to be extended to Hungary.

Chapter III

Soviet Troop Withdrawal from Budapest

The Fight Continues

On October 30, due to pressure from the rebels, Imre Nagy's government demanded that Soviet troops leave Budapest immediately. Our soldiers then stopped fighting all over the town.

At 17 hours Budapest Radio interrupted its program to announce that the Soviet government had complied with Imre Nagy's request and that its troops would withdraw from Budapest.

In accordance with the Soviet government decree, on the evening of October 31, we started to withdraw our troops from the city. On the same evening all our units and higher units left the capital and camped about 15–20 kilometers outside Budapest.

The Special Corps staff was settled in one of our air force formation's bases at Tököl Airport.

In the areas we had occupied the units and higher units put their military equipment and weapons in order; they filled the ranks and supplemented their supplies with ammunition, petrol and food.

The Special Corps staff watched events in Hungary closely, but especially in Budapest.

In that period the armed rebel groups executed communists and state security people in other towns too. Party and state buildings were besieged, and monuments raised to the memory of Soviet soldiers were destroyed. In Budapest they captured the city party committee, mortally wounded the first secretary of the party committee, Imre Mező, and murdered several guards.

Despite their tough declarations Imre Nagy and János Kádár did not manage to prevent armed rebel atrocities. The state and party leadership was not capable of handling the situation.

On October 31 the army, police and the National Guard Revolutionary Military Council delegates met at the Kilián Barracks and elected the Revolutionary Defense Committee. Major General Béla K. Király, a former Horthy officer, was at the head of the Committee, and Colonel Pál Maléter, who had gone over to the rebels.

Maléter had been raised to the rank of general that night and appointed minister of defense.[7]

Maléter immediately ordered headquarters to work out a plan in case the Soviet troops were not willing to leave Hungarian territory.

The organization of the armed forces was led by Király. He set to establishing the National Guard troops, who consisted primarily of rebel armed groups, and started to train and prepare the National Guard for a struggle against Soviet forces. Király was also appointed Budapest city commander.

The Revolutionary Committee accepted an appeal in which one of the points stressed the necessity of withdrawing from the Warsaw Pact. Revanchist elements were also increasingly voluble.

Hungary's fate seemed sealed when, on November 1, the Hungarian government announced that it would leave the Warsaw Pact, declared Hungary's neutrality and demanded that Soviet troops leave immediately.

Nobody thought that Khrushchev and his inner circle would accept these demands. The increasing terror, the capture of the Budapest party committee, and Suslov's, Mikoyan's and Andropov's reports had all helped to shape the Soviet leaders' standpoint. So had pressure from the previous Hungarian leadership, who were in Moscow at the time. Rákosi, Gerő, Révai and the others still hoped that they could return to Hungary.

When Israel, England and France declared war on Egypt, N. S. Khrushchev was given a free hand, as the Western powers were tied up in the Middle East crisis.

On the other hand, the Western powers may have thought that the time had arrived to attack Egypt, as the Soviet Union was preoccupied with Hungary.

But many incomprehensible things happened at the time. In the last days of October, the Soviet government declared that it would not intervene in a friendly country's internal affairs. But two or three days later, in Bucharest and in Yugoslavia–with the participation of China–a decision was made to send military aid to Hungary.

We were informed that two armies from the Carpathian Military District, the 38th field army and the 8th mechanized army, had been sent off to Hungary by General Malinyin, the Soviet Armed Forces chief of staff's first deputy. The paratroop formations had already started to capture airports, including Veszprém Airport, which was invaded by the 31st airmobil guard division's 2nd regiment.

Marshal Ivan Stepanovich Konyev, commander in chief of the Warsaw Pact Member States United Armed Forces, who had arrived in Szolnok not long before, was appointed head of the Soviet troops stationed in Hungary. All signs seemed to indicate that Soviet troops were preparing for a massive military operation.

As these steps were being taken, the Soviet government's declaration that the Soviet Union would not interfere in other countries' internal affairs was received with total incomprehension.

Families of Soviet officers posted in Hungary were continually sent out of the country, out of harm's way. Following the entry of paratroop formations, they crossed Hungary and Czechoslovak territory by rail and road, and then were taken back to the Soviet Union by military planes. As always they tried to evacuate the families of the Special Corps, the Military Court and political workers first.

In order not to provoke panic among families, General Lashchenko arranged that his wife and my family–my wife and two small children– would leave on the last plane.

Before I went up to Budapest, late in the evening of October 23, I telephoned my wife and told her that I was going on a short mission. I did not tell her what was taking place in the capital. The next day, as usual, my wife set off to take our son to school, where he was in second grade. As she came out into the courtyard, she saw the Soviet tanks sent there to defend them and turned back. At that time a Hungarian peasant woman brought milk for our smaller two-year-old son. But when she shopped for bread or other provisions in Székesfehérvár, she often experienced unfriendly looks from the locals.

On the night of November 1, my wife was called into the corps command so they could issue her the necessary travel and financial documents, as if it were impossible to arrange these formalities by day at the airport.

Lashchenko and I did not accompany our families to the airport; we did not even bid them farewell. They traveled to Lvov on the last military plane.

Kádár Requests Military Aid

Late in the evening of November 1, János Kádár and three others, one of whom was a colleague of the Soviet ambassador's, arrived at Tököl Airport, where the Special Corps was camped.

Kádár and his associates seemed exhausted. Kádár's shoes had soaked through. We put them up in our air force's only, and none too big, hotel. We gave Kádár a pair of socks and officers' shoes from the supply depot.

When we asked what the situation in Budapest was, he said that he had left Imre Nagy's government and was now wondering what he should do. When he saw a nice-looking chess set on the table, he became more animated and said something to his colleagues.

Serov arrived soon afterwards, and after a short rest Kádár flew out on one of our planes in the direction of Szolnok–Mukachevo. I only saw him again five days later, when he arrived in Budapest from Szolnok accompanied by tanks.

János Kádár broke with Imre Nagy in order to get into power and requested and accepted military support from the Soviet Union. It is difficult to know why he acted as he did. The desire to be head of state? His commitment to socialism? Or the intention to serve the Hungarian people's interests and improve their living standards? It is possible that all these things played a role.

Before Kádár got to Tököl, his declaration was put out over Hungarian radio in which he announced the formation of a new party, the Hungarian Socialist Workers Party. A few days later it was announced that Kádár, Ferenc Münnich, Antal Apró and István Kossa had left the Imre Nagy government and established the Hungarian Revolutionary Worker-Peasant Government.

In their letter to the Hungarian working people, they wrote the following:

"We are members of a government that is not capable of operating. We cannot remain silent while counter-revolutionary terrorists and bandits, under the banner of democracy, murder with beastly cruelty our best worker and peasant brothers, hold our peaceful civilians in fear, create anarchy in the country and drive our country into the yoke of counter-revolution."

At this time the Revolutionary Worker-Peasant Government published an appeal to the Hungarian people:

"The Hungarian Revolutionary Worker-Peasant Government has appealed to the Soviet troop command in the interests of our people, our working class and our country, to help crush the dark forces of reaction and counter-revolution, to restore people's socialist order and create law and peace in our country."

The leaders of the socialist countries believed that socialism was endangered in Hungary. Thus they not only supported the formation of the new government but–as an essential international step–approved of military assistance to suppress the counter-revolution. The internationalist obligation of providing military aid fell to the Soviet Union.

In accordance with the Hungarian Revolutionary forces' request, Soviet troops had to aid Kádár's government to suppress the forces of reaction and to restore the previous social order and calm in Hungary.

The political leadership still did not rule out the possibility of interference from NATO armed forces, primarily American and West German forces. That is why Soviet troops also prepared to forestall any possible provocations.

Preparations for Combat Operation

On November 2, 1956, Marshal I. S. Konyev, commander in chief of the Warsaw Pact Member States United Forces, summoned General Lashchenko, commander of the Special Corps, to Szolnok to issue the combat order to him.

We set off from Tököl to Szolnok with two tanks and some security. Wherever we went there were crowds and armed groups; twice they tried to hold us up.

We were received immediately by marshal Konyev when we arrived in Szolnok. The duty he gave us was unusual. The marshal greeted General Lashchenko warmly, remarking that they were now working together again for the first time since Lvov. There, in July 1944, Lashchenko, heading the 322nd infantry division, broke through and opened a crack in enemy lines. He held the Koltov corridor through which Marshal Konyev, commander of the 1st Ukrainian Front, led the 3rd and 4th armored guard armies; this played a decisive role in the operations.

Konyev said that he would gladly have come to Tököl personally but that he had been ordered to await directions from the leadership.

Then Konyev asked about the Special Corps' Budapest operations. General Lashchenko reported that our actions were of a special kind, that our troops had to work in very difficult circumstances and carry out, for them, unusual duties. There was no front or enemy in the wartime sense of the term. We had few formations, at the beginning just a single 6000-strong division which was then joined by the 33rd mechanized division from Romania and the 128th infantry division from the Carpathians. These armed forces were not enough to operate in a big city.

Some of the population and the Hungarian army supported the rebels. Our officers and soldiers proceeded with uncertainty and lack of skill. BTR-152 open armored transport carriers and the rubber-tired artillery were not capable of street fighting.

Konyev asked if we had brought in the air force. Lashchenko then said that there were few big centers of resistance and that the air force could not make a precise, effective strike against the rebel centers. This sort of action would cause enormous destruction and provoke even greater outrage from the population.

I informed him that, after our armies had withdrawn, the armed forces had regrouped at the command of Béla Király and were preparing to fight Soviet troops alongside formations formed out of other city commands and garrisons.

A defense ring had been thrown around Budapest, led by Király and Colonel András Márton. Garrisons had been set up reinforced with artillery and armored troops in the settlements around Budapest. The city's main institutions had been seized by rebels, and on the streets soldiers and the National Guard patrolled.[8]

Around Budapest 50 air defense artillery batteries had been placed in firing positions with a total of 400 cannons.[9]

The Hungarian formations in Budapest totalled 50,000 men. They had more than 100 tanks, and there were also more than 10,000 people in the National Guard and the other armed groups.

Then Konyev asked Lashchenko if the Special Corps was strong enough to restore order in Budapest in three to four days. Lashchenko, as an experienced commander, declared that neither our forces nor the time allotted was enough to succeed. The corps had to be reinforced with infantry, assault artillery and armored troops; another division would not hurt although everything depended on how much time we had to prepare. A new division would not know the city or the uniqueness of the operation. If we had to act in the near future, it would be better to reinforce the divisions that belonged to the Special Corps.

As for the time limit, Colonel Malashenko reported that significant forces were gathering in Budapest that showed strong resistance; in addition, the participation of Hungarian formations in the fight could not be excluded. We could destroy the rebels' main forces in three to four days, but certain armed groups would continue to resist. Other troops were to be given the task of defending the Austrian border and fighting the armed groups in other towns, and the Special Corps was to be exempted from these duties.

Following this Marshal Konyev turned to the Corps' duties and outlined them in an unusual way. First he said that the political leadership of the Warsaw Pact states had decreed that Hungary had to be given military aid. The task of destroying the counter-revolutionary forces fell to the Soviet troops.

In accordance with this the Special Corps needed to be prepared within a short time to take part in the operation code-named "Whirlwind," whose aim was to restore order in Hungary.

The Special Corps's task was to destroy armed rebel forces and restore order in Budapest. Those Hungarian People's Army formations that displayed resistance were to be disarmed.

The composition of the Special Corps would remain the same: the 2nd and 33rd mechanized and the 128th infantry guard divisions.

The Corps was reinforced with tanks, artillery and paratroop units. The suppression of the counter-revolution and the restoration of order in Hungary's provincial towns and regions fell to the armies of Generals Mamsurov and Babadjanyan.

Complete combat readiness was set for November 3. The operation was to be initiated by the code word "Grom" or "Thunder."

Finally Marshal Konyev wished us every success and shook our hands; then we departed.

Before departing I had ordered all the division commanders to be at the staff headquarters in Tököl on November 2 at 21 hours.

En route to Tököl we worked out the operation plan and determined the activities of the divisions.

The Special Corps again had to operate in Budapest: it had to seize the city's main objectives, destroy the armed groups and disarm Hungarian People's Army formations.

On reaching Tököl we had finished working out the plan and had defined the problems concerning the establishment of advance details, and the joining of forces of the paratroops with the special groups, as well as the disarming of Hungarian formations and the direction of troops.

When the division commanders arrived, General Lashchenko defined their duties. The combat orders read:

"... the 2nd mechanized guard division should occupy Budapest's northeastern and central areas, the Danube bridges, Parliament, the Hungarian Workers Party Central Committee buildings, the Ministry of Defense, Nyugati Railway Station, and the main police station and surround the Hungarian barracks and should not allow them to approach the city from the north or east.

"The 33rd division is operating south of Rákóczi Road, in the city center.

"The 33rd mechanized guard division should occupy Budapest's southeastern and central areas, the Danube bridges, the telephone exchange, the Corvin base, Keleti Railway Station, the Radio, the Csepel Works, the munitions factory, and surround Hungarian barracks and not allow them to approach the town from the southeast.

"The 128th infantry guard division should occupy Budapest's western region–Buda, the Hungarian People's Army's wartime combat center, Moszkva Square, Gellért Hill–and blockade the barracks and not allow Hungarian military formations to approach the town from the west.

"The Hungarian formations have to be disarmed, in military objectives, in the barracks, where they do not display any resistance and where the arms are seized without violence..."

On the night of November 3 at 3 o'clock, I sent the combat orders in a coded telegram to the division commanders. At the same time I sent them information on the armed groups stationed in Budapest and on the Hungarian formations.

The divisions started to make direct preparations for the operations ahead.

The Special Corps divisions concentrated their forces in exactly the same areas as they had before they had withdrawn from the city and guarded the establishments there. This eased their duties.

One or two special advance details were established, reinforced with a battalion each and 10–12 tanks, with 150 paratroopers equipped with BTR armored transports, in all the divisions in order to carry out special duties and capture main objects.

In these advance details were Serov's KGB colleagues, including Grebennyik, Zurjanov, Korotkov, Klaistov and Sladkevich. Their duty was to capture the rebel leaders and members of the Imre Nagy government.

Details reinforced with tanks, cannons, and engineers were formed to capture the Danube bridges and other objectives.

The higher units and units were in a state of complete combat readiness by November 3 at 24.00; the operation was to be initiated with the code-word "Grom" ("Thunder").

Two tank and self-propelling assault gun battalions from the 2nd mechanized division were grouped with General Obaturov's 33rd mechanized division, which had to carry out the most complicated tasks.

We planned to control the corps' higher units and units at the beginning of the operation from our Tököl base. Later this was transferred to Budapest's eastern districts.

On November 3 the Special Corps Chief of Staff Brigadier General M. G. Shchelbanyin, who had recovered from his illness, arrived at Tököl Airport. He told us that on General of the Army Malinyin's orders he had left Székesfehérvár to take part in the negotiations on troop withdrawal with the Hungarians. When Shchelbanyin mentioned his illness Malinyin replied: fulfill your obligations first, and then you can be ill. General Lashchenko was surprised at this, as none of us knew about the negotiations–even Konyev had not mentioned them. The whole thing was very mysterious; Shchelbanyin was phlegmatic and superficial and did not know either the war plans or the city. He mixed Buda up with Pest. Furthermore, he was not General Lashchenko's official deputy.

Lashchenko decided, "Colonel Malashenko will remain at the head of the operational group controlling operations; you will deal with General Malinyin's group, with information, with communicating with the Embassy and establishing military city commands."

Shchelbanyin asked permission to enter the hospital the next day on account of his poor health.

The Arrest of the Hungarian Delegation

Late on November 3, during negotiations in Tököl, I. A. Serov, president of the KGB, arrested the Hungarian delegation, including Defense Minister Pál Maléter; Major General István Kovács, chief of staff; Colonel Miklós Szűcs, chief of operations; and Ferenc Erdei, former deputy president of the Council of Ministers.

After arresting the delegation, General Zuryanov, one of Serov's colleagues, on orders from the KGB president, gave me the map they had confiscated from the delegation. This map gave the positions of the Hungarian troops and armed formations in Budapest and Hungary. As this map was a working copy with various notes written on it, we could not follow all of it. I was given permission to speak to Pál Maléter, István Kovács and Miklós Szűcs after their arrest. We had the opportunity to clear up a few questions, such as the number of Hungarian troops and armed formations in Budapest and how they had gone across to the rebels.[10]

I now saw Maléter for the second time after meeting him in the Ministry of Defense. In recent days I had run into Kovács and Szűcs regularly, as we had been in the same building.

Now they were all in separate rooms in the prison building, under strict guard. Although they were still in shock from their unexpected arrest, they tried to behave with dignity, and I believe they told the truth. All that they said accorded with reality, and the data on the positions of the Hungarian formations proved correct.

Observing their activities in Budapest at that time and on the basis of personal conversations with them, I can say that I did not consider them guilty.

But Pál Maléter's role and fate remained a mystery to me until the very end. I do not believe that he was an armed rebel leader at the beginning of the events, as people later maintained. At the beginning he vacillated, not knowing what to do. Later he completely supported Imre Nagy, fulfilling his orders just as he did the rebels' demands. Pál Maléter slowly learned the ropes of his role leading the military and did so masterfully, although in the last days he was not able to share power and laurels with Béla Király.[11]

As for István Kovács, he was one of the generals in the Ministry of Defense who knew what was happening, although for various reasons he did not always inform us of the facts. He was a well-trained general who served his country faithfully.

It was not he who organized the struggle against Soviet troops but Béla Király.

But all this is my personal observation, and it is possible that I am mistaken on some points, as I was not to know all the circumstances of the affair.

Maléter, Kovács, and Szűcs were stunned by our betrayal in suddenly arresting them. I tried to calm them as much as possible while talking to them; I told them that we had to keep them there temporarily because of the circumstances, that everything would become clear with time and that afterward they would all be released. I really believed this in regard to Szűcs and Kovács, although Serov and his colleagues had other plans.

I have kept the records of the conversations I had with each of them separately, and I will now quote them in full:

November 3, 1956, notes on conversations with Pál Maléter, István Kovács and Miklós Szűcs after their arrest

Colonel Y. I. Malashenko:

"I have come to speak to you as we are interested in how many Hungarian formations and armed groups there are in Budapest. It would also be good to know when you went over to the rebels."

Major General Maléter, Imre Nagy government's minister of defense:

"I controlled the construction and workers' formations. Before that I was the commander of the security guard for Zoltán Tildy, president of the republic, as well as an army corps commander, and the leader of the Ministry of Defense's statute department.

"On October 23, 1956, I was informed that a group of rebels headed by an army officer had entered the Kilián Barracks, where three construction battalions were posted (Pf. 1221, 1222 and 1226) and were seizing weapons. I sent my deputy to restore order and gave the order to arm the battalion in view of the rebels.

"On October 25 I arrived at the barracks where 700–800 armed soldiers were posted. I left a few of them to guard the barracks and allowed the rest to go home.[12]

"I was informed that two construction battalions (Pf. 1228 and 1229) had disarmed the state security guard and captured the town of Pécs and the uranium mines.

"In Budapest, in the Corvin Cinema and in the surrounding buildings, a large group of armed rebels was posted. Their commander was László Kovács Iván, and his deputy was Gergely Pongrácz.[13] In the same cinema there was also a former Horthy officer with a group of 60 men. Numerous Hungarian People's Army officers went over to the rebels.

"On October 28, when Imre Nagy called the insurrection a revolution and the rebels heroes, I went over to the rebels and reported this to Károly Janza, the minister of defense.

"On October 31 I was elected a member of the Revolutionary Defense Committee and was appointed deputy minister of defense and then minister of defense. The armed troops of the 'revolution' were made up of men from the army, the police and the 'National Guard.' The commander of the police was Sándor Kopácsi.

"General Béla Király relied on the National Guard troops and a few officers; he was probably preparing to take a counter-revolutionary turn. On November 4 I wanted to arrest them and was intending to introduce a tough military dictatorship.[14]

"On October 31 Imre Nagy requested data on the Soviet troops posted in Hungary. I gave the order for the reconnaissance work to be carried out. I demanded that Soviet troops withdraw from Hungary immediately. I believed that we would liberate Hungary by force of arms.

"I cannot answer the question concerning the forces that the Hungarian army has at its disposal in Budapest on November 4, 1956. I believe that the Budapest city command also had formations and institutions, but the 7th mechanized division and one or two regiments were also there. On several occasions I was visited by military attachés from various countries (England, the United States). I asked for moral support from their governments."

Major General István Kovács, Chief of General Staff for Imre Nagy's government, and previously chief of operations:

"I was elected to the Revolutionary Defense Committee in my absence. I only attended a committee meeting once. On October 31 I was ordered by Imre Nagy to report on the situation of the Soviet troops posted in Hungary.

"We received data about this from various towns and institutions. Among others Colonel Tóth, commander of the 8th infantry division, reported on Soviet troop movements and requested permission to attack Soviet troops.

"I mistakenly thought that we were capable of restoring order, and we accepted the demand for Soviet troops to withdraw from Hungary.

"On October 24, 1956, rebels captured the munitions depots of the Lampart and Danubius munitions factories and armed themselves against the police."

Y. I. Malashenko: "How many weapons are there in Budapest?"

Kovács: "I don't know. A few sub-units of the Hungarian People's Army's 7th mechanized division have gone over to the rebels.

"András Márton and Sándor Kopácsi did not carry out orders and did not arrest Dudás. The commander of the 8th mechanized regiment, instead of defending the city party committee, actually helped storm the building.[15] The commander of the sentry battalion, Lieutenant Colonel Sándor Kővágó, did not fulfill his orders and did not disarm the Moszkva Square rebels.

"Béla Király and Sándor Kopácsi had a security guard of 30–40 at their disposal. Király relied on the National Guard, while Kopácsi relied on the police.

"I asked only for moral support from the foreign military attachés who sought me out, and through their mediation I turned for help from the Red Cross network.

Colonel Miklós Szűcs, chief of operations, member of the Revolutionary Committee:

"The 7th mechanized division's 16th and 8th mechanized regiments and air defense units, the Debrecen regiment, a few students from the Zrínyi Military Academy and its commander, Colonel András Márton, joined the rebels from the Hungarian People's Army. After the withdrawal of Soviet troops three divisions–the 5th and 7th mechanized and the 27th infantry divisions–and the garrison's formations and institutions remained in Budapest.

"The question of how many weapons there were in Budapest could be answered by Major General Mihály Horváth, and which air defense batteries were present by the army commanders.

"The operations section collected information on Soviet troops on orders from General István Kovács."

With this the conversation came to an end.

When our troops marched into Budapest, we used the radio stations we had seized from the Hungarians in order to refer the order to the Hungarian commanders not "to open fire on Soviet troops."[16]

Before the start of operations, we received the United Armed Forces commander in chief's Order No. 1, which we then passed on to all our troops. The order contained an analysis of the Hungarian situation and laid down the tasks the Soviet forces had to carry out:

THE UNITED ARMED FORCES COMMANDER IN CHIEF'S ORDER NO. 1

November 4, 1956

Comrade soldiers, non-commissioned officers, officers and generals! At the end of October an uprising was instigated by reactionary and counter-revolutionary forces in fraternal Hungary, in order to liquidate the people's democratic system, destroy the revolutionary achievements of the workers and restore the old landowning-capitalist order.

Events showed that the participation of Horthy elements in this military adventure gave rise to the rebirth of fascism in Hungary and poses a direct threat to our country and the whole socialist camp. We must not forget that Horthy Hungary fought on the side of Hitler's Germany in the last war against our native land.

At the request of the Hungarian People's Republic, on the basis of the Warsaw Pact established between the members of the socialist camp—which says that "it must protect the peaceful labor of our peoples, and defend the borders and territories of our countries from possible aggression and infringement, and there all concerted efforts must be made which are necessary to reinforce the member countries' defense capabilities"—the Soviet troops have started carrying out their allied obligations.

Undoubtedly the working class and peasantry of the Hungarian People's Republic will support us in this legitimate struggle.

The duty of Soviet troops is to extend fraternal aid to the Hungarian people in preserving their socialist achievements, in suppressing the counter-revolution and preventing the danger of the rebirth of fascism.

I COMMAND

the entire personnel of the Soviet forces to display persistence and resolution while carrying out their duties. Aid the local authorities by restoring order and normality in the country.

Preserve the honor and prestige of the Soviet soldier, strengthen fraternal friendship with the workers of Hungary, and respect national traditions and customs.

I am totally convinced that the soldiers, non-commissioned officers, officers and generals of the Soviet forces will fulfill their duties with honor.

The United Armed Forces Commander in Chief
Marshal of the Soviet Union

I. Konyev

Chapter IV

Operation "Whirlwind"

Special Army Corps Troops in Budapest Once Again

Special Army Corps troops, the 38th field and 8th mechanized armies from the Carpathian Military District, and the 7th and 31st air mobil guard division formations (four parachute regiments) took part in Operation "Whirlwind" to restore the existing social order in Hungary.

For the area of operations of the Special Army Corps and the two armies, see the maps at the end of the book.)

On November 4, at 6 in the morning Moscow time, "Operation Whirlwind" began as the code word "Grom" ("Thunder") was given. The main forces of the Special Corps' three divisions set off along their designated routes to capture objectives from three directions. They defeated the armed groups in the suburbs by decisive action, and within an hour, at 5 o'clock local time, they had penetrated the capital.

At 5:20 Hungarian radio put out Imre Nagy's appeal:

"Today at dawn Soviet troops attacked our capital with the obvious intention of overthrowing the legitimate Hungarian democratic government. Our troops are fighting. The government is at its post. I announce this to the people of the country and of the world."

In reality, after Nagy had reported that "the government is at its post," he left Parliament with a few of his associates and went to the Yugoslav Embassy.

Béla Király gave the order to fight, then moved his position to János Hill, from where he attempted to direct the Hungarian formations and to organize the operations of the National Guard and the Budapest garrisons.

At the same time as Nagy's declaration went out, another radio station announced that János Kádár had formed a new revolutionary government and issued his "Appeal and Open Letter to the Hungarian People."

At 7:30 the formations of the 2nd guard division captured the Danube bridges, Parliament, the Party's Central Committee buildings, the Interior and Foreign Ministries, the City Council and Nyugati Railway Station. A battalion of guards was disarmed around the Parliament building, and three tanks were seized.

Colonel Lipinsky's tank regiment disarmed 250 officers and national guard while taking the Ministry of Defense.

The heavy tank-assault gun regiment captured the munitions depot near Fót and disarmed a Hungarian tank regiment.

In just one day this division disarmed 600 people, took about 100 tanks, seized two artillery munitions depots, and captured a further 15 air defense cannons and a great deal of ammunition.

The 33rd mechanized division did not meet organized resistance. It captured the Pestszentlőrinc artillery munitions depot and three Danube bridges and disarmed the 37th Hungarian infantry regiment that had gone over to the rebels.[17]

The 108th parachute regiment disabled five Hungarian air defense batteries who had blockaded Tököl Airport in a surprise attack.

Colonel Gorbunov's 128th infantry division captured Budaörs Airport in the west of the city at 7 in the morning with advance details; 22 planes were seized. It took the signal school's barracks, which attempted to resist.

The 128th infantry division formations' attempts to take Moszkva Square, Buda Castle and the southern residential part of Gellért Hill failed due to fierce resistance.

The closer our troops got to the heart of the city–especially when they approached the telephone exchange, the Corvin Cinema area, the Kilián Barracks and Keleti Railway Station–the more organized and fiercer the rebels' resistance became.

The day's battles proved that just as in the previous conflicts, the rebels were a force to be reckoned with. Their resistance centers had become increasingly bigger, and their numbers had grown. The number of anti-tank weapons had increased, and they were prepared to defend numerous public buildings.

We had to reinforce our troops in the city.

On orders from Marshal I. S. Konyev, the Special Corps was reinforced by another two tank regiments (the 31st tank division's 100th tank regiment and the 66th infantry guard division's 128th tank-assault gun regiment) the 7th and 31st air mobile guard divisions' 80th and 38 1st parachute regiments, an infantry regiment, a mechanized regiment, an artillery regiment, two heavy trench mortar units and a rocket launcher brigade.

The majority of the above formations reinforced General Obaturov's and Colonel Gorbunov's fighting divisions in the central and western areas of Budapest.

To take the resistance strongholds–the Corvin Cinema area, the Budapest Polytechnical University and its environs, Moszkva Square, and Buda Castle, which were all defended by 500 or more armed rebels–the division command had to bring in significant infantry, artillery and armored forces. Assault batteries had to be organized, and bullets, flame throwers, smoke-shells and other explosives had to be used during the struggle. Without any of these, the attempts to capture these strongholds would have meant great losses and would have failed.

It was proposed that Major General Obaturov, the division commander, and Colonel S. G. Kuzmin, the artillery commander, utilize a mass of artillery in these zones.

On November 5, after artillery preparations in which the 11th artillery unit took part equipped with about 170 cannons and trench mortars, General Obaturov's division formations started to besiege the resistance stronghold in the Corvin Alley.

The 71st tank and 104th mechanized guard regiment had to be brought in to battle the centers of resistance around the Corvin Cinema, which included the cinema and surrounding buildings and the nearby Kilián Barracks. These two bases constituted the only resistance intersection. Here there were anti-tank weapons, tanks, artillery equipment, mounted trench mortars, and bazookas; they had also mined the crossings between the houses under the arcades.

There were more than 1000 people in the Corvin area resistance stronghold, which consisted of construction battalion fighters and armed groups who had been fighting since the first days of the uprising.

At 15 hours the assault troops started the siege. The resistance center in the area around the Corvin Cinema and the anti-tank weapons were silently surrounded by our tanks on three sides. The armored units attacked first.

Our assault units destroyed with a decisive attack the resistance center which had been established during the first days of the uprising. More than 300 rebels were killed, 700 were taken prisoner, and five tanks and eight cannons were seized.

Following this they cleaned out the Kilián Barracks. By sunset we had broken resistance in the whole area.

That day the 2nd mechanized division formations had destroyed armed rebels and groups in the northern reaches of the city.

Colonel Gorbunov's 128th division's formations fought that day in Buda. An especially bitter fight was waged around Moszkva Square. The 381st parachute regiment and a tank company fought on the road leading south from Gellért Hill to the Polytechnical University.

First Lieutenant I. J. Karpov received the order to secure the roads leading to Gellért Square and the artillery cannons' positions with his motorcycle unit.

Our reconnaissance troops managed to find a way through the barricades and mined obstacles on the roads leading to the square. They drove towards the square at great speed, and as the reconnaissance troops reached the square they were greeted with machine gun and light machine gun fire from all directions, from windows and attics.

Nearly all our reconnaissance soldiers died in the fight. First Lieutenant Karpov, seriously wounded, was taken prisoner and died of his wounds.

After we had managed to discover the strongholds and hiding places of the enemy in Moszkva Square, Nikiforov's infantry regiment's formations, with the help of the 128th tank-self-propelling gun regiment, started to clear one house after another and destroy the armed groups in them.

A few hours later they took the square and captured the leader of the rebels, János Szabó.

Many Hungarian troops helped us during our operations. They informed us of the situation and actions of the armed groups, and they pointed out leading routes to us.

Because there was no front line during operations, continual reconnaissance, information and observation was especially important.

The armed groups, apart from invading certain public buildings, attacked and captured buildings and fought in many places. It was difficult to distinguish the rebels from the local residents and the Hungarian soldiers.

On November 6 the Special Corps formations continued carrying out their task in Budapest and fighting against the armed groups' strongholds.

The Destruction of Armed Groups in the Country

The action by the two armies brought in from the Carpathian Military District also significantly influenced the general situation and the shaping of "Operation Whirlwind."

The 38th field army under the command of Lieutenant General Mamsurov reached the Nyíregyháza area on October 29 and then received the order to press forward to the western bank of the Danube. They had to secure the Austrian and Yugoslav borders and restore order in western Transdanubia. The army staff, headed by General I. A. Tokaryuk, established its headquarters in Székesfehérvár, from where they directed the operations of the higher units and units with great expertise.

The 8th mechanized army, with General Babadjanyan's armored units at their head, made order in the eastern parts of the country. The army's staff operated out of the military airport in Debrecen. The army's operative group, led by Colonel Lipis, settled in Hatvan.

Nine divisions, field and air defense artillery units, engineers and supply units belonged to these armies. The two armies were filled to 50–60% capacity. Their total number was about 60,000 men.

The formations of the 8th and 38th armies captured the provincial rebel centers of Győr, Miskolc, Gyöngyös and Debrecen and took other county seats in Hungary under their supervision after Operation "Whirlwind" had started. Their authority spread to the main communications centers, including the powerful Szolnok radio transmitter. They captured armament and munitions depots and other military establishments.

They surrounded the main Hungarian garrisons. Our formations captured and closed the roads running along the Austrian border. Higher units and units continued to clear the towns and settlements of armed groups that resisted. They also disarmed Hungarian military formations. During the first days of the operation, two Hungarian infantry corps commands and formations, the 5th air defense and the 3rd anti-tank regiments and the units of a military training center were disabled. We seized all these formations' military equipment.[18]

On November 5, in the woods near Pécs, we crushed several armed groups consisting of 2000 people in all. The uranium mine west of Pécs was taken under our control.

The two armies' higher units and units undertook the reconnaissance work to find and liquidate the remaining armed groups. Altogether about 3500 armed rebels were disabled.

In Dunapentele, 50 kilometers south of Budapest, an enemy Hungarian air defense artillery regiment and several armed groups cooperating with the regiment were rendered inactive on November 7.

Some of the units of the 38th army secured the border; the rest did not allow new rebel forces to reach Budapest. Later these units were subordinated in the Special Corps. During the days that followed we continued liquidating smaller armed groups and collecting weapons from resistents.

The higher units and units of the 38th and 8th armies had to fight armed rebel groups in various towns and settlements. However, these conflicts were limited and occasional, and nowhere near as large as the Budapest operations of the Special Corps.

Two air mobile guard divisions, the 7th and the 31st, also took part in the Hungarian operations, along with four parachute regiments belonging to their units.

The 114th and 381st parachute regiments of the 31st guard division, with Major General Ryabov at their head, landed at Veszprém Airport, where one of our air defense regiments was based, with the division command on October 30. They came to defend the air defense regiment and evacuate their families.

Following the start of Operation "Whirlwind," the units of the air mobile division took part in restoring order in the city of Veszprém.

The division's 381st regiment, whose commander was Colonel Sbitnyev, was subordinated to the Special Corps and fought in Buda.

On November 3 the 7th air mobile guard division was flown into Hungary. The division's 108th parachute regiment landed that day at Tököl Airport, where they surrounded Hungarian air defense batteries. Then, splitting up into sub-units, they received the order to take part in the advanced details belonging to the Special Corps divisions.

The division's 80th parachute regiment, after marching through Makachevo–Szolnok–Budapest, fought in the capital.

The unified operations of the higher units and units belonging to the Special Corps, the 8th and 38th armies, and the air mobile divisions sped up the liquidation of the armed groups and the successful conclusion of the action.

The Direction of Soviet Troops in Hungary

In the press, people who do not know any better often write that the Soviet troops were led by Zhukov, Malinyin, Batov, Grebennyik and others.

But in reality, the commander of the Special Corps, Lieutenant General Lashchenko, led Soviet troops throughout the country in October and in Budapest for the entire course of operations. The operations group under my command directed the higher units and units. I had to deputize for General Lashchenko whenever he visited troops or was called to Parliament, when he rested and at other times. Then it was I who dealt with orders and duties; then it was I who passed on and wrote every order and report.

After November 1 Soviet troops in Hungary were commanded by Marshal Konyev, who had arrived in Szolnok. Subordinate to him was the Soviet Union Armed Forces Headquarters operations group headed by Malinyin and all higher units: the Special Corps, the 8th mechanized and 38th field armies led by Lieutenant Generals Babadjanyan and Mamsurov from the Carpathian Military District, as well as two air force divisions and two air mobile divisions.

The commander of the Carpathian Military District, General of the Army P. I. Batov, did not lead troops in Hungary. He was in Lvov and from there secured the formations' advance to Hungary right up until the Soviet border. This military district's operations group, led by General Tutarinov, based itself in Szolnok.

Budapest's city commander, K. F. Grebennyik, did not take part in troop operations. Grebennyik belonged to the KGB staff led by Serov.

In November 12 divisions, including seven mechanized, two infantry, one tank, and two (four regiments) air mobile divisions belonged to the units of Soviet troops stationed in Hungary. The total number of divisional effectives was about 100,000.

Several division's effectives were under the norms; a few military units remained at their permanent posts.

The Final Destruction of Armed Groups in the Capital

On November 7, the anniversary of the Great October Socialist Revolution, a bloody fight ensued on the streets of Budapest. Obaturov's 33rd division's formations fought armed groups south of Rákóczi Road and captured the Radio buildings.

In the direction of the port, Lebedev's 2nd division formations seized the Danube flotilla of the People's Army.

The regiments of the 128th infantry division besieged the Royal Palace and the Castle District on Castle Hill. More than 1000 rebels were fighting around the Castle. We took 350 sub-machine guns, about as many rifles, a few trench mortars, a lot of pistols and grenades during the fight. Taking advantage of the site's good strategic positions, the armed groups fired on the Danube bridges from here. They reached neighboring districts by using underground passages and terrorized the population. This occured with the Royal Palace and its garrison.

Our formations besieged Gellért Hill and at sunset captured the Citadella and took control of the houses at the foot of the hill.

On November 8 they fought against armed groups hiding in the underground cave passages. The formations of the 128th infantry division continued to liquidate the resistance strongholds that remained. The 381st parachute regiment that was sent to help the division was ordered to capture the Petőfi Barracks.

The 7th air mobile guard division's 100th tank regiment and 80th parachute regiment finished clearing the triangle formed by Fiumei Road–Népszínház Street–Rákóczi Road alongside the 33rd mechanized division's tank regiment.

I had to divide up the duties and organize the cooperation of the paratroops and armored troops working along Rákóczi Road.

The paratroop units worked successfully in clearing this area. They broke into houses from where armed groups had opened fire and with swift, determined action destroyed or disarmed them. Often it was the tanks opened the road by crushing the barricades.

At the beginning of operations the personnel of our troop staff were very resolute. They knew that all socialist countries, including China and Yugoslavia, approved of sending military aid to Hungary, and this helped troops to carry out their obligations thoroughly and in accordance with their orders.

Circumstances were now more favorable than at the end of October. In Budapest there was a state of war, our troops ruled the streets, and armed groups rarely managed to attack us effectively. Our forces and equipment were greater than in October.

The troops' hands were no longer tied by contradictory commands from the Hungarian government (only fire if under attack, shooting and fighting is prohibited, etc.), which had so obstructed troop operations and caused unnecessary losses.

We could not count on cooperation from the Hungarian army, so all our plans were worked out independently, and in accordance with our autonomous circumstances. It also helped that we had significant forces at our disposal. The Special Corps' effectives in Budapest amounted to approximately 30,000 men. And at the same time no fresh forces were joining the armed rebels.

But we did have problems disarming the Hungarian People's Army without incident. The few experiences that our formations had gained contributed to the preparedness of our soldiers and officers. We used the Budapest city telephone exchange to keep in continuous contact. We gave the subordinate staff our command's telephone number and the number of the city's automatic telephone stations, while they gave their own personal numbers to us.

Foreign propaganda, primarily Radio Free Europe, used every means it could, making promises, encouraging, and agitating for the continuation of the armed struggle and the disturbances. But for all intents and purposes, the armed struggle ceased within a few days.

Over the next few days we had further conflicts with the armed groups.

On November 8 we received the news that the Budapest Revolutionary Workers Council was sitting in Baross Street and debating the necessary measures to strengthen the struggle. On General of the Army Malinyin's orders I sent out Colonel Dobrunov's motorcyclist reconnaissance battalion to capture them. During the Budapest conflict the reconnaissance troops managed to carry out several responsible duties very successfully.

The reconnaissance troops, struggling under heavy rebel fire, managed to enter the area, although they did not find the members of the Revolutionary Council. They had arrived too late. When I went after them, I also became convinced of this. Not far from here the reconnaissance troops disabled and liquidated a branch of the National Guard and killed a few rebels.

In the city's southeastern reaches, in the industrial zone of the Csepel Works, armed groups continued to display great force and bitter resistance. It later became clear that their fighting forces had 700 rifles, as well as air-defense and anti-tank weapons, at their disposal. The IL-28 plane sent out to find them was shot down with anti-aircraft weapons.

General Obaturov, the division commander, received the order to clear the Csepel industrial zone on November 9. But before the order even arrived, mechanized infantry formations, accompanied by tanks, had encountered resistance on the northern perimeter of Csepel. The area had been closed off with railway wagon barricades, and the roads were defended with artillery fire.

On the morning of November 9, the mechanized division set off to fight in Csepel. Their units met heavy fire. Air defense automatic guns destroyed four of our tanks, and our infantry suffered severe losses. The attack launched after this exchange of fire was not successful either. The leadership had underestimated the strength of the rebels, and the reconnaissance work was inaccurate.

General Obaturov then decided to launch an attack with a mechanized regiment reinforced with tanks and artillery assault equipment. On November 10 at 3 in the morning he hit the armed groups unexpectedly. They were totally unprepared and did not put up any serious resistance, but dropped their guns and fled.

By morning we had completely cleared Csepel. The 100th tank regiment and the 80th parachute regiment cleared the suburbs, Kispest, Pestszenlőrinc and Üllői Road of armed formations.

The engineering units, who earlier–due to lack of infantry–had been split up into assault detachments, were now called in to break down the barricades and clear the roads, to clear the objectives of mines and to disable missiles.

On the same day the 128th infantry guard division formations destroyed the last armed groups in Buda and its environs. They also disarmed a few air defense batteries who had tried to resist.

The units in the other parts of the city guarded the objectives; they patrolled and combed the occupied areas in order to clear them of any remaining rebels. The rebels–except for the most determined–surrendered one after the other.

The smaller armed groups that were all that remained of the defeated resistance centers did not now bother with holding buildings but used a new tactic. They changed position very quickly and shot from behind the corners of buildings. Sometimes they looted department stores, warehouses, shops and hotels and set many of them ablaze. In the meantime they retreated to the suburbs and beyond the city and later tried to flee to the West. We destroyed Dudás's formations while they were en route near Tata.[19]

Béla Király, Commander in Chief of the National Guard

At the end of October 1956, Béla Király emerged in the military/political arena in Budapest and played a significant role in subsequent events. He had asked Imre Nagy's son-in-law to make use of his "work, enthusiasm and solidarity," and to return him to his post and allow him into the work of the Ministry of Defense's General Staff. He was also supported by Zoltán Tildy.

We know that Béla Király graduated from the Ludovika Academy. During World War II, in the Horthy era, he had worked in the Army headquarters and been awarded a high-ranking medals. At the beginning of the 1950s he was commander of the Zrínyi Academy; later he was arrested and was only released in the summer of 1956. It is obvious that he was a very experienced, well-trained, high-ranking officer.

His personality and activities call for thorough study. On October 31, at the delegate meeting of the National Guard Revolutionary Council in the Kilián Barracks, Király was elected president of the Revolutionary Defense Council.[20] One of the points in the Committee Appeal stressed the necessity of breaking up the Warsaw Pact.

The Revolutionary Defense Committee issued the order to make the state security services unlawful and to disarm all their units. Király took the reorganization of the armed forces and the rehabilitation of those dismissed from the ranks into his own hands. Under the banner of the National Guard, military troop units were formed out of, in the main, armed rebels. Their total number amounted to approximately 15,000.

On October 31 Király was appointed Budapest's city commander; then on November 3 he was elected commander in chief of the National Guard. He oversaw the training of National Guard formations for combat with Soviet troops. A ring of defense was established below Budapest, led by Colonel András Márton.

In the early hours of November 4, when Imre Nagy announced that the Soviet troops had begun the attack, Király summoned the Hungarian rebel formations and troops. At dawn he held a meeting in the main police station on Deák Square and sought out the staff of the American Embassy. Then on that day and those that followed, he patrolled the city and demanded that the National Guard commanders and the officers of the People's Army air defense formations display armed resistance. He did all this certain of aid from the West, about which Radio Free Europe had already spoken.

As we destroyed a significant part of the rebel forces in Budapest, three to four days later the remaining rebels split up into small groups and started to retreat to the suburbs and beyond the city, primarily to the wooded hilly area northwest of Budapest.

On November 8 we were told, perhaps by the border guards, that the National Guard headquarters had resettled its operations center from Budapest to the area around Nagykovácsi and Telki, and that Béla Király was among them. We sent one of our mechanized regiments to the area. A struggle broke out, and we were told by captured national guard that Király had departed to the Austrian border.

On orders from Marshal Konyev, a special group was dispatched to arrest Király, led by Colonel I. I. Skripko, an experienced reconnaissance officer. But they did not manage to either find or arrest Király. As far as we know, he left Hungary and escaped to Austria by helicopter.

I would like to reiterate that after we arrested Pál Maléter at Tököl, he had said that Király, along with a few National Guard officers, had planned a counter-revolutionary uprising. On November 4 he had wanted to arrest him along with István Dudás [József Dudás–editors] and had intended to introduce a military dictatorship. In retrospect it is of course difficult to determine what Maléter really wanted. But it is clear in any case that Béla Király played an important part during those days in November and was one of the leaders of the Budapest operations against Soviet troops.

The formation commanders reported on many prisoners in their reports. Anyone who did not resist was disarmed and released.

One day in November we received the order to disarm all our prisoners and send them to General Grebennyik in the Central Military City Command.

Then things became difficult. It became clear that the commanders had exaggerated the number of prisoners taken in their reports. They listed as prisoners those who had resisted or died in the fight, or who had thrown down their weapons and fled. We actually had hardly any rebel prisoners.

The commander in the corps only sent a few hundred people to the Budapest City Command, and as it became clear later, many of them were captured unarmed and amid suspicious circumstances. They believed that they could clear their names in the City Command with the help of Hungarian agencies.

It is true that, on orders from Serov, more than 1000 people were shut in wagons and sent by rail to the Carpathians. After a while many of them were released and returned home, and a few were handed over to the Hungarian administration.

The deportation of Hungarian citizens by the Soviet KGB naturally provoked outrage among the Hungarian people.

With the destruction of the armed groups in Csepel and Buda, operations in Budapest came to a close.

As a result of Special Corps operations, we broke rebel resistance in Budapest on November 11 and by doing so crushed the armed uprising throughout the country, both in the capital and the provinces.

After the Budapest defeat the rebels broke up into smaller groups and retreated to the wooded hilly region northwest of Budapest. In order to liquidate the groups hiding in the woods, our formations combed the woods and surrounding settlements. The 97th mechanized regiment's sub-units were designated to destroy the group hiding in the woods near Nagykovácsi on the night of November 10. They cleared the area, killed

10 rebels, captured 13 armed people and seized five vehicles and 15 radio transmitters belonging to the National Guard Headquarters.

The final liquidation of the small groups and the restoration of order was undertaken by our formations and the officer law enforcement regiments that had been formed in the meantime. We established city commands in the provincial towns and organized patrols. The patrols cooperated with the police and the Hungarian officers over the following days. Because of this we were able to fulfill our duties to the letter. Hungarian law enforcement agencies, along with our units, secured several institutions, objectives, bridges, railroad stations and main roads.

During the conflict, and following the Budapest operations, we confiscated more than 44,000 guns from the army formations, the armed groups and the civilian population, of these 29,000 sub-machine guns and carbines, 11,500 automatic weapons, approximately 2000 machine guns, 13,500 pistols and 62 artillery cannons, including 47 air defense cannons.

At least 2000 machine guns, automatic weapons, light machine guns and pistols were of foreign manufacture and made after the war. We collected a lot of weapons from the Hungarian military formations.[21]

On November 12, 1956, following the order from the Special Corps commander to collect weapons, we collected a huge amount of weapons from the population. The number of weapons found showed that several thousand people took part in the armed uprising and that most of them were active in Budapest.

Soviet soldiers fighting the armed groups displayed courage, determination and resolution. This explains why we were able to destroy the rebel forces in such a short time. The commander of the independent mechanized reconnaissance battalion of the 2nd mechanized guard division, Lieutenant Colonel G.T. Dobrunov, was awarded the "Hero of the Soviet Union" title and medal in December 1956 for his remarkable combat actions, his heroism and his bravery. In addition 25 other soldiers received this medal.

Many Hungarian People's Army fighters had taken part in suppressing the armed groups and had helped Soviet troops. But the Hungarian army was not able to defend the people's democracy and restore order in the country alone.

But despite this the Hungarian People's Army did not go across to the rebels or act against Soviet troops en masse. Only certain formations

A pair of boots, all that remained of the Stalin statue

T-54s on Üllői Road

Victory of the revolution! Freedom fighters on the T-34s

Kossuth Lajos Square on November 4

A pair of boots, all that remained of the Stalin statue

T-54s on Üllői Road

Victory of the revolution! Freedom fighters on the T-34s

Kossuth Lajos Square on November 4

No photos!
November 4, 1956: the Soviet major promptly reaches for his pistol

October–November 1956: the Soviet coat of arms is taken down from the Soviet monument on Szabadság Square

Major General Pál Maléter, the minister of defense, greets General M. S. Malinyin in Parliament for negotiations on Soviet troop withdrawal on the morning of November 3, 1956

November 3, 1956. Misleading troop movements, troop withdrawal negotiations in Parliament. At the head of the table, Major General István Kovács; to his right Captain V. I. Fomin, instructor to the political section of the Special Corps; General M. S. Malinyin, the first deputy of the Soviet Armed Forces chief of general staff; Major General M. G. Shchelbanyin, the chief of staff of the Special Corps; Captain Shishkin, interpreter; and Lieutenant General F. P. Stepchenko, deputy head of the political section of the Soviet Armed Forces

T-54s on November 7th Square

Üllői Road

Corvin Cinema in October–November 1956

The corner of Üllői Road and Ferenc Boulevard

After the battle of József Boulevard

Fallen Soviet soldiers

Colonel Y. I. Malashenko, the acting chief of staff of the Special Army Corps

P. N. Lashchenko, lieutenant general, commander of the Special Army Corps

I. A. Serov, general of the Army, president of the State Security Forces (KGB)

Colonel Malashenko with his colleagues, October 1956

Retired Lieutenant General Y. I. Malashenko in his study

Y. I. Malashenko, retired lieutenant general, reminisces about 1956 with military historian Jenő Györkei at the Hungarian Embassy in Moscow

Alexandr Mikhailovich Kirov, military historian born in 1956

went over to the rebels. In the capital this meant two mechanized and one infantry regiment, a few construction battalions and around 10 air defense batteries.

Clashes between the two armies took place in the Kilián, Petőfi and Mátyás Barracks and in other Budapest zones, in Dunapentele, Győr, Zákány, Kaposvár, Szolnok and in other garrisons. There were Hungarian soldiers in several of the rebel groups, and a few officers and "advisers" joined the rebels.

The leaders of the People's Army became demoralized during the events and could not influence the troops. But the fact that the Hungarian People's Army prevented mass bloodshed is to the credit of the Hungarian officers and generals.

On November 4 Ferenc Münnich and Gyula Uszta began reorganizing the Hungarian army and forming units to secure social order. In Budapest three law-enforcement regiments were organized, and new units were established in the provinces as well. Thus the Hungarian People's Army was completely recreated.

Soviet Troop Losses in Hungary

Soviet troops suffered serious losses in the 1956 operations. Of the 2170 casualties, 670 were killed and 1500 were wounded.

More than half the casualties were sustained by the Special Corps formations in October, while in the period following this the damage inflicted was slightly less serious. The 33rd mechanized division's units led by General Obaturov suffered great losses too. They were given the most complicated duties; they had to operate in the central districts, where there were more armed groups, and during the first days they did not always succeed in organizing their operations.

The 7th and 31st air mobile guard division had 85 dead, while 12 people disappeared; the number of wounded was 265.

Several of our tanks, armored transports and other military equipment were engulfed in flames and destroyed. The formations of the 33rd mechanized division in Budapest lost 14 tanks and self-propelling assault guns, 9 armored transports, 13 cannons, 4 BM-13 rocket launchers, 6 air defense cannons, 45 light machine guns, 31 vehicles and 5 motorcycles.

The Hungarian population also suffered great losses. In Budapest alone, more than 2000 people died, and 12,000 were wounded.

Approximately 200,000 people left the country.

All this shows that these events were equally tragic for both the Hungarian and Soviet peoples.

The commanders of the Soviet troops stationed in Hungary, particularly the Special Army Corps commander, who had given the orders and commands to carry out duties, tried as much as possible to avoid losses of troops and Hungarian civilians.

Naturally sometimes people died accidentally. The situation was complicated: it was not always possible to distinguish between the rebels firing on our soldiers and those who, abandoning their weapons, fled from the fire. But illegitimate acts and cruelty were not perpetrated against the Hungarian population, and anything tending towards this was immediately stopped.

Recent articles in the press by "eyewitnesses" that report on Hungarian civilians being shot in the head and Soviet troops being executed at the Soviet Embassy after refusing to carry out orders are mere fabrications and lies.

As I wrote earlier, there were cases when the rebels liquidated their state security colleagues, party workers and Soviet prisoners of war.

The Hungarian events have a special place in my life and military service. I was able to lead the operational staff and direct higher units and units during the complicated conflicts that developed in Budapest. I had to gather information about the situation, I had to report to the Command and Headquarters, I had to work out proposals so that decisions could be made, and I had to issue orders to the division commanders. I had to coordinate actions and supervise how duties were being carried out. Every day I had to write reports, coded telegrams and orders. I had to direct the officers of our operational group every day.

My work was full of responsibility, stressful, difficult and complicated.

During the events I had to meet Soviet and Hungarian party and state leaders and other high-ranking military commanders. If I merely listed the names, the meetings and the measures taken, I could prove how important, full of responsibility and stressful my work was at that period.

On November 12, 1956, the Hungarian operations came to a close.

Nikita Khrushchev, Imre Nagy and János Kádár

Nikita Khrushchev, Imre Nagy and János Kádár played the most important role in the Hungarian events of the autumn of 1956. They determined the nature and scope of the Hungarian events in many respects.

After he came to power, Khrushchev declared that relations with the people's democracies would be revised and corrected.

We had to take the uniqueness of these countries and their national factors into account more. But events came to a head with extraordinary speed in Poland and Hungary. The situation that developed, often with some prejudice, was approached on an ideological basis. Furthermore our political leaders' opinions on the Hungarian situation were not unanimous.

At the beginning of June 1956, Suslov, who had just come to Budapest, observed "The atmosphere of the workers and peasants is good; there is no comment on the crisis within the party or the uncertainty of the party leadership." His advice was, in essence, to strengthen party unity and to preserve Rákosi's prestige.

One month later, in July 1956, Mikoyan, who was visiting Hungary, said just the opposite: "The crisis has sharpened in the country, power is slipping from the Hungarian comrades' hands, and the hostile elements are forming a parallel center which is active and decisive." He believed that Rákosi should be replaced by the young András Hegedűs.

The Hungarians–making an unfortunate choice–supported Ernő Gerő and the continuation of the Rákosi policy. In September and October, the Soviet Embassy in Hungary informed Moscow that the situation in Hungary was deteriorating, that "our friends" could not take the necessary measures after the July plenum.

The situation became serious not just in the party but in the entire country. All this prompted Khrushchev to take the appropriate steps.

Khrushchev and his followers were compelled to take tough measures against the opponents of the Rákosi regime who wished to make great changes, and against the danger that Hungary would split from the socialist camp.

Khrushchev's initial good will soon petered out.

After the condemnation of Stalinism, taking into account the internal political situation in our country, Khrushchev knew that the people would not support steps which would result in the breakup of the Soviet camp.

Hungary's withdrawal from the Warsaw Pact would have meant the end of the postwar status quo and a strengthening of NATO's position. Thus Khrushchev decided he would not let Hungary go over to the West.

He was afraid of the consequences of unpopular measures, including the army's reaction; this was one of the reasons for his actions. Khrushchev said: "We cannot agree with such a turn in events, neither as communists and internationalists nor in the name of the great power of the Soviet Union." He believed that NATO would do nothing more than express its outrage at the Soviet intervention.

On the first day of the events, on October 23, a decree was issued on the Soviet troops' entry into Budapest to restore order.

On October 24 Imre Nagy returned to power as the head of the Hungarian government.

Between 1953 and 1955, when he was still prime minister, Imre Nagy drafted a program for the restoration of the country's independence, the democratization of society and an increase in living standards which was received with great enthusiasm by Hungarian intellectuals and among the masses. But Rákosi tried to manipulate Khrushchev against him, saying that Nagy was a pursuing a "revisionist course" and seeking the approval of the nationalists.

And now Nagy had returned to power. At the beginning he thought that order would be restored by force. In Moscow they trusted him, as did Mikoyan and Suslov, who had arrived in Budapest.

But the situation in Budapest became increasingly complicated. The opposition demanded further concessions–the creation of a coalition of parties, the introduction of a multi-party system in the country, etc.

Imre Nagy tried to stay in the saddle, which is why he began to unite with the rebels. He reevaluated the events throughout the country, and at their request he broke up the state security services. He announced the withdrawal of Soviet troops from Hungary and withdrawal from the Warsaw Pact, and he requested help from the UN.

On the last day of October, Suslov and Mikoyan reported on the deterioration in the situation. The party's leading organs were racked by incapacity, and the party organs were falling apart.

The district party committee was seized by hooligans, and communists were murdered. The units of party members were slow to organize. Factories stopped working. The population sat at home. The railways did not operate, and students and other rebels could not be stopped.

Suslov and those around him drew the appropriate conclusions and asked that Marshal I. C. Konyev be sent to Hungary and be entrusted with the leadership of Operation "Whirlwind" to restore order and the people's democratic authorities.

It stands to reason that Imre Nagy had to be replaced, as he did not intend to leave voluntarily. A new government had to be set up, and for this Soviet troops had to be sent in. Initially they planned for Ferenc Munnich to head the government, but the Yugoslav comrades suggested that it would be better if Kádár was leader.

At the end of October, on October 29–30, 1956, Moscow headquarters drafted the plan for Operation "Whirlwind."[22]

The plan was to introduce 12 divisions and called for the disarming of the untrustworthy Hungarian People's Army so that they would not act against the Soviet troops and János Kádár's government.

The report on the further strengthening of the friendship and cooperation between the Soviet Union and other socialist countries which was published on October 30 in the Soviet press condemned postwar relations between these countries and expressed the Soviet Union's willingness to construct equal, friendly relations in the future. We soldiers believed that we would not have to carry out a military operation in Hungary. But three days later fresh Soviet troops arrived in Hungary.

Later we thought that all this was to cover up the operation, so that we could attack the country unexpectedly.

But most likely it was because the foreign policy apparatus, headed by an unofficial leader, A.T. Sepilov, did not adjust its proposals in accordance with the Soviet Ministry of Defense about who should do what. The Central Committee Presidium, however, had not kept the military preparations secret from the Foreign Ministry.

During the events of November 1956 and later, indeed for many years, János Kádár played the main role in shaping political events in Hungary.

When he became the HWP Central Committee's first secretary on October 25, János Kádár supported Imre Nagy and his October 28 declaration, in which Nagy reevaluated the events and announced the withdrawal of Soviet troops from Hungary and Hungary's withdrawal from the Warsaw Pact. Kádár, in order to get into power, broke with Imre Nagy, supported the Soviet Union's military aid, and announced the formation of the revolutionary government and party. With the cooperation of Soviet troops, the anarchist armed groups and troops were crushed.

The struggle with the opposition forces was founded on this aid. In the end the previously existing order was restored. It is difficult to judge what prompted Kádár's actions. It was probably not just ambition to be head of state but also anxiety for the fate of Hungary. Kádár was a realist; he saw that Imre Nagy had lost and that power was on the Soviet side.

Kádár's rule was doubtless preferable to Rákosi's return. Kádár's government–at the sacrifice of concessions and repression–took on many of the opposition's proposals. He was able to stabilize the situation in the country relatively quickly and break out of international isolation.

He skillfully managed to consolidate forces in Hungary and start and develop manufacturing once more.

He praised the Soviet Union and socialism in order to avoid a counterattack from the Soviet party, but Kádár gradually realized his own aims and carried out a series of social and economic transformations in the country which served the broadening of democracy and the improvement of living standards in Hungary.

At the Twenty-second Congress of the Soviet Communist Party, János Kádár summed up the significance of Soviet aid: "We are deeply grateful to our Soviet brothers for the aid they extended to the Hungarian people during difficult times. This aid played a decisive role in the Hungarian people's defeat of the counter-revolution..."

We must not forget these words when we evaluate Hungarian events.

János Kádár managed to realize numerous social-political and economic transformations and thus to complete the period of "realist socialism" in a peaceful way.

After Kádár's death the Hungarian people were not content with these achievements, and Hungary took a new path to development.

The Historical Tragedy

1. After World War II the Soviet Union imposed on Hungary, and on a few other countries, its own path to development. Some of the peoples of these countries accepted this path and set to creating the conditions for "people's democracy." When an armed uprising broke out in Hungary in the autumn of 1956 that threatened the existing social order, the Soviet Union sprang to its defense.

Leading Soviet politicians agreed that they would extend military aid to Hungary on request from the Hungarian government. This decision was supported by all the leaders of the member states of the Warsaw Pact, who indeed saw it as the Soviet Union fulfilling its internationalist obligations.

The Soviet troop march into Hungary was necessary to defend the existing order and was intended to prevent Hungary from breaking from the socialist camp, withdrawing from the Warsaw Pact and making peace with the West, and to prevent the United States and NATO from encroaching on Soviet borders.

Our political leadership and our ideologists announced that our fraternal ally, Hungary, was in danger, and we believed this and saw events in this light.

In those years our ideologists exercised very great influence, and we believed that we were supporting the Hungarian people on request from the Hungarian government, that we were helping the workers to restore and maintain the existing order. We were convinced that we were fulfilling our international obligations.

We believed that our socialist social order was progressive, that in our countries no kind of anti-state movement could be allowed and that all transformations had to be realized by the highest authorities. The assemblies and protests, and especially the armed uprising against the given social order, were simply unacceptable in our eyes.

Soviet troops helped restore calm and the existing social order in Hungary.

Officers and soldiers fulfilled their combat duties; they did not wonder whether their actions were legitimate, and they did not question orders. Furthermore, many remembered that Hungary had fought on the fascist German side against our country in the last war, and when they saw the cruelties of the counter-revolution, they saw their own actions as a continuation of that previous struggle.

Despite this the Hungarian people's action against the Rákosi–Gerő clique and the mistakes they had committed, the many legitimate demands, and the heroism which the people displayed during the struggle for freedom awoke a certain involuntary sympathy in us.

2. But it would not be right to show all the events in 1956 in a rosy light.

Looking back today, the decision of Soviet and Hungarian leaders to bring Soviet troops into Budapest seems completely wrong. Unlawful acts should have been prevented, the reactionary forces should have been fought, and social order should have been restored, but all this should have been done by the Hungarians themselves.

The entry of Soviet troops into Hungary to restore law and order was an intervention by the Soviet Union into Hungary's internal affairs and violated international law.

In 1849 Czar Nicholas I ran to help the Habsburgs and contributed to the suppression of the revolution in Hungary. More than 100 years later, in 1956 Khrushchev sent Soviet troops to restore order in Hungary. The Hungarian events in 1956 were tragic for both the Hungarian and Soviet peoples.

3. The 1956 events in Hungary showed once again that the liquidation of political conflict, the end to a crisis in the country is only possible if we remove the social-political and economic reasons and this is not a military problem.

The solution to such problems, the restoration of law and order, as history reveals, is much more effective if done by political means and negotiations.

The use of force, military operations, play a subordinate role and are not capable of solving all problems alone. In addition the use of an army causes great losses among the population and is accompanied by destruction and devastation; it limits the use of military force and makes resolving problems more difficult.

Finally, it is unacceptable for the troops of other states to be used for such aims.

The 1956 events in Hungary were the first painful symptoms of the beginning of the postwar crisis of the socialist system.

On October 22, 1992, in Moscow, at a reception in the Hungarian Embassy, I was introduced to the president of the Hungarian Republic, Árpád Göncz, who was on an unofficial visit to our country.

The president asked me if I had been in Hungary in 1956 and how I saw the events today. I told him that I played an active role in the events and that, as a colonel, I had fulfilled my duties as the Chief of Staff of the Special Corps during Budapest operations.

My evaluation of the Hungarian events is ambivalent today as it was earlier.

This was not simply the Hungarian people's revolutionary uprising and freedom fight.

The destruction of the capital and district party committees, the cruel executions, and the way rebels treated communists, state security personnel and believers in the existing system, all bear the marks of counter-revolution.

Today people who know nothing of the facts blame Soviet officers and soldiers for committing illegitimate acts while simply carrying out their duties.

The Soviet politicians, primarily Khrushchev and his followers, and the Hungarians who requested military aid are all responsible for the subsequent historical tragedy.

As events unfolded the Hungarian people's numerous legitimate demands and their uprising against the Rákosi–Gerő clique, awoke our respect and sympathy.

Without this struggle perhaps the celebration which you are now commemorating would not be held.

At the reception Árpád Göncz gave a speech in which he said that not everybody sees the 1956 events in the same way: Hungarian leaders, our people and Soviet generals all see the events differently.

After his speech Árpád Göncz told me that during the war he had fought against fascism, had taken part in the underground movement, and in fact had been wounded by a bullet.

I also told him that I had fought in the Soviet army against the Germen and Hungarian troops during those years. In the zone next to us, in Szajava, General Béla Miklós, commander of the 1st Hungarian Army, had come over to our side.

During the Budapest operations in the autumn of 1956, we tried as much as possible to avoid mass bloodshed. Of course he could imagine how many victims there would have been if only one of our tanks or light machine guns had opened fire on the protesters or the assembled crowds. We did not bring in the air force either. [In the combat at Nagykovácsi, fighter bombers attacked us, using air to ground missiles. That could not have happened without Malashenko's knowledge.–Béla K. Király] "That is true," said the president. I continued, "It is natural that there are different ways of looking at 1956. We were on the other side of the barricades. You became president of the republic, in part because of your participation in these events, and you have your own official accepted view of events which you present.

"My views and evaluation of events are not the same as yours, although concerning many factors and events, we agree on a lot. Your ambassador and his staff, who represent the Hungarian people and their reconciliation- and peace-seeking country, know this," I said.

President Göncz said that the Hungarian and the Russian people did not go to war against each other, but that one fought for its leaders and the other against its leaders.

I did not challenge this very questionable statement.

Between our peoples reconciliation, understanding and peace should prevail.

Afterword

The History of the History

This book, *The Soviet Military Intervention–1956*, looks back over a long period. This subject was shrouded in dense fog for years. We did not know much about the suppression of the revolution and freedom fight.

From 1969 until 1972, I was a post-graduate student in Moscow at the Soviet Academy of Sciences' World History Institute. I built up good relations with Russian historians, several of whom were so-called "alternative thinkers." In 1990 I returned for a short study trip to this institute. I was looking for documents related to the Comintern in the Spanish Civil War.

My friend Péter Gosztonyi, knowing of my trip, asked me to look for the 1956 Soviet military interveners–to find out who the commanders were, what forces they employed, what military techniques they used, how big their losses were, and so on.

This trip really was "long-distance reconnaissance work." Officially they would never have accepted such a research subject. Therefore I was doing "illegal" work. I sought out "wise" people who would tell me their secrets in a credible way.

At that time Lieutenant General Lashchenko, the commander of the Special Corps, was still alive. I would have liked to have met him, but I was told he was gravely ill, and he died in 1992. The second man in the corps, the leader of the operational group in the Budapest operations, retired Lieutenant General Malashenko, was not willing to speak about anything.

Finally some sort of picture came together from all the conversations I had had, which I reported on in my article "Who the Commanders Were," which appeared in the newspaper *Magyar Nemzet* (Hungarian Nation) on February 2, 1990.

In March–April 1992 I returned to Moscow. This time the circumstances were more favorable. At a reception in the Hungarian Embassy in Moscow, Péter Gosztonyi and I met Yevgeny Ivanovich Malashenko, who talked to us over a glass of wine in the Embassy salon. But even then he was very close-mouthed, and it seemed he would not open up for us.

A few days after the reception, we had come to the end of our mission, when our "general" phoned us and said he wanted to talk to us.

We sat down once more in the Embassy salon. We had the feeling that this man did not want to take to the grave all he knew about 1956. He spoke honestly when he said he wanted to review all the previous viewpoints about 1956. After this, in the evening, when I phoned him his wife told us in a desperate tone that her husband had become ill on coming home and been taken to hospital. His state was said to be grave. One man, a Russian colonel, even accused us of poisoning him.

In September 1992, on a mission from the Hungarian Foreign Ministry along with my colleague, the historian István Vida, I selected documents on 1956 from the Russian Federation's Foreign Affairs Archive. We learned only later that the basis for our work was the "Yeltsin dossier." (The Hungarian language publication of these Soviet archival materials President Boris Yeltsin presented to the Hungarian government during his 1992 visit of Hungary.) I again met Yevgeny Ivanovich, who promised to finish his memoirs.

In March 1993 I spent 10 days in Moscow. Péter Gosztonyi and I got into the Armed Forces Headquarters Podolsk archive. I was able to read some interesting division reports on 1956, but we were not allowed to take notes. The fruit of this trip was when we became acquainted with important witnesses to the events such as Colonel Tsapenko, the 1956 Budapest military attaché.

I also got to know Lieutenant Colonel Kirov at that time, the young military historian born at the time of the Hungarian Revolution, who was writing his doctoral thesis about 1956.

In March 1994 I returned to the Russian capital. I was shooting the film "Secretive Ones" along with Miklós Horváth, my fellow military historian, and the film director Anna Geréb. I also persuaded Lieutenant General Malashenko to stand before the camera and talk. He said that he would be finished with his memoirs very soon. In June 1995 I traveled to see him to get the manuscript and settle the publishing contract.

We would have liked our author, Yevgeny Malashenko, to come to our book launch. He wanted to do so, but his deteriorating health prevented him from coming. Instead he sent the letter below, which shows what a long path this man has traveled. This man, who at the very beginning, in 1990, was not willing to speak about the 1956 events, has now come out self-critically in 1996.

I have never heard Soviet soldiers or generals speak so openly about 1956. Yevgeny Malashenko deserves all our respect as a result.

Budapest, 1996

Jenő Györkei

To Dr. Jenő Györkei
Military Historian
Budapest

Dear Jenő Györkei,

Due to the state of my health I'm afraid I cannot avail myself of your invitation and take part in the book launch.

You, of course, know that in the autumn of 1956 I led the operational group of the Special Corps staff posted in Budapest. I recall those problematic events in my memoirs. Perhaps with the help of the memoirs the image of events will be even more objective and complete, and they will give a broader look at history, especially concerning the activities of the Soviet troops.

The time that has passed since then allows certain generalizations:

1. The events in Hungary in the autumn of 1956 played an important historical role in several Eastern European countries. This was the first instance of a mass armed uprising against the existing totalitarian regime.

The Hungarian people rose up against the Rákosi-Gerő clique and initiated a fight for the freedom and independence of their country.

The Hungarian uprising took on mass proportions; it was not inspired by the West, although the West did support it.

History reveals that in the long run, ideas cannot be forced onto a people who do not accept them.

2. The Soviet Union's top leadership, citing the Hungarian government's request for aid, with the support of the leaders of the socialist countries, went to the defense of the system they had imposed on Hungary and sent Soviet troops to Budapest.

The entry of Soviet troops in Budapest and then into the entire country was an interference in Hungarian internal affairs.

The restoration of law and order in the country should have been left to the government and the Hungarian people.

3. Soviet troops carried out the orders of their government and Ministry of Defense; they did not fight on their own initiative.

Soviet officers and soldiers did not reflect on whether their actions were lawful or not.

We were told that troops were extending aid at the request of the Hungarian government and on the basis of the Warsaw Pact and that they were fulfilling their internationalist obligations.

At that time it was not easy to see events clearly.

Political leaders, including Imre Nagy and János Kádár, called the uprising a counter-revolutionary rebellion, called the rebels rioters and counter-revolutionaries, and asked for armed aid.

The cruelties perpetrated against Hungarian party activists, state security personnel, and Soviet soldiers captured in Budapest, Várpalota and a few other towns, as well as the reprisals, terror, and revanchist appeals, reinforced our belief that these were signs and elements of counter-revolution.

Some of our soldiers were also sometimes cruel; they opened fire, accidentally killed civilians, and took food and wine.

Yet despite all this, we did not feel hatred towards the Hungarians, even when we witnessed cruel killings more than once. Our soldiers had also not forgotten that, in 1941, Hungary had attacked the Soviet Union with Germany and that Hungarian soldiers had destroyed our land.

Despite all this, some instances of rebel bravery earned our respect. The command of our troops tried to avoid the mass destruction of the Hungarian civilians. As is well-known, our troops did not break up demonstrations or mass meetings, did not open fire on the protesters, did not bring in the air force against armed units and did not take part in arresting the Hungarian negotiating delegation or deporting Hungarian citizens.

4. Now, four decades on, I view the 1956 events as a historical tragedy.

Short-sighted politicians managed to turn our peoples against each other.

Today Hungary and Russia are following a new path of development. Long years are still necessary to reconcile our peoples.

I hope that the appearance of this book based on individual impressions and personal experiences, along with the other events to commemorate the 40th anniversary of 1956, will contribute to the reconciliation of our peoples and the expansion of cooperation between our countries.

Yevgeny Malashenko
Lieutenant General, Retired

Notes

¹ The points were drafted not by the Petőfi Circle but at the big assembly of the Budapest Construction and Transport Technical University MEFESZ, held on October 22.

² The paper was signed by András Hegedűs on October 27, and on October 28, Andropov sent it to the Soviet Central Committee Presidium.

³ Mainly political prisoners were released from the jails after October 25. Criminals were only released from jails and forced labor camps until October 28. Reports of a wave of armed émigrés are not true.

⁴ In the unsuccessful attack on the Corvin Alley, officers from the Zrínyi Military Academy and the officers ordered to the Academy after the radio appeal, as well as those from the Kecskemét 12th mechanized regiment, were led by Colonel András Márton, commander of the Zrínyi Miklós Military Academy.

⁵ The attack on the Corvin Alley groups was initiated by Soviet troops, but due to great losses of reconnaissance tanks, the attack went wrong. Imre Nagy's prohibition did not reach the commander of the Soviet division involved. Gergely Pongrácz did not take part in the negotiations between Nagy and the leaders of certain rebel groups.

⁶ Imre Nagy was in a prisoner-of-war camp when the Winter Palace was besieged [János M. Rainer].

⁷ The event mentioned by Malashenko, the election of the Revolutionary Defense Committee, did not take place in the Kilián Barracks but at dawn on October 31 in the building of the Defense Ministry. Pál Maléter did not take part at this meeting; he was elected to the Committee in absentia, without his knowledge. Pál Maléter was appointed first deputy to the minister of defense on October 31, major general on November 2 and minister of defense on November 3. Major General Béla Király led the meeting called by the Revolutionary Committee for Public Safety's Temporary Operational Sub-Committee to debate organizational and technical problems concerning the National Guard.

⁸ The organization of Budapest did commence but, by November 4, was not as organized as Malashenko thought. Colonel András Márton was appointed commander of the outer defense ring, but he did not take up his new appointment until November 4.
⁹ The air defense troops were not placed in firing positions around Budapest at this time. Budapest's airspace was already defended by army air defense troops before October 23.
¹⁰ Despite the source quote, the data on the contact between Pál Maléter and Malashenko is inaccurate.
¹¹ There is no basis for assuming Pál Maléter and Béla Király were hostile to each other. The news that Maléter had about Király after November 4 cannot be verified.
¹² The construction battalion soldiers in the Kilián Barracks were not armed. The weapons of the barracks' guards had been taken by the protesters and then rebels on October 23. On October 25, when Pál Maléter arrived at the Kilián Barracks, there were seven or eight weapons in all.
¹³ Gergely Pongrácz was not László Iván Kovács's deputy but on November 1–according to some sources, on November 2–after a commander election he became the commander of the Corvin Alley groups. His predecessor, László Iván Kovács, was elected one of his deputies.
¹⁴ The military dictatorship that Pál Maléter was planning would have sought to fulfill the demands of the revolution.
¹⁵ The 8th mechanized division did not defend the Budapest Party Committee headquarters. On October 30 the 33rd Esztergom tank regiment sent six tanks to help defend the building. A sub-unit of the regiment, mistaking the objective, helped capture the party headquarters.
¹⁶ Malashenko, at the time he wrote down his conversations with the arrested officers, did not recall that, apart from sending a telegram calling on the army to surrender in Pál Maléter's name and without his knowledge, Colonel Miklós Szűcs helped with data on the amount of forces in Budapest and that István Kovács, in his letter to Major Generals Gyula Uszta and Gyula Váradi, called on the armed forces to cease resistance.
¹⁷ The 37th Hungarian infantry regiment did not cross over to the rebels. This regiment took part in active combat against the rebels–often on their own initiative. That is why they received the "Revolutionary Regiment" title from the Kádár government after the revolution.
¹⁸ The anti-tank artillery regiment mentioned by Malashenko did not exist. Of the Hungarian People's Army's two anti-tank artillery regiments, the 36th Kiskunhalasi regiment laid down its arms on October 24 without putting up resistance, while the majority of the 8th Tab independent anti-tank artillery regiment also gave themselves up peacefully on the same day. Soviet tanks

destroyed the six anti-tank cannons taken from the regiment by the local sentry sub-unit. The 5th air defense artillery regiment's barracks in Miskolc was invaded by two Soviet tanks, which destroyed two of the cannons set up in the barracks yard. The Soviets fired on the regiment's 2nd battery, which was in firing positions, without warning, and one soldier was wounded.

[19] Malashenko and Kirov both overstate József Dudás's role in the armed struggle. Before October 27 Dudás did not take part in any revolutionary movement. He first came onto the scene on October 29 in the editorial offices of the *Szabad Nép* newspaper, where he then organized his central base. Dudás's armed group, after being obedient to him at the beginning, soon became independent of him. Thus he did not direct the activities of the armed groups or the subsequently formed National Guard formations. Until November 3 leading rebel circles felt strong hostility toward Dudás. Imre Nagy issued an order for his arrest. This order was carried out by Béla Király, but after he became convinced that the accusations against Dudás were baseless, for example capturing the Foreign Ministry building, he released him. Dudás sought refuge in the Zrínyi Military Academy on November 3, where he was again arrested on orders from Colonel András Márton, then released again for similar reasons.

[20] Major General Gyula Váradi filled the post of president of the Revolutionary Defense Committee. This sitting was not in the Kilián Barracks. The Revolutionary Defense Committee was formed not on October 31 but on October 28, when Imre Nagy broke up the state security services. Béla Király had just started the process of rehabilitation of purged officers. The November 4 aggression prevented this operation.

[21] We have found no documents testifying to these 2000 foreign weapons.

[22] According to the latest sources set out in the introductory essay, the drafting of Operation "Whirlwind" was started on October 31 after the decision by the Soviet Central Committee's Presidium.

Appendices and Maps

Soviet troops deployment in Hungary and their routes to Budapest
October 24, 1956

The Special Army Corps Command (Székesfehérvár)
4th mechanized regiment (Székesfehérvár)

The 17th mechanized guard division (Szombathely)
56th mechanized regiment (Szombathely)
57th mechanized regiment (Győr)
58th mechanized regiment (Körmend)
39th tank regiment
27th heavy tank-assault gun regiment
83rd tank regiment (Hajmáskér)

The 2nd mechanized guard division (Kecskemét)
4th mechanized regiment (Székesfehérvár)
5th mechanized regiment (Kecskemét)
7th mechanized regiment (Szolnok)
37th tank regiment (Sárbogárd)
87th heavy tank-assault gun regiment (Cegléd)

195th fighter air division (Pápa)
1st fighter air regiment

177th bomber air division (Debrecen)
2nd pontoon bridge regiment (Komárom)

33rd mechanized guard division (Timisoara)

128th guard infantry division (Mukachevo)

Soviet troops' operational zones during Operation "Whirlwind" November 4, 1956

United Armed Forces Chief Command (Szolnok)
7th, 31st air defence guard divisions

8th mechanized army command (Debrecen)

38th army command (Székesfehérvár)

Special Army Corps Command (Tököl)

8th mechanized army
11th, 32nd, 35th mechanized divisions
60th air defence artillery division
70th infantry guard division
31st tank guard division

38th army
17th, 27th, 39th mechanized guard divisions
61st air defence artillery division

Special Army Corps
2nd, 33rd mechanized guard divisions
128th infantry guard division

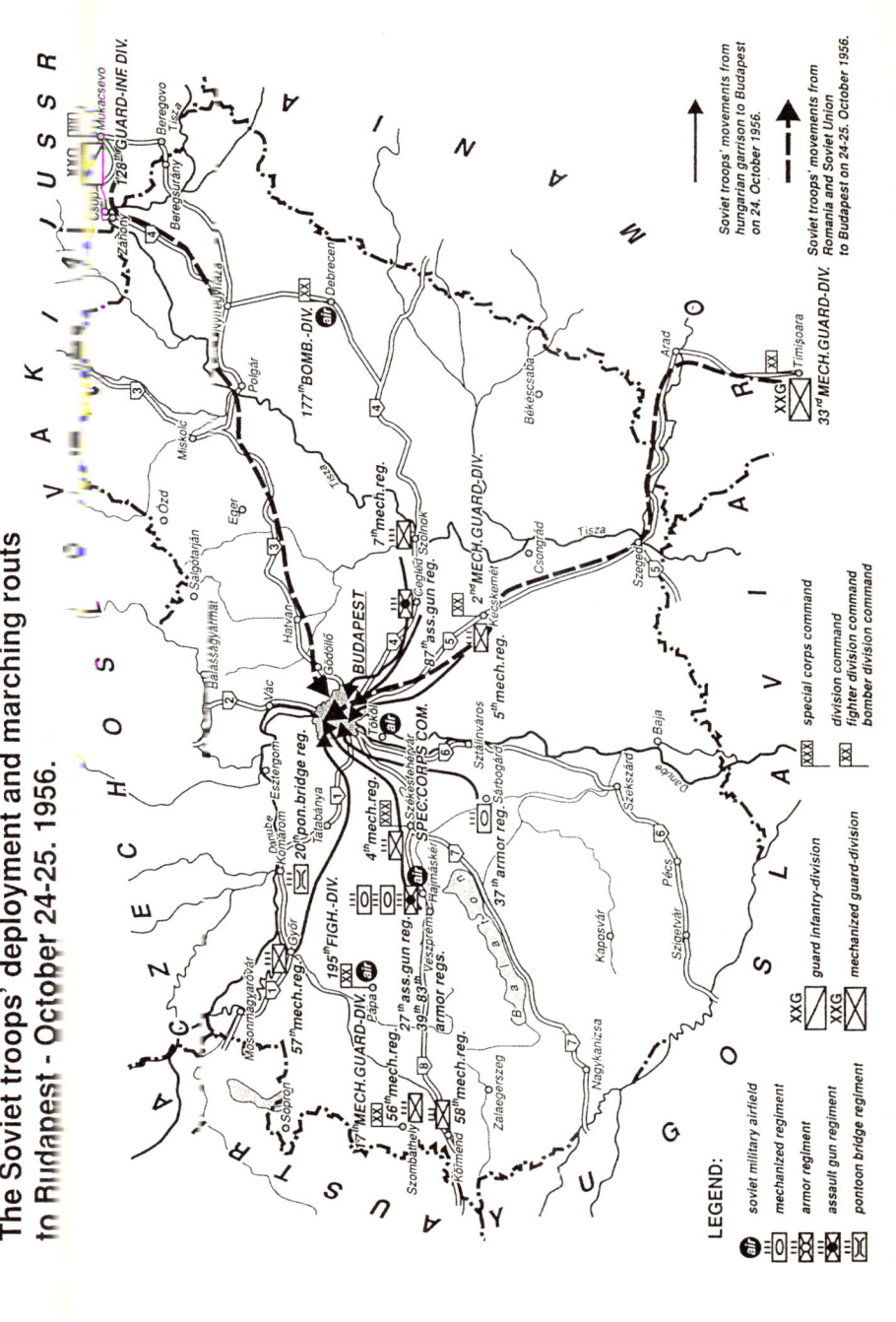

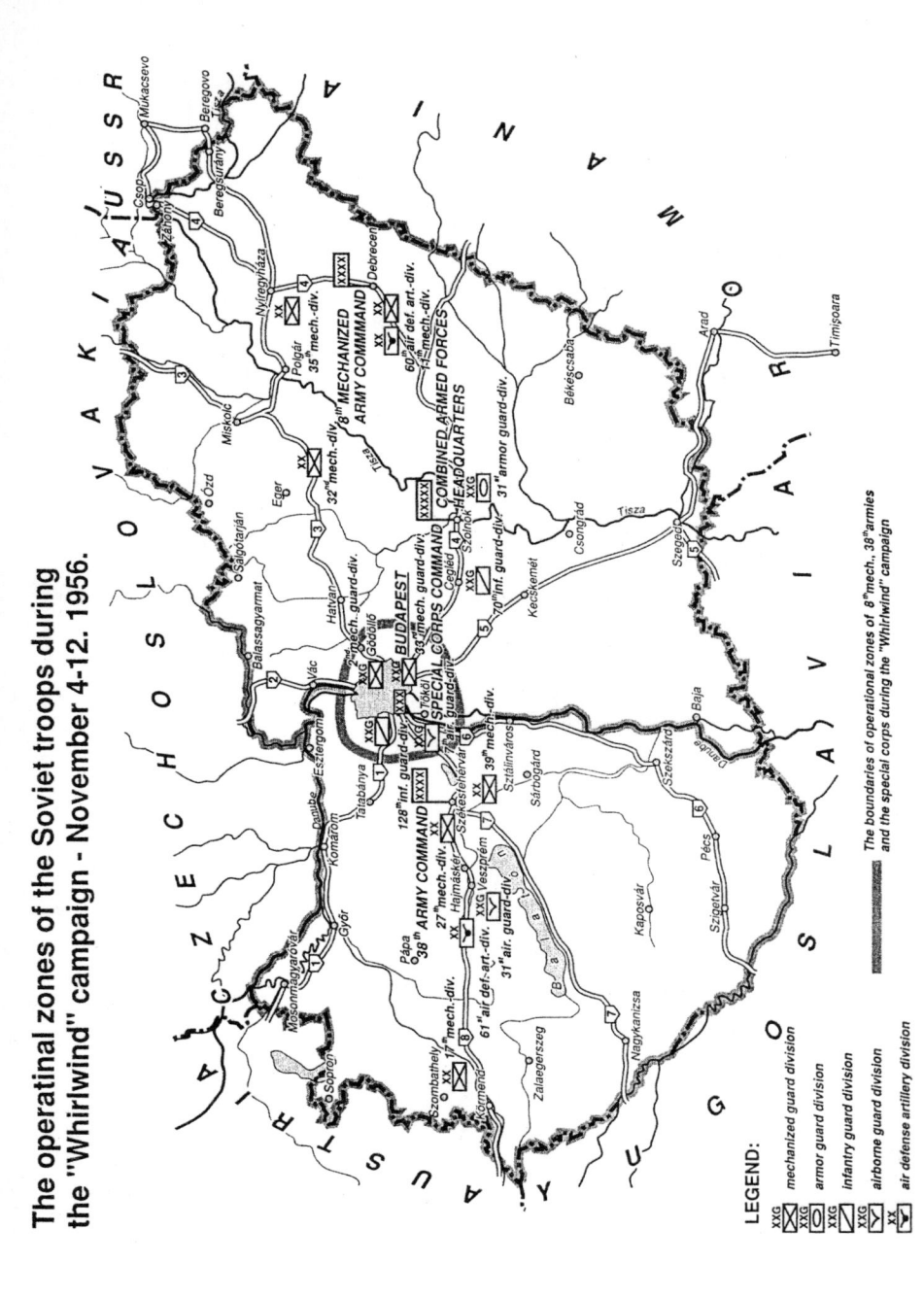

The operational zones of Special corps' troops during the "Whirlwind" campaign - November 4-12. 1956 at Budapest

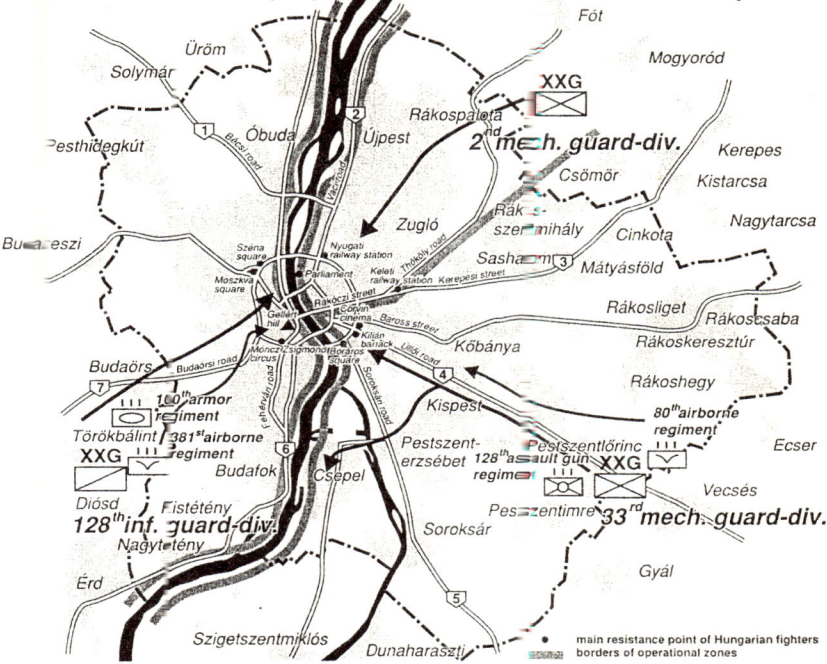

Biographical Notes

Ács, Lajos (1922–1968)–Communist politician, between 1953 and October 1956 a member of the Central Committee and Politburo, secretary of the Central Committee.

Andics, Erzsébet (1902–1986)–Historian, communist politician; between 1954 and 1956 HWP Central Committee member and section chief. From 1950 until 1972 head of department at ELTE, member of the Academy of Sciences.

Andropov, Yuri Vladimirovich (1914–1984)–Soviet politician. From July 1953 adviser to the Soviet Embassy in Budapest, then from July 1954 until March 1957 Soviet ambassador to Hungary. From 1957 Soviet Communist Party Central Committee section chief, from 1961 member of Central Committee, from 1962 until 1967 secretary to Central Committee. Between 1967 and 1982 president of the KGB. From May 1982 secretary to Central Committee, then from November chief secretary. From 1983 president of the Soviet Union's Supreme Council Presidium, head of state.

Antonov, Alexei Innokentevich (1896–1962)–General of the Army, from 1955 until his death chief of staff of the Warsaw Pact United Armed Forces.

Apró, Antal (1913–1994)–Communist politician. In 1956 deputy president of the Council of Ministers, founding member of the Hungarian Revolutionary Worker-Peasant Government, deputy prime minister until 1971.

Babadjanyan, Amazasp Hachaturovich (1906–1977)–Marshal of Soviet armored forces, of Azerbaijani nationality. From 1950 to 1959 army commander in the rank of colonel-general, deputy commander of the Carpathian Military District. From November 1, 1956, was active in Hungary at the head of the 8th mechanized army.

Babyak (?)–Soviet lieutenant.

Bajkov, Vladimir Sergeyevich (1922–)–In 1956 on the staff of the Soviet Central Committee's foreign section, from November 3 Kádár's permanent escort, then adviser to the Soviet Embassy in Budapest.

Bata, István (1910–1982)–Communist politician, colonel-general, HWP Politburo substitute member.

Batov, Pavel Ivanovich (1897–1985)–General of the Army. Served in the Red Army from 1918, from 1936 to 1937 a military adviser in Spain, army commander in World War II, between 1955 and 1958 commander of the Carpathian Military District.

Bebrits, Lajos (1891–1963)–Railway worker, communist politician, transport and communications minister between 1949 and 1956. From May 1957 the Hungarian ambassador to Sweden.

Berei, Andor (1900–1979)–Economist, husband of Erzsébet Andics. From 1954 until the end of October 1956, president of the National Planning Office.

Bibó, István (1911–1979)–Philosopher, sociologist, university lecturer. In 1956 representative of the National Peasant Party/Petőfi Party, between November 2 and 4 minister of state in Imre Nagy's government. In 1957 was arrested, in 1958 sentenced to life imprisonment. Released in 1963. Librarian at the Central Statistical Office until his retirement in 1971.

Bichan (?)–Colonel, Soviet tank regiment commander.

Bobrosky, Alexander Andreyevich (1922–1956)–Soviet captain.

Bogár, János (1934–1956)–Miner, soldier.

Bognár, József (1917–1996)–Economist, university lecturer. Smallholders Party politician. Between October 26 and 31, 1956, deputy prime minister in the Imre Nagy government.

Bohlen, Charles–U.S. ambassador to Moscow in 1956.

Borishenko (?)–Soviet lieutenant.

Boriskin, A.–Brigadier general, held leading position in the Russian Federation's military supreme prosecutor's office.

Biographical Notes 299

Bulganyin, Nikolai Alexandrovich (1895–1975)–Soviet politician, marshal. Between 1953 and 1955 minister of defense, from 1955 until 1958 prime minister. From 1948 until 1958 member of the Soviet Central Committee Presidium.

Burmistov, Y.V.–Soviet soldier.

Csergő, János (1920–1980)–Communist politician, from 1954 until October 31, 1956, then from 1957 until 1963 metal and engineering industries minister.

Czottner, Sándor (1903–1980)–Communist politician. From 1950 until October 31, 1956, mining and energy minister. From 1957 until his retirement in 1963 minister of heavy industry.

Darvas, József (1912–1973)–Writer, public personality. After 1945 president of the National Peasant Party, president of the Writers Alliance.

Davidov (*)–Chief of staff of the 33rd mechanized division.

Dobi, István (1898–1968)–Smallholders Party politician, from 1952 until 1967 president of the Presidential Council.

Dobrunov, Grigoru Timofeyevich (1912–)–Soviet army colonel, served in the army since 1939. Company and battalion commander in the war. After the war battalion and regiment commander. In October–November 1956 commander of the Special Corps 2nd army's independent mechanized reconnaissance battalion. In December 1956 was awarded title Hero of the Soviet Union. From 1962 colonel, retired.

Dögei, Imre (1912–1964)–Member of HWP Central Leadership, then of HSWP Temporary Central Committee, agricultural minister to the Hungarian Revolutionary Worker-Peasant Party.

Dogopolov (?)–Soviet captain.

Donáth, Ferenc (1913–1986)–Communist politician, after 1945 state secretary for agriculture, section leader of the HWP Central Leadership, member of Central Leadership since 1945. At the beginning of 1951 was arrested on trumped-up charges, was in prison until 1954. After his release deputy director of the Hungarian Academy of Sciences Economic Sciences Institute. From October 24, 1956, again member of HWP Central Leadership, worked directly with Imre Nagy. On November 4, fled to the Yugoslav Embassy, then was deported to Romania. In April 1957 arrested, in 1958 was sentenced to 12 years at the Imre Nagy trial. Released in 1960.

Donchenko, L.A.–Soviet guard major.

Dudás, József (1914–1957)–Engineer, participant in the anti-fascist resistance movement, in 1944 member of delegate on cease-fire negotiations. After 1945 was politically persecuted. In 1956 leader of the Hungarian National Revolutionary Committee. In 1957 sentenced to death and executed.

Dulles, John Foster (1888–1959)–Between 1953 and 1959 the U.S. secretary of state.

Eden, Sir Robert Anthony (1897–1977)–British Conservative politician, foreign minister between 1951 and 1955, prime minister from 1955 until 1956. Chief architect of the attack on Egypt.

Egri, Gyula (1923–1972)–Communist politician. Member of HWP Central Leadership from 1954, secretary of Central Leadership in 1955. From November 1956 until March 1957 lived in the Soviet Union. First county secretary from 1957.

Erdei, Ferenc (1910–1971)–Sociologist, Peasant Party politician. In 1955–1956 deputy president of the Council of Ministers, leader of the Tököl delegation. Arrested with Maléter and then released a few weeks later. Later general secretary of the Patriotic People's Front, secretary of the Hungarian Academy of Sciences.

Erdélyi, Károly (1928–1971)–Diplomat. In 1956 adviser to the Hungarian Embassy in Moscow, then worked on the staff of the Foreign Affairs Section of the HSWP Central Committee, later its chief. Personal Russian interpreter and adviser to János Kádár.

Farkas, Ferenc (1903–1966)–Peasant Party politician. On October 31, 1956 elected general secretary of the party. Minister of state in Imre Nagy's last government.

Farkas, István (1935–1956)–Soldier.

Farkas, Mihály (1904–1965)–Communist politician, member of the HWP Central Leadership, secretary of the Central Leadership. From 1948 until 1953 minister of defense. In 1955 he was relieved from the highest leadership, in 1956 he was expelled from the party. In 1957 he was sentenced to 16 years imprisonment for breaking the law; in 1961 he was pardoned.

Fedorov (?)–Soviet major.

Firyubin, Nikolai Pavlovich (1908–1983)–Between 1955 and 1957 the Soviet ambassador to Belgrade, then deputy foreign minister.

Földes, László (1914–)–Communist politician.

Fomin, Vitali Ivanovich (1925–)–Soviet captain, instructor to the Special Corps political section. Retired colonel and military historian.

Furseva, Yekaterina Alexseyevna (1910–1974)–Between 1954 and 1957 Moscow first secretary to the Soviet CP, 1951–1961 secretary to Soviet Central Committee, then from 1960 cultural minister.

Gáspár, Sándor (1897–1982)–Communist politician, trade union leader. Between 1945 and 1956 member of Hungarian Communist Party and HWP Central Leadership.

Gerő, Ernő (1898–1980)–Communist politician; in November 1944 he returned home from Moscow. Member of the Hungarian CP and then of HWP Central Leadership and Central Committee. Minister for transport, finance, then minister of state until 1952, then until July 30, 1956, deputy prime minister. From July 18, until October 25, 1956, first secretary of the HWP Central Leadership. On October 28, fled to Soviet Union, where he stayed until 1960. In 1962 he was expelled from the party.

Golikov, Philip Ivanovich (1900–?)–General of the Army. Between 1950 and 1956 commander of the Soviet mechanized army stationed in Romania, from 1961 marshal of Soviet Union.

Gomulka, Wladislav (1905–1982)–Polish politician. Between 1956 and 1970 the first secretary of the Polish CP.

Göncz, Árpád (1922–)–Writer, translator. In 1944 took part in the anti-fascist armed resistance in the Táncsics battalion. In 1945 member of the Independent Smallholders Party, managing editor of the paper Nemzedék (Generation). In 1948–49 a laborer, then a welder and locksmith. In 1956 during the revolution he worked in the Peasant Alliance. In 1958 he was a second-degree defendant in the Bibó trial and sentenced to life. In 1963 he was freed with the amnesty. In 1990 he was an

MP, president of the Parliament, then he became the president of the Hungarian Republic.

Gorbunov, N. A.–Colonel, commander of the 128th infantry division.

Grachov, Pavel Sergeyevich (1948–)–Graduated at the Riazan paratroop military college in 1969, of the Frunze Military Academy in 1981 and the General Staff Academy in 1990. In 1982–82 paratroop regiment commander in Afghanistan. Hero of the Soviet Union. In 1985–1988 paratroop division commander. In 1990 commander and colonel-general of paratroops. During the coup d'etat attempt in August 1991 he played a wait-and-see game with his paratroops, then refused the order to take the "White House." From May 1992 until June 1996 minister of defense, general of the Army.

Grebennyik, Kuzmin Yevdokimovich (1900–1974)–Served in the Red Army since 1919. Graduated at a high-grade border guard officer school. Battalion and regiment commander in the army. During the war infantry corps commander. After the war until 1961, until his retirement served as a lieutenant general in the interior staff on the border guard services. In October–November 1956 he was under Serov in Hungary; on November 4 he was Budapest city commander as a brigadier general.

Gyenes, Antal (1920–1996)–Communist politician, between 1946 and 1949 president of NÉKOSZ (National Alliance of People's Colleges), then its general secretary. From October 27, until November 2, 1956, minister for collecting [agricultural] surplus in Imre Nagy's government. From November 1956 until July 1957 member of HSWP Central Committee. From 1957 worked on staff at the Hungarian Academy of Sciences Economic Sciences Institute.

Habsburg, Ottó (1912–) Head of the Habsburg family, politician and writer. Member of the Pan-European Union from 1936, between 1940 and 1944 Washington representative. From 1957 until 1973 vice president of Pan-European Union, then its president from 1973.

Hammarskjöld, Dag Halmar (1905–1961)–Swedish head of state, from 1953 secretary general of the UN, died in an an air crash in 1961.

Haraszti, Sándor (1897–1982)–From 1948 until 1951 deputy section leader in the party apparatus. Sentenced to death in show trial in 1951. The sentence was not carried out; he was released in 1954. One of the leading figures in the Imre Nagy group. On November 4, 1956, he fled to Yugoslav Embassy, then was deported to Romania. In 1957 was arrested, sentenced to eight years in 1958, in 1960 released with amnesty.

Hazai, Jenő (1921–) Between 1950 and 1957 deputy head of the main political section of the Hungarian People s Army, then head of the main section, major general.

Hegedűs, András (1922–)–Communist politician, sociologist. In 1956 president of Council of Ministers, member of HWP Politburo. On October 28, 1956, fled to Soviet Union, came home in 1958.

Hidas, István (1918–)–Communist politician, from October 1954 until October 1956 vice president of Council of Ministers, a member of the HWP Politburo.

Horváth, Imre (1901–1958)–Mechanic, fighter in the workers' movement. In 1919 worked in the political police during the Hungarian Soviet Republic. Interned after the Soviet Republic fell, released in 1920, in 1921 arrested again and sentenced to 10 years of penal servitude. In an exchange of prisoners, got to the Soviet Union where he completed mechanics' college, and in 1932 completed a mechanical engineering degree. In 1933 he returned home on an illegal mission and was arrested and sentenced to 10 years. In 1944 he was taken from Szeged Csillag Prison and interned in Dachau. From 1946 he was a diplomat; from November 4, 1956, until his death he was foreign minister.

Horváth, Mihály (1914–1995)– Major general, from November 1950 was chief of logistical planning for the main section of the General Staff.

Iván Kovacs, László (1930–1957)–Haulageman, then mine ambulance man. On October 23 took part in the siege of the Radio. From October 24 fought in the Corvin Cinema. From October 25 recognized leader of the Corvin Cinema fighters. From November 1, according to other sources from the 2nd, deputy commander in chief. Arrested on March 12, 1957, sentenced to death and executed on December 30, 1957.

Jánosi, Ferenc (1916–1968)–Calvinist priest, Russian prisoner of war, fighter in the anti-fascist resistance movement. Chief of educational section in the new democratic Hungarian army, from 1948 deputy chief of main political section of the Ministry of Defense. During 1954–1955 general secretary to the Patriotic People's Front National Council. Son-in-law of Imre Nagy, with whom he was interned in Romania. In 1958 sentenced to prison for eight years, released with amnesty in 1960.

Janza, Károly (1914–)–Professional officer, colonel from 1949, major general in 1950 and lieutenant general in 1952. Deputy chief of the Logistical Services, then its chief. From October 26 to 31, 1956, minister of defense.

Kádár, János (1912–1989)–From July 1956 secretary, from 25 October 1956 first secretary of the HWP Central Committee. President of the Hungarian Revolutionary Worker-Peasent Government. First secretary of the HSWP.

Kaganovich, Lazar Moseyevich (1893–1991)–Soviet politician, deputy prime minister, member of Soviet Central Committee.

Kalistov (?)–One of Serov's staff in Budapest in October–November 1956.

Kállai, Gyula (1910–1996)–Communist politician; from 1945 member of Hungarian CP and HWP Central Committee. In 1951 tried on trumped-up charges, released in 1954, again Central Leadership member from July 1954.

Kána, Lőrinc (1914–)–Laborer since 1949, professional army officer, major general. From 1951 until 1955 chief of National Air Defense Command. From 1955 commander of air defense artillery division.

Kardelj, Edvard (1910–1979)–Yugoslav politician of Slovenian origin. Next to Tito he was the second figure in the party leadership, the party's leading ideologist.

Karmisin, Dimitri Dimitrevich (1926–1956)–Soviet captain.

Karpov, J. Y.–Soviet lieutenant.

Kelemen, Gyula (1897–1973)–Social Democratic Party politician. In 1948 sentenced to life in a show trial. In 1956 general secretary of the newly formed SDP in 1956. On November 3 and 4, minister of state in Imre Nagy's government.

Kéthly, Anna (1896–1976)–Social Democratic Party politician, in 1956 president of SDP, minister of state in Imre Nagy's government, after 1956 president of the Hungarian Revolutionary Council in exile.

Khrushchev, Nikita Sergeyevich (1894–1971)–Soviet politician. After Stalin's death, from September 1953 first secretary of the Soviet Central Committee, from 1958 until 1964 president of the Council of Ministers.

Kicska, János–Lieutenant.

Király, Béla (1912–)–Professional army officer, graduated from Ludovika Academy in 1935. 1940–42 at the Honvéd [General Staff] Academy, 1942–1945 general staff officer. In 1945 went over to the Soviets with his brigade. Escaped from Soviet prisoner-of-war camp. In 1946–1947 chief of staff of 1st division. In 1948–1949 the deputy commander of the army infantry, then in 1949–1950 the commander. In 1950 major general and the founding commander of the Zrínyi Military Academy. In 1951 he was sentenced to death on the trumped-up charge of conspiring against the state, which was then commuted to life imprisonment. In 1956 he was released but not rehabilitated. Commander in chief of the National Guard. Continued fight against the Soviet aggressors. On November 11, directed the combat at the town of Nagykovácsi (northwest of Budapest). In late November emigrated first to Austria, then to the United States. He returned home in 1989. Promoted to colonel-general in 1990. In 1990–1994 served as member of Parliament.

Kirichenko, A. I.–Soviet politician, in 1956 member of the Soviet Central Committee Presidium. First secretary of the Ukrainian Communist Party.

Kis, Árpád (1918–1970)–Engineer, between 1950 and 1954 minister of light industry, then until October 23, 1956, chemical and energy minister. From 1956 until his death member of HSWP Central Committee.

Kiss, Károly (1903–1983)–Communist politician, member of HWP and then HSWP Politburo. Between 1946 and 1957 president of the party's Central Supervisory Committee. From February 1957 secretary of the HSWP Central Committee.

Kiss, Lajos–Sándor Sziklai's father-in-law.

Kő, András–Historian, fact-finder on the Kossuth Square "Bloody Thursday" on October 25, 1956.

Köböl, József (1909–)–Communist politician, between 1948 and 1956 member of HWP Central Leadership, on October 24, 1956, elected member of Politburo.

Kochnyev, S. T.–Soviet major.

Kohanovich, E. N.–Soviet colonel.

Koltai, Vilmos–Colonel, the Kossuth Artillery School commander.

Kőműves, József–Social Democratic Party politician.

Kónya, Albert (1917–1988)–Physicist, member of the Hungarian Academy of Sciences. From July 30 until October 31, 1956, minister of education, from 1957 lecturer at the Budapest Polytechnical University.

Konyev, Ivan Stepanovich (1897–1973)–Marshal of Soviet Union. From May 1955 until 1960 commander in chief of the Warsaw Pact United Armed Forces.

Kopácsi, Sándor (1922–)–After 1945 police officer. From 1952 until 1956 police colonel, Budapest police chief, follower of Imre Nagy, one of the organizers of the National Guard, member of Revolutionary Defense Committee. In 1958 sentenced to life imprisonment in the Imre Nagy trial, released with amnesty in 1963.

Korotkov (?)–Worked with Serov in October–November 1956.

Korzenyevich–Major general, Soviet military adviser to the Hungarian army headquarters.

Kossa, István (1904–1965)–Communist politician, member of the HSWP Central Committee, on November 4, 1956, founding member of Hungarian Revolutionary Worker-Peasant Government, minister of finance. Later transport and communications minister.

Kovács, Béla (1908–1959)–Smallholders Party politician. In 1945–1947 general secretary of Independent Smallholders Party, minister of agriculture, then after spending eight years in prison in the Soviet Union, from October 26 until 31, 1956, agriculture minister in the Imre Nagy government, minister of state from November 3 to 4, 1956.

Kovács, István (1911–)–Communist politician, member of the HWP Politburo, from November 1955 secretary to the Central Leadership. From 1956 until 1958 lived in the Soviet Union.

Kovács, István (1917–)–Clerk, professional army officer from 1948, major general. In 1948–1951 student at the Frunze Military Academy. From November 1, 1951, chief of main operational section of the General Staff. From October 31, until November 4, 1956, chief of General Staff of the Hungarian People's Army. On November 3, 1956, the KGB arrested him at Tököl as one of the members of the Hungarian negotiation delegation, in 1958 sentenced to six years, released on April 4, 1960.

Kóvágó, Sándor–lieutenant colonel, commander of Budapest guard battalion in 1956.

Kovalenko (?)–Soviet lieutenant colonel.

Kozlov, Frol Romanovich (1908–)–Soviet politician, in 1956 secretary to the Soviet Central Committee.

Krivoseyev, Anton Vasiliyevich (1909–)–Brigadier general, served in Soviet Army since 1931. Graduated from Armored School. During the war tank battalion and regiment commander. After the war mechanized division commander. In 1955–1956 commander of the Special Corps 17th mechanized division, then until his retirement in 1967 deputy commander of the tank army.

Kromsov (?)–Soviet colonel, military adviser in the Hungarian People's Army.

Kuzmin, Sergei Yevdokimovich (1910–1989)–Colonel, the Special Corps artillery commander. From 1969 brigadier general, then retired.

Kuzminov, Mikhail Yakovlevich (1910–1988)–Guard colonel, Hero of the Soviet Union, in 1955–56 city commander of Budapest subordinate to Lieutenant General Lashchenko. Retired in 1961.

Kuznyecov (?)–Soviet colonel.

Kuznyecov, Vasili Nikolaiovich–Soviet politician, engineer, diplomat. In 1956–1957 first deputy to the foreign minister, Soviet delegate at the UN General Assembly's XI session.

Lashchenko, Piotr Nikolaiovich (1910–1992)–General of the Army. Served in the Soviet army since 1930. In 1955–1956 commander of the Special Corps station in Hungary in the rank of lieutenant general.

Lassó, Károly–Police captain.

Lebedev, Sergei Vladimirovich (1908–1965)–Commander of the Special Corps 2nd mechanized division. Served in the Soviet Army since 1928. Fought as a tank sub-unit and unit commander in the war. After the war regiment and then division commander. After 1957 deputy army commander, retired in 1959.

Lipinsky (?)–Soviet colonel. Commander of the 2nd mechanized division's tank regiment.

Lipis (?)–Soviet colonel.

Liu Tsao-chi (1898–1969)–Chinese politician, member of the permanent committee of the Chinese Politburo. In 1968, at the time of the Cultural Revolution, was arrested on trumped-up charges and died in prison.

Losonczy, Géza (1917–1957)–Journalist, senior correspondent on the newspaper *Magyar Nemzet* (Hungarian Nation), member of the inner opposition circle around Imre Nagy, minister of state in Imre Nagy's government. Interned in Romania, then while his case was being reviewed in Budapest, he went on hunger strike and died.

Lukács, György (1885–1971)–Philosopher, university lecturer, member of Hungarian Academy of Sciences. In 1956 higher education minister in the Imre Nagy government, member of the HSWP Temporary Executive Committee, interned with Imre Nagy in Romania, returned home in 1957.

Lukács, Matvey–Private in the 32nd mechanized division, Hungarian in origin, born in the Carpathians. On November 3, at 19 hours he deserted as his formation crossed the border at Békéscsaba. As a result he was expelled from Komsomol, court-martialled and executed.

Madarász, Ferenc (1921–1967)–Major general, from May 1, 1949, professional army officer in the Hungarian People's Army. During October–November 1956 commander of the National Air Defense Command.

Malenkov, Georgi Maxsimilianovich (1902–1989)–Soviet politician. From 1946 until 1957 member of the Soviet Central Committee Presidium. Between 1953 and 1955 president of the Soviet Union's Council of Ministers. In June 1957 expelled from the Soviet Central Committee and the Presidium for party disciplinary reasons.

Maléter, Pál (1917–1958)–Professional army officer, in November 1956 defense minister in Imre Nagy's government, major general. In the Imre Nagy trial he was sentenced to death, executed on June 16, 1958.

Malin, Vladimir Nikiforovich–From the Khrushchev era until 1956 leader of the Main Section in the Soviet Central Committee's apparatus.

Malinyin, Mikhail Sergeyevich (1899–1960)–General of the Army. From 1919 soldier in the Soviet Red Army. In 1933 graduated from Frunze Military Academy. As a chief of staff of the higher units, took part in the Russo–Finnish War. During World War II fought in the battles of Moscow, Stalingrad and Kursk and was brought into Berlin. From 1952 until his death first deputy to the chief of General Staff of the Soviet Armed Forces.

Mamsurov, Kadzi U. D. (1903–1968)–Soviet lieutenant general of Ossetic nationality, commander of the 38th field army.

Marity, László (1931–1956)–Young person from Budakeszi who was shot by Sándor Sziklai.

Marosán, György (1908–1992)–Social Democratic, then communist politician. From July 1956 the vice president of the Council of Ministers, on November 4, 1956, founding member of the Hungarian Revolutionary Worker-Peasant Government, then minister of state. Between 1957 and 1959 first secretary of the Budapest Party Committee.

Marosy, Ferenc (1893–1986)–Diplomat, in 1920 started his career in the foreign office. Worked in Geneva at the League of Nations, then in Budapest at the Foreign Ministry. Served in the embassies in London, Bucharest and Madrid. On the eve of World War II, was consul in Cairo and then in Zagreb. In 1943–1944 he represented Hungary in Finland. Lived in Madrid from 1945. From 1949 until 1969 led the Madrid Hungarian Royal Consul–represented the Hungarian National Committee which sat in New York and its leading figures Tibor Eckhardt and György Bakách-Bessenyei.

Márton, András–colonel, commander of the Zrínyi Military Academy in 1956, sentenced to 10 years in 1958.

Medvedev, Igor Nikolaievich–in 1956 leader of the Soviet Central Committee's Foreign Affairs Section.

Mekis, József (1910–1984)–Communist politician. From 1948 until 1956 member of HWP Central Leadership.

Miklós Béla, Dálnoki (1890–1948)–professional soldier, colonel-general. From August 1, 1944, commander of the 1st Hungarian Army, on October 15 went over to the 4th Ukrainian Front command. From December 22, 1944, until November 15, 1945, prime minister of the Provisional National Government.

Mikno (?)–Soviet lieutenant.

Mikoyan, Anastas Ivanovich (1895–1978)–Member of the Soviet Central Committee's presidium, vice president of the Soviet Union's Council of Ministers. From 1946 president of the Supreme Council's Presidium.

Mikunovich, Velko (1916–1983)–Yugoslav politician, diplomat. Between March 1956 and October 1958 ambassador to Moscow.

Mindszenty, József (1892–1975)–Catholic cardinal, archbishop of Esztergom from 1945, Hungary's Prince Primate. Sentenced to life in a show trial in 1948. Released on October 31, 1956. On November 4, took refuge in the U.S. Embassy in Budapest, where he lived until 1971, then went abroad.

Molnár, Erik (1894–1966)–Lawyer, historian, philosopher. Between 1954 and 1956 minister of justice.

Molotov, Vyacheslav Mikhailovich (1890–1986)–Soviet politician. From 1939 until 1949, then between 1953 and 1956 foreign affairs commissar and foreign minister.

Münnich, Ferenc (1886–1967)–Communist politician. Ambassador to Belgrade in 1956, interior minister in the Imre Nagy government. After November 4, 1956, founding member of the Hungarian Revolutionary Worker-Peasant Government, minister of the armed forces.

Munos Grandes, Augustin (1896–1970)–Spanish general. During World War II, between 1941 and 1942 commander of the voluntary Spanish "Blue" division at the Eastern Front. In 1951–1957 Franco's defense minister, then between 1962 and 1967 deputy prime minister.

Nagy, Imre (1896–1958)–Communist politician; between 1953 and 1955 and October 24 and November 4, 1956, prime minister. Member of the HWP Politburo, member of the HSWP Temporary Executive Committee. Interned in Romania, then sentenced to death on June 16, 1958, and executed.

Nagy, Jenő Lambert (1931–)–Fact-finder, researcher on the October 25, 1956, Kossuth Square "Bloody Thursday" events.

Nagy, Mrs. József (1921–)–Communist politician. Light industry minister from September 1955 until October 31, 1956, then again from December 1956 until 1971.

Nezvál, Ferenc (1909–1987)–Communist politician, from 1956 until 1966 minister of justice.

Nikifor, N. S.–Soviet lieutenant colonel.

Nógrádi, Sándor (1894–1971)–Communist politician. Between 1949 and 1956 Chief of main political section in the People's Army, first deputy to the Minister of Defense, colonel. Between November 1956 and April 1957 section leader in party headquarters, then ambassador. President of the HSWP Central Supervisory Committee.

Nonn, György (1918–)–Communist politician. Between 1946 and 1956 member of Hungarian CP and HWP Central Leadership.

Nyers, Rezső (1923–)–Printer, politician, economist. From 1940 member of Social Democratic Party, subsequently leading member of the Communist Party.

Obaturov, Gennady Ivanovich (1915–1996)–Brigadier general, commander of the 33rd mechanized division in 1956. Soldier since 1930, military district commander after 1956, commander of Frunze Military Academy, deputy inspector general of tank and armored troops, General of the Army. Retired in 1973.

Orbán, Miklós–State security colonel, commander of the Interior Ministry State Security Authority's interior law-enforcement troops.

Ostapenko, Ilya–Soviet captain, Budapest truce bearer. Propaganda spread the false story that he was shot by Germans after carrying out his duties. The truth is that he lost his life on the way back to his post by his own side's trench mortar.

Östör, János–Police captain.

Ostoros, Dr. Gyula–Regional politician of Budakeszi in 1956.

Pálfy, György (1909–1949)–Professional army officer, graduated from the Ludovika Academy in 1932 as a lieutenant, in 1939 graduated from General Staff Academy. In 1939 left the army, member of Hungarian CP since 1942. After 1945 colonel, leader of the Ministry of Defense's military political section. Lieutenant general in 1948, inspector general of Hungarian Army, sentenced to death and executed in show trial in 1949.

Pavoli, M.J.–Major general on the staff of the Soviet Armed Forces headquarters.

Pervukhin, Mikhail Georgiyevich (1904–1978)–Soviet politician. Between 1952 and 1957 member of the Soviet Central Committee, first deputy to the prime minister.

Petrochenko (?)–Soviet captain.

Petrov, Vladimir Ivanovich–Soviet lieutenant colonel.

Pidliteychuk, P.S.–Soviet private.

Pineau, Christian–French foreign minister in 1956.

Piros, László (1917–)–Communist politician, major general, commander of the ÁVH border guard. In 1953–1954 first deputy interior minister, leader of the ÁVH, interior minister until October 24, 1956.

Pongrácz, Gergely (1932–)–Born in Gherla (Szamosújvár) in Romania. After the war he moved with his parents to Mátészalka and then to Soroksár. Before November 1956, he was an agronomist. From October 25, fought in Corvin Alley. On November 1–according to some sources, on November 2–elected commander in chief of the Corvin rebels. They held out until November 10 at dawn and then retreated. Left the country on November 28, 1956. Lived first in Spain and then in the United States. He returned home in 1990.

Pospyelov, Piotr Nikolayevich (1898–1979)–Soviet politician, secretary to Soviet Central Committee until 1961.

Pronykin (?)–Soviet lieutenant.

Rajk, László (1909–1949)–Communist politician, sentenced to death in a show trial in 1949 and executed.

Rajk, Mrs. László, née **Földi, Júlia** (1914–1981)–Widow of Rajk who was executed in 1949, active participant in opposition circle around Imre Nagy. Interned with Imre Nagy in Romania, returned home in 1958.

Rákosi, Mátyás (1892–1971)–Until 18 July 1956 first secretary of the HWP. After he had been relieved from this function by the central committee of the party, he left the country to live in the Soviet Union until his death. In 1962 he was expelled from the HSWP.

Rámiás, Pál–Lieutenant.

Rankovich, Alexander Leka (1909–1983)–Yugoslav politician of Serb origin. Interior minister from 1948 until 1953, chief of the intelligence service. Deputy prime minister from 1953 until 1963. President of the republic from 1963 until 1966. Was relieved of all his posts in 1966 and then expelled from the party.

Révai, József (1898–1959)–Communist politician, ideologist. From July to October 1956 member of Politburo. From end of October 1956 until April 1957 lived in the Soviet Union.

Ribnyánszki, Miklós–Minister in the Imre Nagy government.

Rónai, Sándor (1892–1965)–Social Democrat, Hungarian communist politician.

Rukavsev, A. A.–Soviet colonel.

Ryabov, P. M.–Major general, commander of the parachute division.

Saburov, M. Z. (1900–1977)–Soviet politician between 1952 and 1957, member of the Soviet Central Committee presidium, deputy prime minister.

Saluhin, A. V.–Soviet guard major.

Sbitnyev (?)–Soviet colonel.

Sepilov, D. T. (1905–)–Soviet politician. Between June 1956 and February 1957 foreign minister. Secretary to the Soviet Central Committee, member of the Presidium. He was relieved of his post for party disciplinary reasons at the 1957 June plenum and expelled from the Central Committee. Expelled from party in 1962. In 1976 his membership was renewed.

Serov, Ivan Alexandrovich (1905–1990)–From 1925 until 1928 student at the Leningrad Military Technical College. Party member from 1926. Between 1928 and 1935 served in the Red Army in various commander positions. In 1935 started his studies at the Kubishev Military Engineering Academy, which he finished in 1939. Member of the Ukrainian Communist (Bolshevik) Party Central Committee and Politburo. At this time came into close contact with Khrushchev, who was the Ukrainian Party's first secretary. When Khrushchev came to power and became the Soviet CP's leading figure, his main confidante was Serov. In 1941 he was deputy to Beria, the Soviet state security commissar. Between 1941–1945 he was deputy internal affairs commissar. He directed the deportation of the Chechens, Ingush, Kalmuk and Crimean Tartars in 1944. In 1945 adviser to the Polish government's State Security Ministry. Between 1945 and 1947 deputy commander in chief for the Soviet Military Administration in Germany, from 1954 until 1958 president of the KGB. In October–November 1956 he directed the state security services in Hungary and as a result was awarded with the Kutuzov order in December 1956. From Tito's and Khrushchev's negotiations in Brioni we know that the Soviet leadership's conception was that in Hungary a situation had to be created in which Imre Nagy was faced with chaos and disturbances and could not see how to go forward. The aim was that there should be no government before the Soviet intervention, and that Imre Nagy should resign. Serov worked to this end; he was in Budapest by October 25 on personal orders and with personal powers from Khrushchev. From December 1958 until the end of 1962, he led the Armed Forces State Reconnaissance Administration (GRU). At the beginning of 1963, one of the members of his staff, Colonel O.V. Penkovsky was accused of being an Anglo–American spy; this also meant the fall of Serov. He was relieved of his post, his rank was demoted to brigadier general and his "Hero of the Soviet Union" medal was taken away from him. From then on he worked as an adviser on higher educational questions for the commander of Turkestan, then the Volga Military District. In April 1965 he was expelled from the party and sent into retirement by the Soviet Central Committee Party Supervisory Committee for his lack of political vigilance, the mistakes he made in selecting GRU cadres and the great infringement of socialism he had shown in the NKVD–KGB, as well as the abuses he perpetrated in Germany.

From this time onwards he spent a lot of his time in his dacha near Moscow and had a pretty unpleasant time during the Brezhnev era. As a fallen leading party commissar, he was under constant surveillance. After a long and grave illness, he died of sclerosis.

Shchelbanyin, G. A. (1905–1962)–Major general, chief of staff Special Corps. Served in the Red Army since 1922. Retired in 1958.

Skripko, I. I.–Colonel chief reconnaissance officer with the Special Corps.

Sladkevich–Member of Serov's staff, October–November 1956.

Sobolyev, A. A.–The Soviet Union's UN delegate at the November 5, 1956, extraordinary sitting.

Sokolov, V. Y.–Soviet captain, interpreter.

Sokolovsky, V. D. (1897–1968)–Marshal of the Soviet Union (1946), Hero of the Soviet Union. From June 1952 until 1960 the Soviet Armed Forces chief of General Staff. In October–November 1956 one of the controllers of the Soviet troops' operations in Hungary.

Soldatić, Dalibor (1909–?)–Yugoslav diplomat, between 1953 and 1956 ambassador to Budapest.

Solymosi, János–Lieutenant colonel.

Stepchenko, Fyodor Petrovich (1909–1978)–Served in the Red Army since 1927. On November 3, 1956, as deputy political section chief of the Soviet Armed Forces, took part in the troop withdrawal negotiations led by General of the Army Malinyin. In 1971 retired as a colonel general.

Suslov, M. A. (1902–1982)–Soviet politician, the party's leading ideologist. Party member since 1921, worked in the party apparatus from 1931. From 1941 member of Soviet Central Committee, between 1952–1953, then from 1955 member of the Soviet Central Committee Presidium.

Svernyik, Nikolai Mikhailovich (1888–1970)–Soviet politician, between 1953 and 1956 president of the Soviet Union's Trade Union Central Council, member of the Soviet Central Committee Presidium.

Svoboda, Jan–Secretary to the Czechoslovak Communist Party's Central Committee.

Szabó, Gergely (1921–)–Chemical engineer, communist politician. In 1946–1947 general secretary of NÉKOSZ, from 1952 until October 31, 1956, chemical industry minister. From 1957 company engineer-in-chief.

Szabó, István B. (1893–1976)–Smallholders Party politician. Vice president of the Smallholders Party since 1945. From 1944 until 1946 political secretary of state in the Ministry of Defense. Minister of state in 1946. Took part in the reforming of the Smallholders Party in 1956, between November 3 and 4 minister of state in Imre Nagy's government. Arrested in 1957, sentenced to three years, released in 1959.

Szabó, János (1897–1957)–Driver, commander and leader of the Széna Square rebel group. In January 1957 sentenced to death and executed.

Szál, Albert–Lieutenant.

Szalai, András (1917–1949)–Communist movement fighter, member of the Hungarian Youth Communist League since the age of 15. After 1945 leader of the Hungarian CP's Cadre Section. In 1949 arrested on false charges and sentenced to death in Rajk trial.

Szalai, Béla (1922–)–Communist politician. Between October 1953 and 1956 member of HWP Central Leadership and of Politburo since 1954. From May 1957 leader of the Berlin trade legation.

Szántó, Zoltán (1893–1977)–Communist politician. HWP Central Leadership member, in October 1956 Politburo member.

Szigeti (?)–State security lieutenant.

Sziklai, Sándor (1895–1956)–Agricultural laborer, cobbler. In 1915 was made Russian prisoner of war. Took part in the Russian Civil War and remained in the Soviet Union. In World War II he led one of the anti-fascist schools for Hungarian prisoners of war in the Soviet Union. After 1945 he was a colonel in the Hungarian People's Army, from 1953 director of the Military History Institute. On October 26, 1956, in his Budakeszi apartment, he killed himself after murdering two people.

Szilágyi, József (1917–1958)–Active participant in the circle around Imre Nagy. Leader of Imre Nagy's prime ministerial secretariat. In 1958 sentenced to death and executed.

Szőnyi, Tibor (1903–1949)–M.D. major of the Communist movement, MP after 1945, head of the Cadre section of the CP. In 1949 on the basis of fabricated charges he was arrested and executed.

Szűcs, Miklós (1920–)–Professional army officer, graduated from Ludovika Academy. Lieutenant in the Royal Hungarian Army. Colonel in the Hungarian People's Army. Graduated from the General Staff Academy in Moscow, chief of the operations section of the General Staff. On November 3, 1956, member of the troop withdrawal delegation led by Ferenc Erdei.

Takács, László–Major.

Tausz, János (1911–1988)–Social Democrat, then Communist politician, in 1955–1956 interior trade minister.

Tikhonov, M. F. (1900–1971)–Lieutenant general, in 1956 the Hungarian Defense Ministry's chief adviser. From 1918 soldier in the Red Army. Graduated from Frunze Military Academy in 1930. Before the war commander of sub-units and units. From 1941 division and corps commander. After the war first deputy commander of the Frunze Military Academy, then in military diplomatic service. Retired in 1957.

Tildy, Zoltán (1889–1961)–Calvinist priest, Smallholders Party politician. Between 1945 and 1948 prime minister and president of the republic. In 1956 minister of state in Imre Nagy's government. In 1958 sentenced to six years in prison.

Tito, Josip Broz (1892–1980)–Yugoslav politician. From November 29, 1943, marshal, president of the National Liberation Committee. Between 1945 and 1953 president of the federal government, from 1953 until his death president of Yugoslavia.

Tóth, István–Lieutenant colonel.

Tóth, Lajos (1917–)–Laborer, professional army officer from 1949, from May 1, 1951, major general, deputy commander of the Armored Officers School, then division commander. From November 20, 1954, until October 30, 1956, the Hungarian People's Army chief of General Staff.

Tóth, Zoltán–Lieutenant colonel.

Treper, Ivan–Colonel.

Tutarinov, I. V.–Brigadier general, chief of staff of the Carpathian Military District.

Ushakov (?)–Soviet lieutenant, officer in the 60th air defense artillery division's 419th regiment's 3rd battery. He accompanied János Kádár and the Revolutionary Worker-Peasant Government from Szolnok to Budapest on November 7, 1956, with his unit.

Vas, Zoltán (1903–1983)–Communist politician. From 1945 member of Hungarian CP and of HWP Central Leadership. In October 1956, during Imre Nagy's government, he was an adviser to Nagy. On November 4, 1956, he took refuge in the Yugoslav Embassy, was then taken to Romania and returned home in 1958.

Végh, Béla (1922–) Communist politician. From 1953 until October 24, 1956, secretary of the HWP Central Leadership. From May 1957 worked on the District XIII HSWP committee.

Virág, Ede–Colonel, in 1956 leader of the Hungarian People's Army Foreign Affairs Section.

Yartsev, Vladimir Yegorovich–Soviet lieutenant.

Yudin, Pavel Fyodorovich (1893–1991)–Philosopher, member of Academy of Sciences. Between 1953 and 1959 Soviet ambassador to Beijing.

Zade (?)–Egyptian extraordinary envoy to Budapest in 1956.

Zherebcov, G. I.–Soviet colonel.

Zhukov, G. K. (1896–1974)–Marshal of the Soviet Union, member of the general headquarters during World War II, the highest commander, deputy to Stalin. From February 1955 until October 1957 minister of defense. From 1953 member of Soviet Central Committee and in 1956–1957, of the Presidium.

Zólomy, László (1916–1990)–Colonel. Chief of Operations Section of the General Staff in 1956. Arrested on November 7, 1956, sentenced in 1957. In 1989 he was rehabilitated and promoted to the rank of brigadier general.

Zuryanov (?)–Brigadier general. In October–November 1956 worked with Serov.

Also Available from CEU Press

"The Prague Spring '68"
Chief editor: Jaromír Navrátil
Preface by Václav Havel

"The Prague Spring '68 helps answer the question of why the Soviets invaded Czechoslovakia, as it had Hungary, while it overlooked insubordination elsewhere."

The New York Times

This widely acclaimed book is the first to document a Cold War crisis from both sides of the Iron Curtain. It is based on unprecedented access to the previously closed archives of each member of the Warsaw Pact, as well as once highly classified American documents from the National Security Council, CIA, and other intelligence agencies.

Presented in a highly readable volume, the book offers top level documents from Kremlin Politburo meetings and transcripts of KGB recorded telephone conversations between Leonid Brezhnev and Alexander Dubcek.

The Preface is written by Václav Havel, President of the Czech Republic, and the editors have a unique perspective to offer since they are members of the commission appointed by Havel to investigate the events of 1968–1970.

Contents
  Preface
  Foreward
     Prelude to the Prague Spring of 1968
  2. From January to Dresden
  3. Revision Reform, Revolution
  4. The July Crisis
  5. August–The Month of Intervention
  6. The Aftermath
  Documentary Epilogue
  Bibliography

ISBN 963 9116 15 7
Cloth • 596 pages • **Price:** USD 59.95 / GBP 38.00

Available at ALL good Bookshops
  Distributed in the UK by Plymbridge Distributors Ltd., Estover Road, Plymouth PL6 7PZ
  Distributed in US by Cornell University Press Services, 750 Cascadilla Street, Ithaca, New York 14851-6525, USA
  Further Information: CEU Press, Tel: 361-327-3014 Fax: 361-327-3183